TITLE FIGHT

TITLE FIGHT

The Battle for Gay News

Gillian E Hanscombe · Andrew Lumsden

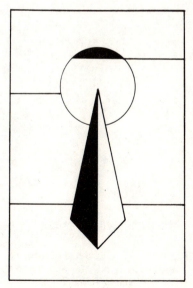

Brilliance Books

First published by Brilliance Books 1983
Copyright © Gillian E Hanscombe and Andrew Lumsden 1983

BRILLIANCE BOOKS 14 CLERKENWELL GREEN
LONDON EC1

ISBN 0 946189 60 9

Typeset by MC Typeset of Chatham Kent.
Printed by Nene Litho and bound by
Woolnough Bookbinding
both of Wellingborough, Northants

CONTENTS

Part One

THE TITLE

Winter 1981–82

BLISS IN THAT DAWN

It is January 13, 1982, a Wednesday. The twenty one staff of Britain's national gay newspaper are at work, as usual, in the clerical, production and editorial departments of the paper they bring out every fortnight.

The editor Denis Lemon is absent, as he has been for some time now. He is sick with hepatitis, and is shut away at home in North London, forbidden by doctors to go out of doors.

It is a unique organisation. Other than 'Scotty', the retired woman and practising Anglican who comes in four days a week as assistant to the editor, everyone present in the office is homosexual.

There are fourteen gay men, working in the advertising room, in the art room, in the editorial department, on reception, in accounts and finance, on distribution, subscriptions and mail order. There are six lesbians, working in typesetting, in the editorial department and in advertising.

They work in a rabbit-hutch of an office, a small, white, two storey building in West Kensington. It sports 'For Sale' boards, which have been there for more than six months. The windows wear grilles, protection not only against burglary and vandalism, but also against anti-gay violence. For the same reason, the windows are made out of expensive, unbreakable plastic. Inside, the floor coverings are in a state of ruin far beyond any hope of repair, but it hardly matters, since only the barest minimum is left free to walk on; the rest is covered with shelves, machines, boxes and surfaces – with mail order stocks, back issues of the paper, files, mail sacks, stationery, and books. Wall space, like floor space, is severely restricted, but here and there hangs an old postcard from a colleague or lover on holiday, or an ancient poster advertising some long past gay event.

The ground floor houses a tiny reception area, where Mike Allaway takes all incoming phone calls and sorts replies to classified advertisements. Next to him, crammed so close that the two can never stand up at the same time, sits Bob Stratton – when he is not out delivering the paper – doing the distribution paperwork. Some half dozen steps away is a cubby-hole called the 'kitchen' – so small that only one person can stand in it and two only if they're feeling specially intimate – where the kettle boils nearly without ceasing and people avail themselves of their only 'perk': free tea and coffee.

Downstairs, also, is the art room, boasting three drawing boards, one desk and a collection of boxes, bins, cabinets and shelves. Here the three art room workers – Jean-Claude Thévenin, Glen Platts and Tony Reeves – design, paste up and provide the graphics for the newspaper. Squashed into the corner, at the one desk, sits Jo Hodgkinson, with file cards, drawers and trays full of information sheets and newsletters, a telephone she shares with Alison upstairs, and a host of pens, pencils, scissors, staplers, clips and tapes. In addition to her main function, Jo is responsible for co-ordinating the production schedule of the paper and for proof-reading it, which she either does herself or arranges for a part-time worker to do. Here, single handed, Jo somehow performs her main task, which is the compilation of the Gay Guide and the Diary of Events. For many, Jo's contribution is the heart of the paper, providing a central storehouse of information about gay groups and activities nationwide. Because of Jo's work, lesbians and gay men can know that they are part of a network which spans age, gender, class, interests, tastes and convictions.

Next to the art room is a dark room, where the valuable copy-camera produces prints of photographs to the required size and where the headliner makes the headlines. Apart from the equipment, the dark space is littered with Letraset, photographic and other discarded materials. Outside the dark room is some four square feet of space, chock-a-block with a photocopier, franking machine, large safe and huge piles of envelopes and Jiffy bags. Here Alisdair Clarke must work as best he can, coping with the subscription list and with servicing the mail orders for books, jewellery, T-shirts and other items on offer in the paper. He is hardly ever seen sitting down. A chair, after all, takes up more space than two standing legs.

Next to the reception area is a room shelved all the way round, where more book stocks are kept. Here Robert Palmer, the business manager, sits on his three legged stool at a bench. He seems always to be poring over scores of columns of figures, all tidily and minutely written. He shares his telephone line with the editor upstairs. And his room has a door, which is nearly always shut.

Tucked at the end of a tiny corridor – which is also shelved full to overflowing and where some of the shelves, broken by the weight, stick jaggedly between the books which will never fall, since the great pressure of their weight keeps them jammed together even without support – tucked away out of sight or sound is a room some six feet square where four people must work on the advertising and accounts needs of the paper. In addition, part-time workers and occasional clients must somehow squash into this little box of a room. Nor can it be quiet; most of the work done here is done on the telephone.

Downstairs a good carpet is not missed. That upwards of fourteen people can spend half their lives in such cramped conditions is something of a wonder. That they do their arduous jobs so well and so cheerfully is nothing short of a miracle. They do not need a decent carpet; and they even manage with broken chairs to sit on, typewriters that are always breaking down from overuse; lack of proper ventilation and lack of natural light. Their working conditions are truly appalling, but they hardly ever grumble. It is only when the threat of tea, coffee, milk and sugar running out occasionally arises, that a temper or two might fray at the edges.

Upstairs staff fare no better. The stairs themselves are so narrow that no-one may pass on them and anyone wishing to go up or down must peer and see if they are free. There are three rooms and two lavatories upstairs. The first room houses the typesetting department, where Wendy Simpson and Lesley Jones process the entire written contents of every issue. They each have a valuable machine, but they must nevertheless suffer too, from inadequate old chairs and benches. No money has been spent on making their job more comfortable. In their small room the noise of their machines is deafening. But they do, at least, have a window.

The next room along is the news room, which has no space to

spare for direly needed shelves and cabinets, other than a few high, narrow shelves already filled. The room is entirely covered with four desks and chairs, telephones, typewriters and trays. Here the news team – news editor Andrew Lumsden and reporters Chris Kirk and Gill Hanscombe – sit and work, telephone and type. Here, too, is the editor's desk, chair, telephone and tray. He has no better office facilities than anyone else, but does some of his work from home.

All the inhabitants of the news room smoke, which is a constant assault on the two occupiers of the last upstairs room. Scotty sits in here at her small desk and large typewriter, dealing with all the editorial records – the paying of contributors, the filing of names and addresses, the sorting of editorial post, the typing of anything and everything the editor requires of her. She is everyone's dream of a secretary, protecting – as she does – the editor from all and any outside incursion on his time and interests and even from his own workforce. Scotty, to many, appears to be nothing short of a saint. She is not incapable of making a mistake, and she most certainly is not without humour. Her saintliness consists in her utter reliability, her capacity to remain aloof from conflicts, to resist being needled or nettled, and her unspoken reassurance that really the editor isn't so dreadful 'once you know how to handle him'.

At an only slightly bigger desk in the same room sits Alison Hennegan, who is styled Assistant (Features) Editor and Literary Editor. No-one knows what the brackets around Features mean. There is something between her and the editor. He hardly ever speaks to her. And she seems to have no Features work to do. But hers – without doubt – is the Literary Supplement which she does single-handed. On shelves above her, crammed and hanging over her, on the floor in heaps and piles around her, on every inch of her desk – are books and more books, catalogues, publishers' leaflets, trade journals, magazines and papers. Alison is probably England's expert on what is being published by, or about, or of interest to, lesbian women and gay men.

Off this room is the building's only other lavatory, used sometimes by the desperate but more often thought of as 'Scotty's loo'. Though she hotly denies any proprietorial right to a loo of her own, Scotty understands the delicacy behind the joke. Alison and Scotty keep their door closed in a valiant effort to keep out the noise and smoke of the newsroom next to them. The upstairs staff – like their downstairs colleagues – try not to complain or grumble, despite the horrendous nature of their working conditions. Indeed, Alison is sometimes heard to point out that the health and safety people would probably find the offices illegal, if they came to investigate.

January 13, 1982, is two days from press day with issue 232, which will appear in the London gay clubs and pubs on Tuesday January 19, be round the rest of the country by Thursday, and be in the hands of foreign subscribers – in Saudi Arabia, Hong Kong, Israel, Germany, North America, South America – in the last days of the month, or in February.

Jean-Claude Thévenin (called JC), who was once the absent editor's lover and who has been at *Gay News* since its second issue in June 1972, is designing the cover. The deputy editor, Andrew Lumsden, who has been at the paper since the previous year, has chosen for the cover: "HUNGER STRIKE IN BELGIUM" "LOVERS: ARE THEY WORTH IT?" "Brrrrr! To warm you up we bring you HOT SAPPHIC NEWS FROM THE FORESTS OF LICHTAART p 8 THE SLOW BURN OF YOUTHFUL SEXUALITY p 12 and we put the heat on THE LONDON LISTING MAGAZINES p 15 and on THE TIMES p 20".

The art room have commissioned a cover drawing from artist Sue Dray to illustrate the main feature, "Lovers: are they worth it?" by Felice Picano, reprinted from an issue of the Los Angeles gay paper *The Advocate*. The feature has been chosen by the editor, despite his absence and despite a feeling amongst his staff that too much North American material is reproduced in *Gay News*. But the illustration – a line drawing of two youthful gays, one in shorts, the other in sailor T-shirt, to be printed in blue and white – is much admired.

Uniquely among Britain's national newspapers, *Gay News* is carrying material written exclusively by and about lesbian women and gay men. The paper's staff – like other workers everywhere – belong to unions, pay PAYE, handle as much turn-over as many another small business and prove their competence and reliability by bringing out their product every two weeks, on the dot, year in, year out.

But lesbian women and gay men – according to the public stereotypes made of them – are supposed not to be able to do such things. The men are assumed to be frivolous and unreliable, the women hostile and neurotic. It is further assumed that both groups need heterosexual men, themselves made stable by commitments to wives and children, to make them behave responsibly.

It would be unthinkable in much of the world, but here in Britain, in 1982, social conditions allow at least that this group of lesbian women and gay men can work together without concealment and that they can sell the results on a wide scale. Yet the *Gay News* staff – and much of their readership – are aware that this freedom of assembly and this right to recompense for labour are elementary civil rights and should be unsurprising; the very least to be expected from a Britain proud of its 'democratic' tradition.

Other than Scotty, the *Gay News* staff know each other as lesbian women and gay men. Most, but not all, have 'come out', are open, that is, about their sexuality to intimates, acquaintances, colleagues and officials; to anyone, indeed, who may enquire.

That a viable gay paper exists is astonishing, in a curious sense, even in Britain, where the paper has been coming out for half a generation. No magazine editor, no television producer, ever asks to make a feature article or a documentary out of an office which, after all, is culturally and sociologically unique. *New Society*, for instance, has never been near it, the *Gay News* production enterprise is 'invisible', even though the *Gay News* that it produces is visible on news stands.

Some of *Gay News*'s uniqueness lies in misapprehensions that homosexuals have about their own newspaper.

Most suppose it to be a form of community service, like the 'voluntary' organisations, such as the Gay Switchboards around the Western world which take phone calls from anxious gay men and women. They suppose, too, that the paper is 'collectively' owned and run, the property of the workforce; or held in some kind of trusteeship, and essentially charitable in its nature and aims.

It isn't. Lock, stock and barrel it belongs to the absentee editor. He is regarded by the longest serving members of staff, and by some in the London gay world who are unusually well informed about *Gay News*' affairs, as a hard-faced man who has done well out of the Gay Liberation wars, and proposes, it is suspected, to do even better.

The paper was formed out of the homosexual protest movement

that swept out of America in the late 1960s – the Gay Liberation Front consciously modelled on the disobedience tactics of blacks, students, 'hippies', women, and other 'non-conformists'; and which fought its wars in the USA, Canada, South America, Britain, continental Europe and Australasia, during the early 1970s.

From 1968 on, the word 'gay' has become familiar usage, not only in English, but also in many other languages, ceasing to be a private code and becoming a public proclamation of homosexuality. To say of someone that he or she was gay now meant that he or she saw it as important to be acknowledged by friends, family and employers as homosexual. It might mean no more – nothing overtly political – but it meant at least that. Then the press and media in general, picking up on the word more because it's short and fits a headline than for any better thought out reason, muddied the usage again.

They used it, and still use it, as a simple synonym for 'homosexual', so that a homosexual who has been keeping his nature a secret and yet, like the Queen's Bodyguard in 1982, is suddenly discovered, is referred to as 'gay'. Further, the press generally mean a homosexual man, leaving homosexual women out of it, when they refer to a gay or gays.

Most of these complications were yet to come when *Gay News* developed from 1971 meetings of the GLF in London. The proposed title of the paper, which was some eight months in preparation, was at that time flamboyant and assertive. The very word 'gay' was still causing outrage in the correspondence columns of national newspapers, and there were those, including its future owner–editor, who wanted it called something less flagrant.

Other newspapers launched in America and Canada in the same era – *The Advocate*, in Los Angeles, and *Body Politic*, in Toronto – were more sophisticated, or more discreet, in their choice of title. Only *Gay Community News*, of Boston, first issue 1973, was equally extrovert, daring the readers to define themselves at once as 'gay'.

By January 1982 any semblance of shock in the title of the British paper has long since faded away for most of the 18,000 who buy it twice a month, or the 50,000 or so, it is estimated, who finally get to read borrowed copies of each issue. And the owner–editor is known to most on staff and to a handful of the well informed to be

9

bored with it and longing to go.

On this particular Wednesday the tension is almost unbearable. The issue is going well. There's no particular production problem. The news-staff – reporters Chris Kirk and Gill Hanscombe and news editor Andrew Lumsden (who doubles the job with deputy editor) – are working flat out on the 16 pages, out of a 48 page paper, which they have to have finished and away by Friday evening.

There's a story on a Belgian teacher, Eliane Morissens, who was dismissed from her post after 'coming out' on Belgian TV as a lesbian on October 22, 1980, and is now (as will be referred to on the cover) starting a hunger strike.

There's an analysis of the handling of gay news and issues by the London 'listings' magazines, *Time Out, City Limits,* and *Event,* which finds they do the job badly, and stories about Poles in London, about police *agents provocateurs,* about the Archbishop of Canterbury wanting to retain the criminal offence of blasphemy, about the Kincora 'boy's home scandal' in Northern Ireland . . . .

There are news features about gay doctors, about the first sexual experiences of gay men and lesbians, and about a conference of the International Lesbian Information Service held at the start of the year in the woodlands of Lichtaart, near Antwerp . . . .

Jo Hodgkinson has completed work on revisions to the 6-page 'Gay Guide – Where to Go in Gay Britain and Ireland'. And she is writing the last of the 4-page Diary of Events (discos, cabarets, rambles, theatres, conferences, meetings, benefits, around the nation).

Now in her fifties, Jo has been at the paper for three years. She has developed the Diary from less than half a page to its present four, and the Guide from four pages to six. She's at her desk in the crowded art room, checking entries for accuracy.

The existence of these pages, which carry no advertising, is widely mistaken as the proof that *Gay News* is a possession of 'the community', a communal property of the country's gay population, administered – as it were, in trust – by the editor and staff. The Guide and Diary link people across the country. Often, they're referred to as a 'lifeline'.

The main feature, 'Lovers: Are they Worth it?', has been laid down. So has the 5-page *Gay News* Literary Supplement.

Alternating between five pages and three pages an issue, the 'LitSup' is another single handed job, covering the flood of publications of direct concern to homosexuals.

The script of a play about Lord Alfred Douglas, a book proclaiming 'bi' to be better than gay, letters by Wilhelm Reich, a critique of Ingmar Bergman, the autobiography of Elizabeth Wilson, *Faces of Feminism* by Olive Banks, are among this issue's reviews. And there's a feature article about the New Zealander, Charles Brasch, whose life work, says the intro, 'was a quiet critique of heterosexual society'.

Alison Hennegan, now in her thirties, joined the paper in 1977 as assistant features editor (the brackets came later) and literary editor, after doing 'voluntary' work at the national gay counselling service 'Friend'. She has built up the 'LitSup' from two pages to an occasional peak of eight.

With long brown hair and a weakness, as she admits herself, for too much junk food, Alison, like Scotty the assistant to the editor, is Christian, a cross glittering below her throat. She is a celebrity in her own right in the gay movement in Britain, both for her work on the 'LitSup' (which has no equivalent anywhere else in gay publishing, in Britain or abroad) and for appearances as an 'out' gay woman on 'Gay Life', a British television series.

She is committed to the ideal that gay women and gay men can co-operate in enterprises that combat the chauvinist heterosexuality of society – one of the two most publicly committed such gay women in the country, together with the only paid worker in the Campaign for Homosexual Equality, Anna Durell. (CHE is a law-reform body).

Alison also has the title Assistant (Features) Editor, but has for a long time been fed up with its meaninglessness, while being reluctant to ask that it be struck out. The editor chooses each issue's main general feature without consulting her, and the news editor only consults the news team, if anyone, about news features.

Seven other pages of the new issue have gone down: they are the night life and general consumer spending pages, written and prepared by a freelancer, Peter Burton, and the arts reviews and regular columns have also been seen to press for two issues now by Peter, in the absence of *Gay News'* editor, who usually runs them. Peter's main item this issue is an appraisal of a gay men's bar,

Harpoon Louie's in the Earl's Court Road, London, where the bar staff, most unusually, are all women.

But he has also written a feature about the changing gay scene in the South Coast resort of Brighton – 'suddenly the gay scene in Brighton has become much friendlier' – and edited a page of new paperbacks: Nancy Cunard, Katherine Mansfield, Jim Jones' *People's Temple, Women at Work* . . . Jean-Claude Thévenin, of the art-room, has done his usual column, 'Sounds', about pop music.

With dyed hair, the colour of which (like Wendy Simpson in typesetting) he's always changing, Peter Burton always has a cigarette hanging from his lip, lighting them from a box of kitchen matches. He lives in Brighton by choice, coming to London for a maximum of four days a week to see and be seen at the gay clubs and call in with his copy at the *Gay News* offices.

He's written for almost every gay magazine Britain has seen for the last fifteen years (before *Gay News* they were timid picture magazines, which came and went, none lasting for long). He has been secretary to the writer Robin Maugham, a short-story writer and a roadie for Rod Stewart. He's short and chubby, and when he wears a pair of pale blue and white dungarees has an eerie resemblance to a one time children's character on British TV, Andy Pandy.

Unflaggingly efficient, everything he does is in on time, and typesetters say his copy is the 'cleanest' they get from anyone. The editor, who, when he's well, dines with Peter once a fortnight – but socialises with no-one else on staff on a regular basis – has warned the deputy editor that Peter is hasty, and needs watching or the quality will start slipping. But then the editor has had warnings to give about the general tendency of everything to deteriorate, if unwatched . . . .

The gossip column, 'Bosie' (after Wilde's nickname for Alfred Douglas), is in place on the inside back cover, as is the astrology column by 'Merlin': '1982', says 'Merlin', 'is going to be a mixture of uncertainty, unease, and brinkmanship . . . .'

All the display ads are in place. As will be the five pages of classified ads as soon as typesetters have finished the last of them: 'Hertfordshire, near Ware, thirty-three, slim, seeks guy with own place for friendship. Box 232. 119'.

The new issue is going all right, but still the tension is unbearable. Snow is falling, in light gusts, outside the office windows. It's going to be a trudge home through the slush. And the business manager has warned everyone that he may have to make a very important announcement the next day.

Thursday, January 14. By pushbike (Bob Workman, the staff photographer), by motorbike (Peter Coell and Peter Jones and Sandy Murdoch, respectively financial manager, assistant to the financial manager, and advertisement manager), by car (Gill Hanscombe, staff reporter), they come through the winter's gloom to Normand Gardens, London W14.

By tube they come, and bus: Jo Hodgkinson, of the Guide and Diary, Scotty, Assistant to the editor, Chris Kirk, staff reporter, Mike Allaway, of reception and box replies, Alisdair Clarke, mail order and subscriptions (who has been homeless recently, and sometimes sleeps in the office), Amanda Price, classified ads, typesetters Wendy Simpson and Lesley Jones, Tony Reeves, art assistant, Glen Platts, one of the paper's two art directors.

The other art director, 'JC' (Jean-Claude Thévenin), walks from his home one street away. Alison comes late to the office this morning. Like Peter Burton she has a home outside London – hers is in Cambridge. She has been staying at the North London home of one of the paper's reviewers.

Peter arrives by taxi from the flat he stays in when in London. Andrew Lumsden, deputy editor and news editor, comes by another taxi, from his flat in Ladbroke Grove. And in the company van, which every fortnight delivers a new issue, hot from the press, to the London gay night spots, comes van driver Bob Stratton, who has plastered the sides of the van with nuclear disarmament posters.

'No Cruise', one of them reads. Which is enough to make a gay man blink, seeing it on the flanks of the *Gay News* van; for 'cruising' is what gay men call it when they are out on the town trying to pick one another up.

The tiny kitchen does an even sharper business than usual, for people are cold, and they are worried, and though the art room and the news room get on with pages still to be done for the issue that is almost to bed, there is a good deal of excited gathering in knots by everyone else, to warm hands and stomachs on coffee, and talk about what may be to come.

The rumour is out, out among the staff if scarcely wider than that, that from his sick-bed in Islington the editor is organising his own retirement; and may be announcing the fact today.

All small offices seem to contain the extremes of human nature; and twenty people (the business manager, yet to arrive, would make twenty-one; the editor, twenty-two) is not so small an office as all that. The fact that virtually everyone is homosexual would seem, to those who don't know gays, to limit the range of personalities. But it doesn't.

Sandy Murdoch, the display ads manager, a broad shouldered six-footer who has been with the paper nine months, is entitled to a car at *Gay News*' expense, under the deal he made, but rarely appears on anything but his motorbike, in full black leathers; he's a freak for bikes.

Wendy Simpson has been a typesetter at *Gay News* for two years. One of the most careful dressers on staff, she, alone of the women, sometimes wears a Dietrich-style suit and tie, coming nearer to one of the classic lesbian 'looks' than any of the others. It's only seven months since she chose to become a lesbian. She is one of two women on staff with a child – a fourteen year-old skinhead. She gets furious about the constantly bad publicity given by newspapers to skinheads – kids with their hair shaven to the skull – 'as if they're all going round beating people up'. The boy's not only showing pronounced heterosexual tendencies, but is also driving Wendy mad with the sexist language he picks up at school. She jokes that he's heterosexual but that maybe it's just a phase he's going through.

The other woman on staff with a child, is the news room's Gill Hanscombe. Australian-born, Gill has lived in England for thirteen years and has a young son. In her thirties (as Wendy is), Gill joined *Gay News* only seven months ago, driven by the costs of supporting her son and her home to apply for the job of reporter, which she'd never done before. Nor had she even heard of *Gay News*, much less read it, until – knowing of her penury – Jo Hodgkinson offered her the part-time proof reading job. She is already a published author, co-author of a book on lesbian motherhood called *Rocking the Cradle*, and of many poems and articles. Her first novel, *Between Friends*, is about to be published in the USA.

There are others on staff who have university degrees, but she, uniquely, is entitled to be called Dr Hanscombe – she is a doctor of philosophy of Oxford University.

None of the fifteen gay men at *Gay News*, including the editor and the business director, has children. Only one, Andrew Lumsden, has ever been married – and both he and his wife knew him to be homosexual. Nine of the male staff, however, are 'married' in the other sense, sometimes jokingly used by gays: they have live-in lovers.

One such is Mike Allaway, who does box replies (the forwarding of answers to classified ads) and sits in the entry way of the office as receptionist. He and his live-in lover are in their early twenties, and both are campaigning monogamists. They object strongly to what they see as the pressures in the 1980s male gay world to be 'non-exclusive', to sleep around, to have an 'open relationship'.

Mike longs to write. He's been on one magazine already, on the clerical side, hoping to break through to journalism. Here he is on *Gay News*, and no nearer; for the paper is very compartmentalised, there is little space, other than the occasional book review, for anyone who wants a share in the editorial side.

Chris Kirk, just turned thirty, is lucky, by Mike's standards: he is in the news team, he writes prolifically for the paper. Another of the office's careful dressers, he is something between camp and punk, with a variety of ear-rings and brooches and badges. He seems always to be in love with someone, even though he has two permanent relationships already. 'I'm emotionally promiscuous', he says.

In his time he's worked in wardrobe – for the famous Granada TV production of 'Brideshead Revisited', among other shows – and on a business magazine. He joined the paper less than a year ago, a few months before Gill and a few weeks before Andrew, and all too often has the air of the White Rabbit, frantically studying his watch: for him, the story will never get written, the edition will never come out.

An expert on the rarely open, frequently submerged, references to homosexual love in popular music of the last thirty years, he's something of a hero worshipper. Besides being greatly impressed by the currently absent editor, he's much taken, just now, with Glen Platts of the *Gay News* art-room. Everyone can see it . . . .

Tall Glen, with traces of the Northern accent of his background has worked at the paper for eight years, longer than anyone other than his colleague in the art-room, 'JC', and the editor. Now thirty-three, he's the most punctilious and untemperamental of workers, his rare irritations – usually to do with people gossiping in the art-room and disturbing the work – the more striking.

He tends to wear 'flying' suits, 'boiler' suits, the loose clothing of male occupations. His portable radio tuned to a popular channel on the shelf over his head ('will you please turn it down', says Jo at intervals, from her desk in the other corner of the room, trying to hear herself speak to gay organisations down the phone), he shares the preparation of the main editorial art-work with 'JC'.

'JC', who came to the paper nearly ten years ago at the age of twenty-two, is another who outfits himself with style each working day – but why say so? Of the fifteen men on staff, only two could be said to verge on the slovenliness and near hostility to style of most men in a predominantly heterosexual British office.

They are Tony Reeves, the art-room 'junior', who has been full-time on the payroll for a year, though a closely involved freelancer for *Gay News* for five years before that, and news editor Andrew Lumsden. Oddly enough, exceptionally inartistic in their appearance though they both are, they are in fact practising artists, selling their work away from *Gay News*. Andrew has pretty well given it up, under the pressure of news-and-deputy editing, but Tony finds time to carry on.

Tony is more taciturn even than Glen – only 'JC', out of the art-room threesome, is voluble, 'very French', in his fluent but strongly accented English. Besides laying out the advertisements carried by the paper, Tony is in-house cartoonist and frequently does line drawings for features, more often than 'JC' or Glen, though both, of course, are capable of it.

Tony, thirty-one, has the distinction of having drawn a banned illustration in *Gay News*. It appeared with an allegedly blasphemous poem, in 1976; the poem about a centurion's erotic reverie on the crucified Christ which was first prosecuted by Mary Whitehouse in the British Courts and then by the British Government at the European Court of Human Rights.

Andrew is one of the heavy smokers in the office (the news room all smoke heavily) and, at forty, one of the three oldest members of

16

staff. An experienced journalist who in the past has worked in Fleet Street, he is very reclusive about his life away from work, and seems uninterested in forming any friendships from *Gay News*, after eight months working there.

His arrival in 1981 was out of the blue, so far as everyone else but the editor was concerned. Known as a personal friend of the editor, it is suspected that he, if anyone on the existing staff, will know what it is that's to be announced by the business manager if the latter, still not arrived, ever gets in this January morning . . . .

Deeply suspicious, of anything and everything that may be about to occur, is staff photographer Bob Workman. He has been full-time on the paper for five years, and is on the worst possible terms with the editor. Each, if possible, tries not to speak to the other. Since the photographer's work is mainly, though not exclusively, for the news room, and since the editor, even when well, spends no more than a few hours each day in the office, and on many days doesn't come in at all, that's possible.

Bob is a foot-in-mouth specialist. Andrew calls him a big softy, but it's true that he gets up the nose of one person or another on staff almost every day, usually by criticising their work. He's on especially bad terms with the art room. Like Mike, he is professionally frustrated, having no features editor to work with, and indeed, in the whole office, it's the two of them who most often cause annoyance in other people; and to each other.

Every office, like every school, has the boy the master can't stand, and one or another of whose school mates, at any one time, can't stand either. Bob is *Gay News*'s.

Yet in the surrounding gay world of London, he's one of the best known people at the paper, not just because his photographs appear there credited to him, but because he's indefatigable in getting on his push bike, day after day, including weekends, to attend the gay events and take the photographs that tell as much of the story as the words.

In his thirties, he lives in a Crescent five minutes away, with his lover Tim, and does all his photographic processing there – developing the pictures that others take for the paper, as well as his own.

Lesley Jones has him taped. It sometimes seems that Lesley Jones the second typesetter who works alongside Wendy, has everyone taped. At twenty-four, she came to the paper two years before, to work on subscriptions, now Alisdair's job, and has only recently moved into the typesetting room to learn the skill. She doesn't say much, but when she does, it's impatient and pointed, and quite indifferent to whether or not the listener wanted to hear it.

Just now, it's almost impossible to go into the typesetting room without finding the two typesetters entwined in one another's arms – the only physical demonstration of affection going on just now in an office that seems to be blessed or cursed, as perhaps most are, with some kind of spontaneous incest taboo, preventing people, even if they do rather fancy one another, from doing much about it.

There have been exceptions over the years, but just now *Gay News* isn't notably amorous. Even at the last Christmas office party – held in a gay pub, and not among the filing cabinets – no hidden longing came drunkenly and disreputably to the surface.

(But then, few had enjoyed it. The pub, the Edward VI in Islington – named, eccentrically, for the boy-king of England who may well have died of hereditary syphilis – had been the unilateral choice of the editor, and had been so unpopular with a number of staff that one at least, Gill, had asked if attendance was compulsory.)

The prettiest member of staff, to use disgracefully sexist terminology, is by universal consent Amanda Price, aged twenty-one, who has been doing the classified ads for a year. Daughter of a father in the Foreign and Commonwealth Office, she's 'public school' educated and works as a female outpost in the cramped corner office of the building that also houses Peter Coell and Peter Jones of accounts, and advertising manager Sandy Murdoch.

She is virtually the office censor. For the 'men's personals', the classified ads in which Hertfordshire man seeks guy with own place for friendship, attract ads that are outrageously sexually explicit in the eyes of British law (though not American), and she has to tone them down. If she didn't, *Gay News*, even in 1982, would risk a police prosecution for 'conspiring to corrupt public morals'.

But perhaps Alisdair is the prettiest member of staff. Very tall, very thin, twenty years old, Alisdair Clarke is struggling to learn the complexities of the subscription and mail order operations of the paper. A Londoner born and bred, who is lifting himself by sheer willpower from a schoolboys drug-circle which as he says himself nearly finished him off, he works long, hard, conscientious hours.

Curt with nervousness over the phone, when talking to readers, he's repeatedly in trouble with complaints about subs not having arrived, books apparently missing, readers offended on the phone or by letter. Almost always in skin tight trousers and singlet, he wears metal studded wristlets and a cartridge belt slung low on the hips, and gay male visitors tend to say: 'Who's that?'.

Apart from the Peters, of accounts, everyone is now accounted for. 'Accounts' always has a slightly separate air from the rest of the *Gay News* organisation, a separation resented by some – by those, Wendy, Bob, Alison, Lesley, Gill, who attach most importance to regular staff meetings, with all that that implies by way of comment and criticism on the paper's financial, as well as editorial or internal, policy.

The Peters rarely attend staff meetings, pleading that they're too busy, that such meetings are a waste of time, and that – besides – they ought to be chaired and have an agenda. On one Friday of particular exasperation, Peter Coell demands to know why he should inconvenience himself and oblige others by coming to a staff meeting, given that in all the time they've worked at the paper, Wendy has never once acknowledged the 'good mornings' he's tried to give her (though Wendy would say that she never says good morning to anyone). There are tensions at *Gay News* . . . but where are there not?

Peter Coell, financial manager and company secretary, has been at the paper since 1978. In his late thirties, without formal training in accountancy, he gets in at 7.30 am every weekday, to supervise the opening of the post and the money orders and other forms of cash that come in for subscriptions, mail order, and ads. He leaves, undeviatingly, at 4 pm. This disjunction in working hours from most other people's may be one of the reasons why he and his assistant, Peter Jones – who follows the same routine – seem to have little part in the general communal life of the office.

There is also a 'political' dispute between Peter Coell and the editorial decision takers at the paper. He accuses *Gay News* of cowardice in its neglect of the 'man–boy love' issue (paedophilia) which takes up a lot of space in the Canadian, American, and

Western European gay press, and which has provoked a major trial – the Tom O'Carroll case – in the UK.

Peter Jones has been at the paper for a year. Another big man, like Sandy, he wears his dark hair in a page boy cut, and has a lover, an air line steward.

The morning is going by. People look out of the windows, to see whether they can spot the repellently coloured British Leyland Metro (which is always breaking down) – it is a sickly yellow green – in which the business director should be turning up. Like the advertising manager, he has the use of a company car.

Gay News fronts onto a suburban street in a highly residential district of London's West Kensington. Opposite is a big parish church, St Andrew's. GN's own building is a freehold, so no landlord can ever turn the newspaper out. It is recessed from the pavement, with a small forecourt of its own. White painted and tiny, it's been home to the paper for six years and 'home' is the word – for there are private residences, homes to unknown families, on either side.

It was originally acquired as a lease in 1976, and converted into a freehold – at an advantageous price – following the bankruptcy of the former owners. The 1970s property values inflation in the UK has taken the selling valuation of the building up to somewhere in the region of £70,000, despite the squalor within.

Apart from its grilles and reinforced windows, it has few other defences; there is an alarm system to be operated by the receptionist, if the police raid, but it's just been discovered that the system no longer works. The police haven't raided yet. It's assumed that the phones are intermittently tapped. Any homosexual in a 'sensitive' position in the Civil Service – or in the police force itself – is encouraged to make phone contact elsewhere.

The car has arrived. People move towards the usual 'conference room' – the *Gay News* art room – which is soon crammed to overflowing. He's short, chubby and thirty-three years old, the business director of *Gay News*. Clutching his three legged, tall stool, he plonks it down in the only remaining space, by the doorway, and grins as people hush each other into silence.

Squatting on upturned wastepaper baskets, squeezed between drawing boards and the wall, sprawled on the floor, people go quiet, faces expectantly turned. There is no sign of the editor, thirty-four year old Denis Lemon. Plainly he is still shut away indoors on his doctor's orders. Or else – the impression rises, intensifies before anything is said – or else he is never coming in again . . . .

The business director looks at a clipboard he holds in his lap and in the unnatural voice of someone very sure he isn't articulate, begins his announcement: 'I'm very glad to be able to tell you that Denis has agreed to leave *Gay News* . . . .'

There's a roar of applause and jubilation.

Time to introduce the business manager.

It isn't only revealed this January 14, 1982, that the editor of *Gay News* has decided to leave after spending half his working life at it – and the whole of the paper's life. It's also revealed that he's selling it, and the person who is buying the paper is the man making the announcement.

Scotty knows what he's going to say because as assistant to the editor she's done the secretarial work for both parties to the sale. Since he is a personal friend of the editor, Peter Burton also knows. And the company secretary – Peter Coell – knows.

Three other staff members have had some idea for a while, but have only known for certain over the last twenty-four hours. On the previous evening they were called to the editor's flat to be told in broad outline about the deal but not to be told in detail. One day business manager Robert Palmer's solicitor will bluntly inform the staff that 'a company exists for the benefit of its shareholders'.

The three called to the editor's flat were Andrew, the deputy editor; JC (Jean-Claude Thévenin) who – for years – has been a director of the holding company, Gay News Ltd – the company which owns the paper – and who is also the longest serving member of staff; and Peter Coell, who does *Gay News*'s accounts. These three had gathered the general nature of the documents: a coming transfer of all the shares in Gay News Ltd from the editor to Robert Palmer, the business manager.

The 'cast list' – printed on page two of every issue of the paper – detailing the employees and their functions, shows Robert Palmer in early 1982 as it has shown him since he came on to the newspaper in January 1981, in the double capacity of business director and marketing director.

While in his twenties he worked for a succession of famous large companies: American-owned international advertising agency Young & Rubicam, British-owned advertising agency Lintas (Walls Ice Cream Etc), American grocers General Foods (Maxwell House). His experience and particular business interest, he says is in 'product development'.

He has wavy dark hair, and with his short stature, chubbiness, and a mixed air of diffidence and desire to be liked, inspires protective feelings in his generally taller gay male friends. Few people radiate harmlessness, but Robert certainly does so, or tries to.

There's a schoolboyish air to him even now, as he announces that he's to take on the ownership of 'The world's largest circulation newspaper for homosexuals', as page two of each issue also proudly proclaims. American gay men would call him 'preppy'.

Yet he's not quite that, with all the implications it carries in America and in the rag-trade of high spending on punctiliously collegiate jackets and ties and shoes and sweaters – après-boating wear. Unlike the other men on the staff, with the occasional exception of the editor, he does indeed wear jackets and ties, but the message is one of social dependability, rather than 'preppy' sexiness.

There's no discredit in that, on a spectrum so wide that very little attracts discredit, and where very few are completely without diffidence. Where there is so much competition, or at any rate pressure to be seen to compete, Robert gives many of his friends a feeling that here is somebody agreeably warm, full of the affection that so many men are too tense or too uninterested to display.

He's one of the many more or less monogamous men on staff, with a lover whom he met six years before. Each has his own flat, but they're thinking that perhaps now, after all these years, they'll set up home together. The idea is for Alan to sell his own flat, and move in with Robert, but nothing has come of that as yet in January 1982.

By a peculiar coincidence, the British stream of pop singers has thrown up one called Robert Palmer, described, quite unlike the Robert Palmer of *Gay News*, as being 'a cool, distant man'. Every now and again vast posters appear in London blazoned with the words 'Robert Palmer', which is very disconcerting for everyone.

Perhaps Robert will invite him to a party. A great party giver, the business director of *Gay News*, but not the kind of party, with men only, designed to start with social conversation and end, as the law puts it, with criminal conversation. He has a liking for celebrities, and for a couple of hundred guests at a time.

His two-floor flat in London's rather fashionable Little Venice has a garden at the back, and politicians tolerably sympathetic to the civil rights of gays can be found drifting into it from the opened ground floor rooms during one of Robert's summer time parties.

He is a self-effacing host, a maker of introductions, whose pleasure it is to know that he has arranged it all, and that people know he has, rather than to be the obvious focus of attention. He has a remarkably comprehensive index of gay names and addresses, and adds to it indefatigably, a 'hostess with the mostest' of London gay life. (There are higher social reaches of male gay life in London, where the homosexual merchant bankers and hereditary rich meet in congenial circumstances, but these are indifferent to civil rights campaigners, indeed afraid of them).

The flat belongs not to Robert, who rents it, but to the Church Commissioners, the Church of England's agents for its vast properties in North London and elsewhere. Tenants of the Commissioners can be of any religion or none, though some effort is made that they should be tolerably 'respectable'; but as it happens Robert is one of the few whose credentials to be in such a flat could be called impeccable.

Not only does his surname signify a pilgrim. His father is a canon in the Church of England, and formerly a vicar in Oxfordshire. He himself was a chorister in the St Paul's Cathedral Choir School – he has a photograph of himself in a line up of other choirboys being smiled at by a bouquet-carrying Queen Mother.

Something of Barchester Towers, of the Victorian England of deaneries and modest property owning – an England currently being extolled by the Prime Minister, Margaret Thatcher, who wants a return to its 'values' – hangs about Robert and his background. He can scarcely be Mr Slope, Trollope's arriviste chaplain to the Bishop of Barchester. But he might yet become the bishop, in manner.

He has already headed an organisation: the Campaign for Homosexual Equality (CHE), the fifteen years old English and Welsh pressure group for improvements to the laws affecting homosexuals. In 1978 he became its Chair (the title invented to · avoid the cumbersome 'chairperson') and ran it for two years. He wasn't the delighted choice of CHE's executive, which had hoped for someone more extrovert and 'starry', but no-one else had offered.

An organisation which had moved its premises from Manchester to London, and which had branches all round the country, CHE was in decline from its most exuberant days when Robert took over. A quiescent not to say acquiescent, self-help enterprise for homosexual men and women in the 1960s (when it was *Committee* rather than Campaign, for Homosexual Equality), CHE had been galvanised in the early 1970s by the imported American-style movement, Gay Liberation Front (GLF).

GLF had run out of energy by about 1973, whereupon CHE, chaired by a woman, Glenys Parry, had an extraordinary creative spurt attracting considerable publicity and providing reams of entertaining news stories for *Gay News*. CHE had begun to run out of steam by about 1977 – so much so that internal debate, about lack of appeal, failure to interest gay women, hazy campaigning targets, became the main preoccupation of many involved.

Robert had become Treasurer in 1977, an unpaid 'charitable' task like all the others at CHE, other than the part-time worker appointed in 1981. His energy and assiduity in an undertaking where others on the executive were often erratic if not downright lazy, impressed everyone. When he put his name forward for Chair, people told themselves that though someone more articulate and leaderly would be wonderful, Robert at least would he hard working.

Hard working he was. After its development by Tyneside CHE he pushed an information package about homosexuality for schools, called the CHE Tape/Slide kit, which many schools allow into their classrooms, and organised the membership supervision to such effect that the numbers of gays belonging to CHE rose from about 3,500 to 4,500, where they plateaued, beginning to sink again after he left.

Opinions divided about whether he'd been a good Chair or a poor one. It wasn't easy to form an opinion, for like his successor, Professor Mike Jarrett of Cardiff University, he had to do the job at a time when gays in Britain, like all in Britain, had had the exuberance knocked out of them by deepening economic recession.

He retired in 1980 with many close friends in CHE, a well-known name in the small circle of British gay politics, without having made any mark on the wider stage, or on the general media.

In January 1982, after a year on the paper, he's still very little known to the editorial and production staff – but then *Gay News* is very much a matter of sub-groups who get on with their craft-skill but have little social contact with fellow workers. Small though the staff is, there is no regular forum at which people could ask what others are up to.

It was the editor who invited him on to the paper, in a negotiation which resulted in Robert arriving with a seat on the Board and a company car. He's been exceedingly energetic ever since, though to what ends isn't all that clear, given the extreme compartmentalisation of the paper's internal workings.

The two Peters, in accounts, have the most detailed picture, and seem to respect him, and to be fond of him. He has been altering the accounting procedures, shifting them from a monthly basis to a four week period (thirteen to the calendar year), and, more significantly, preparing the way for computerised data-processing, first for the payroll and invoicing, next for the subscription lists and mail-order customers. The system is just being installed in January 1982.

Under his marketing hat he has organised a Readers' Survey, through a questionnaire carried in *Gay News*' own pages shortly after getting to the paper early in 1981; and in the course of 1981 has argued the editor into retaining the services of a small advertising agency, both to advise on the marketing uses of the Readers Survey results, and to advise on advertising the paper itself in the general media.

Tackling the perennial distribution problem of the paper (the reluctance of Britain's near-monopolistic and frequently moralistic distribution companies to 'handle' something outrageously styled *Gay News*), he has begun to make approaches to W H Smith and to Menzies, two of the leaders in the field (and in moralism), to see whether they will reverse their decision not to handle *Gay News*.

That 'schoolboy' look and manner of his is probably useful to the paper in its dealings with a perpetually suspicious 'straight' world. If he can be so assuaging in his approach to fellow gay men and women on the paper, how much more mollifying, and safe, might he appear to businesses which may be full of homosexuals, but never of 'out' ones, and which could find their worst prejudices confirmed if they encountered Wendy in her dyed hair and Dietrich suit, or Alisdair in his studded wristlet and cartridge belt.

He is the acceptable face of gaiety, no doubt about that, and it could be argued that with twenty-one people on the payroll, a product to get out all round the country, and bills to be collected or paid to the tune of some £450,000 per year – and all this during a national slump – such a buffer between 'marginalised' homosexuals and heterosexual orthodoxy is needed.

The editor, Denis Lemon, though preferring the hardline, overtly male gay look that Alisdair goes in for, suits up and gets into jacket and tie, in order to move without too much comment in the more respectable areas of life. He has done so more and more in recent years. Denis Lemon's move towards respectability is sufficiently strong for him to declare himself – on occasion – to be bisexual.

With his 'customary belligerent stare', he tells Gill Hanscombe that he sometimes 'lays women' and impresses the same point on Wendy Simpson to whom he says – during an encounter on the stairs when she was still heterosexual – 'I've had my moments of perversity. I can be very perverse.' 'I'm not homosexual', he insists, 'I'm really bisexual.' But he has told the same thing to Alison almost shyly, saying that sexual relationships with women have proved an unexpectedly pleasurable and emotionally satisfying experience.

Unknown to staff, it has been Robert's intention, throughout the whole of his year on the paper, to become at least a part-owner of *Gay News*. He arrived seeking ways and means to bring this about.

The effort, crowned publicly as a total success on January 14, 1982 (complete ownership), rather than a partial success (as the acquisition of a minority shareholding would have been), is presented as a public service to readers, to the staff of the paper, and to the movement for gay self respect and gay civil rights throughout the country.

Such is the description of his targets which Robert gives to staff, and which arouses applause from many of those present, as he makes his announcement that the editor of *Gay News* is leaving.

He strikes a willing chord, for there are those who have worked a long time at the paper, and others who have had close knowledge of its affairs, who take the dimmest view of the man who is going; who indeed, has gone.

Denis Lemon is unquestionably one of the two best known homosexuals in Britain, in the eyes of the press – the other being Maureen Colquhoun who is 'notorious' for having publicised herself as a lesbian while a serving Member of Parliament. Many well intentioned and reasonably well informed heterosexuals in the media would take for granted – at the beginning of 1982 – that if gays in Britain acknowledge any hero at all, that hero would be Denis Lemon.

He is certainly a celebrity to many in the gay world, but, more than that, he truly *is* a hero to many of those who assiduously read – and save – each copy of *Gay News*; and also to those who are still impressed by what they saw as dignity and courage when he was taken to court at London's Old Bailey in summer 1977 because of publishing in *Gay News* the poem which attracted the extraordinary charge of 'blasphemous libel'.

Yet others – owing, no doubt, both to the nature of the male gay ghetto and to the reluctance of the British media to treat the subject of homosexuality with any degree of ongoing seriousness – others, both gay and straight, have never heard of him. Not knowing that he was a celebrity, Gill Hanscombe – new to his employ – has found him to be an arrogant and bullying employer. Those who feel kindly towards him might describe his style as 'presidential', but others might find the word 'dictatorial' more appropriate. Something of the mood among the sceptical can be guaged from the accusations levelled at him in an interview with one of his staff, a year before Robert's success. News reporter Graham McKerrow, invited to take the job of news editor shortly afterwards accepted by Andrew, said no, and gave Denis Lemon the benefit of his considered opinion of his recent performance as editor and owner of the paper.

It was a 'curiously friendly' meeting, yet Graham listed every fault he saw in the paper – such as editorial content, staff/management relations ('divide and rule' policy), general lack of vision, and no contact with readers or understanding of them – and blamed these on Denis. He told Denis that, for the sake of *Gay News*, Denis ought to go. For his own part, Graham couldn't work with Denis any longer and certainly not as news editor to Denis's editor.

A popular performer in gay pubs and at the occasional conferences of the gay movement, Eric Presland, who briefly had a job at *Gay News*, has been performing a satirical song aimed against the editor of *Gay News* for a couple of years. The theme is that the *Gay News* editor has 'sold out': that so far from feeling any passion for the needs of gay people, as represented by readers at home and abroad, Denis Lemon has become preoccupied with winning personal approval in the 'straight' world; and with high living.

Eric Presland sings the song on the campus of Durham University at a CHE Conference in August 1981, just five months before Denis in fact decides to leave. Some of the dozens of gay men and women listening, who have travelled from all over the country, are plainly bemused by what sounds like a personal vendetta. Others, who regard themselves as having a clearer insight into the nature of *Gay News'* editor–proprietor, whistle and cheer their approval. *Gay News* reporters in the room are silent. Soon afterwards, Denis instructs Jo to remove from the Diary of Events any of Eric's performances on the grounds that as he is so fond of 'running down' *Gay News* he is not entitled to any publicity from the paper. Jo removes the entries for a few issues, but then decides by herself to reintroduce them, since they meet the Diary's criterion of being gay events.

The song, with its crystallisation of animus against the some-time hero, had been written the year before, for CHE's 1980 Conference. That one had become briefly legendary, for editorial staff of *Gay News*, other than the editor, had been in tears under the emotional pressure of attacks on Denis's behaviour in firing a *Gay News* news editor, Harry Coen. Graham McKerrow, who joined *Gay News* as a reporter under Harry's news editorship, remembers the news room as being in 'chaos'. It seemed to Graham that Harry couldn't control it, but also that he had no support from Denis. Before he began his job, Graham recalls meeting Denis to discuss various things; and Denis warning him of Harry's 'incompetence'.

Denis flatly asserted that Harry Coen had been no good, and brushed aside the criticisms as being those of a self-interested

CHE-based clique, more concerned about their friend Harry than about the requirements of a properly run newspaper. (Harry Coen, for his part, moved on to a contract with the London *Sunday Times* news-desk, and by January 1982 is shortly to be offered a full-time job on that paper.)

A tone of contempt for CHE and for the 'gay movement' in Britain as well as for many past and present employees of the paper, certainly marks the conversation of the editor–owner of 'The world's largest circulation newspaper for homosexuals' by the start of the 1980s.

At the same time he insists increasingly that the policies of the paper, and his decisions, are 'private'.

Bony in the face from illness, his hair cropped as short as a military recruit, Denis is on his feet in January 1982, but very weak. A slim (just now, gaunt) six-footer, he's a good looking man with large eyes and an attractive smile. As an 'advertisement' for the modern male homosexual, when photographed for the general media during the 1977 trial, he couldn't be bettered.

He was in at the conception of the paper, in late 1971; found its first, tiny, offices near London's Paddington Station; put into the launch costs the tiny amount of savings he then had; became its editor in August 1972, and has remained so ever since, doing – at one time or another – virtually every job, other than printing, required on a newspaper.

Like the other members of staff, he personally went out selling copies of the paper outside pubs and clubs in London in the early 1970s. He wrote very 'camp' film reviews in the early numbers, under the self-mocking pseudonym of 'Denis Grinspoon'. He was at the centre of the growth of the paper from a minute circulation to nearly 20,000 – higher than that of many famous British speciality periodicals such as *The Spectator* and the *New Statesman*.

And then came the Old Bailey trial.

In the summer of 1976, four years after the birth of the paper, he came into the art room, where a poem which was to become notorious was already pasted-up on the boards.

'That'll get the Christians going . . .' one of those present remembers him saying.

Indeed it did – the 'Moral Majority' ones, though the phrase had yet to be invented. It was the poet James Kirkup's ruminations, through the erotic homosexual viewpoint of a centurion, on the body of the crucified Christ. A Mrs Mary Whitehouse, not herself homosexual, was shown the issues of *Gay News* containing the poem, and asked her solicitor if there was any way of prosecuting it.

He came up with a charge of blasphemous libel, not used in England for fifty years. Under its provisions, Denis was found guilty at the Old Bailey jury trial in 1977, fined, and very nearly sent to prison. The bizarre nature of the charge, and the shock it gave to the whole British 'liberal' establishment, made Denis for a time a national and in some degree international figure.

He had the curious experience that year of seeing at a nearby restaurant table, in the fashionable Joe Allen's, a face that he *knew* he'd seen somewhere before, and which he suddenly realized was that of an actor who played Denis himself in a television reconstruction of the trial: a *doppelgänger* of a kind that few can hope, or fear, to experience.

After the verdict, some of the American gays, who had watched the antediluvian events in far off Britain with appalled fascination, invited Denis to recuperate in the USA. News editor Michael Mason edited the paper in his absence, as indeed he had done through much of the endlessly time consuming legal preparations for the 1977 trial.

It seemed for a moment in 1977 as if Denis Lemon was going to become a new permanent personality in the British national consciousness, an archetype for late twentieth century homosexuality much as Germaine Greer had become an archetype for new developments in women's liberation, a figure in chat-shows, newspaper magazine supplements, one-liners on comedians' scripts.

But it was only for a moment. He had long since ceased to write, for *Gay News* any more than anywhere else. And though talkative, and uninhibited when secure in private company, he felt himself inarticulate – and was inarticulate, speaking heavily and uneasily – if asked on to radio or TV or to a speaking engagement. Older people on the paper saw him as a man still unable to shake off past insecurities.

He didn't rise to the opportunity; or fall to it, if that would have been the effect of being able to accept the briefly proferred role of fame. Celebrity waned, other than on the network of the gay world, as fast as it had come. But Denis personally, and *Gay News* as a paper, remained fixed in the recollection of the media as names which might be referred to and be recognised by a general, predominantly heterosexual, public. Cartoonists could use the title '*Gay News*' if they were drawing some joke about reactions to one of the more or less annual homosexual 'scandals' dear to the British media.

For the 1977 trial, and for all the press photography that went with it, Denis carefully wore suit and tie and had his hair cut in a socially conformist manner (in the early days of the paper, it had been shoulder length, and he wore the wildly colourful clothing of the 'alternative society'). All this was obedient to the recommendations counsel always make when a Briton is due to be prosecuted before a jury of 'equals', and it made a very good impression on a heterosexual public unused to knowing that a gay man can look 'like anyone else'.

Fame, however, had its dubious effect. There were those watching who thought that the admiration of well disposed heterosexuals had more impact on Denis than the admiration of fellow-homosexuals. He had known relative celebrity in the 'sub-culture' for five years, since *Gay News* made its appearance in the hands of gay readers, but the respect of non-gays on such a scale was quite new.

It was genuinely new. Respect for the achievement of a homosexual in the arts – Hockney, or Britten – is commonplace, but respect for a gay man or woman in full *propria persona* as, first and foremost, homosexual, is still almost unheard of, even though a Kate Millett can be admired for her concentration on herself as woman among other women, or a Martin Luther King for his concentration on himself as a black among other blacks.

People on the paper which had brought Denis to his celebrity, together with people active in the British gay movement, began to see Denis as dismissive of the constituency from which he came. They said he was adopting the values of 'straights'. If he was something of an ambassador out into the world of 'straights', then – in the disapproving language of the Foreign Office – he had 'gone native': he was putting the aspirations of 'straights' before those of the 'gay country' from which he came.

To his new reporter, Gill Hanscombe, he repeatedly explained that *Gay News* was assuredly *not* an 'alternative' or 'radical' paper and that it was not a part of the gay movement. It was, he insisted, 'a newspaper', pure and simple.

He arranged for Gay News Ltd to buy him a company car, a Rover for some £7000 and, by 1981, had changed it for a TR7 sports car. He was paid some £15,000 per year; nothing by the measure of a Fleet Street national newspaper, where a young reporter could soon expect as much, but some three times more than the least well paid members of staff – this on what was regarded as a semi-charitable 'community' newspaper. In addition, in his final full year on the paper, 1981, he charges, so at least Robert tells his staff in January 1982, £17,000 in expenses.

Admirers invited him to join a 'gentlemen-only' club of quite a different sort to those familiar in urban gay male life; The Reform A mansion near Buckingham Palace, by the same architect as the Houses of Parliament, it was once the headquarters of 'Whiggery', of the aristocrats who favoured the Reform Acts of the early nineteenth century.

By the 1970s, it had lost all associations with either aristocracy or reforming politics, but was instead a central London haven for the successful professional classes – for judges, for businessmen, for public relations and advertising people (Robert, too, joins The Reform in the early 1980s), for men wanting moments of elegance and civilisation as a break in the working day.

When Denis joins, it has just liberalised its rules enough to allow women guests of members a rather greater access to the premises, and is about to break tradition, and allow women membership itself – few apply. (The reasons are primarily economic: the club is having trouble covering its overheads).

All of this is far removed from the daring of *Gay News* when it began some ten years before; from the rebelliousness of many gay people; and from the kind of lives led by almost everyone else on staff.

It seems after 1977 that the obsessive and aggressive capacities which were needed when Denis forced the paper into successful existence have turned against the paper itself, and those who work on it.

The *monstre sacre* has become *monstre* pure and simple, the revolutionary is devouring his children. The hero of Toulon has become the emperor of the French. Excessive phrases? Yes – given the small arena of events – but by the end of 1981 he is seen by many as looming over the gays' best known paper, stifling it; and resisting all change with the assertion that it's *his* paper (a legal truth), and that everything from finances to policy-making is at his own discretion, and no business of anyone else on staff or off.

The latest news editor, Andrew, renewing an older acquaintance with Denis in 1980 (and well before either man has any thought of his joining the paper) is astounded by the extent of the hostility towards the *Gay News* editor that he finds both on the paper and in otherwise sane-seeming individuals in the gay movement.

Knowing Denis only in private life in 1980–81, he has found him a generous friend, with a very likeable live-in lover. Having known him at an earlier stage of his life as well, before *Gay News* started, Andrew is struck by how self-confident Denis has become in private life; and again in private life, by how open a formerly very reticent person has become.

He sees Denis at work cultivating a new contributor to the features side of the paper, and sees him also when preparing an article for press – and is not only admiring of how punctilious and careful Denis is, but moved by the respect with which a man who had little formal education (Denis left school at fifteen) regards both the standards which should be met by the paper, and the sensitivities of the writer.

Andrew is also, it is true, taken aback by the flashes of arrogance he sometimes hears Denis use in talking of well-known people on 'the gay scene', and somewhat surprised by the standard of life *Gay News* seems able to afford its editor–owner. But he can remember Denis as a poor twenty-five year-old, with few apparent prospects and knows well what an unlikely creation a national fortnightly homosexual newspaper seemed when Denis got to work on it in 1971.

There are other dissidents from the view of Denis as so much of a good thing as to have become a very bad thing. Some of them are in the art-room on the day Robert describes his pride in procuring the means for the editor's departure.

News reporter Chris Kirk feels depressed. Like others on staff he has known, in his year on the paper, what it is to get short shrift from Denis and the curt rejection of an idea; but he admires him nevertheless and likes working for him.

Advertising manager Sandy Murdoch has found him 'a bastard, but straight' (Sandy meant 'honest'). In fact Sandy, at this meeting, decides to go, and does indeed leave the paper shortly afterwards. He keeps the full extent of his opinions to himself, but he doesn't care for Robert whom he has experienced as marketing director.

Peter Burton, on the editorial side, has for years been a friend of Denis, and shares many of Denis's feelings about the shortcomings of people involved in the gay movement, besides having a temperamental horror of rows or confrontations, and an instinct to walk away from them while they're going on.

Scotty, above the fray by virtue of her years and her four-day working week, wishes that people could just get on together. She feels that it's only necessary to make up your mind what you will or won't stand for to bring Denis into line. But, then, in her own phrase when she wants to be uninvolved in the demands being made by others, 'at my time of life' she finds almost everyone on staff, including Denis, very young.

Having made his dramatic announcement that he has bought the paper, Robert takes questions. Now that the news is out, the excitement radiates from him, but he keeps very visibly containing it, trying not to say too much.

Partly it's that his sense of being inarticulate is warring with the pleasure of being a centre of attention at such a moment – the sentences about the service he hopes he has rendered by 'getting rid of Denis' are the most excitable of all, as he plainly feels he is capturing the hearts of most of his audience. (After the meeting some express doubts and suspicions, but only to each other.)

But the effort to contain his excitement has another cause. He can't, he repeatedly says, answer many of the questions immediately put to him, because the contract of sale won't be completed, and become legally binding, until February 22.

And if he disobeys Denis's injunctions to tell staff, and anyone else, the barest minimum, 'then Denis is quite capable of tearing up the arrangements, and coming back as owner and editor in full charge'.

Trust me, is the message. Or you will find yourselves groaning for eternity under 'Denis Lemon' – four syllables which by now have the power of an evil spell, of an anathema, evoking the equivalent of a hasty telling of rosaries and muttering of Hail Marys. If any one face typifies shock at the notion that Denis might reappear, after coming so close to permanent disappearance, it's the staff photographer's, Bob.

'I hate him', he has been saying in his customarily intemperate fashion – but then for months Denis has been telling people, and his words seep back, that some sackings are overdue at *Gay News*. And Bob Workman's is one of the names he most often mentions.

Bob looks white in the face at the idea of Denis returning. Nevertheless, he says, immediately, to Robert Palmer 'I wonder if this is the last time we shall be able to speak as friends?' Bob is one of the very few on the staff who is not naive about the effects on anyone – however seemingly benevolent – of the power which accrues to sole ownership. And he asks, straight out, of Robert, how much he has paid Denis for the paper. Robert regrets that he is unable to answer, saying that the terms of the deal must be kept secret. He intimates that this is Denis Lemon's dictum, rather than his own.

Under the strictest injunctions from Denis (Robert says, and there's no reason to doubt him) Robert asks that no member of staff confirm to outsiders that control of the paper is changing hands, until the February 22nd deadline is past.

The only publishable fact (and it goes into the issue just going to bed, as a late-minute news-flash) is that Denis has decided to retire as editor. It can be added and published that Andrew is to become *Gay News*'s editor in Denis Lemon's place.

This is unpopular with a number of members of staff, some of whom, such as Wendy, out of her political convictions, have long been committed to a desire for general staff participation in editing – an editorial collective – others of whom have long felt that if Denis were ever to go, Alison has the seniority and the outside reputation to be offered the editorship of *Gay News*.

'Is Andrew's appointment not open to discussion?' someone asks. 'Have we just got to accept it?'.

'Is Andrew's appointment as editor one of the secret terms you're not allowed to discuss?' asks someone else.

'No, it's not one of the conditions in the sale documents', answers Robert, 'but Denis has made it plain he wants Andrew as editor'.

He omits to mention (perhaps he is flustered, or feels he has given the simplest answer to the question) that he has himself, as incoming owner, invited Andrew to edit the paper.

As it happens, Andrew has quite frequently, in the last few months, found himself encouraging Robert to accept that on newspapers, or in offices, the occasional confrontation is unavoidable: 'Better to have the row at once, if there's one looming, than forever try to get round it.'

He has given the advice when Robert has been at odds with Denis over some policy, or feared being at odds with any member of staff.

At this key meeting for the future of the paper, he is shaken to find that Robert appears, by omission, to be trying to deflect sharp questioning of his choice of editor by stressing only that the unpopular Denis is in favour of it.

(That night Andrew describes the incident to a well known Fleet Street journalist, and she says: 'That man is going to be a disaster. He's going to be weak, and he'll try to leave you in the firing line'. Andrew replies: 'Oh, he'll learn. As owner he'll *have* to live with making himself unpopular'.)

The other editorial announcement is that Peter Burton is coming on to the staff full-time, with a responsibility for arts and entertainments coverage, in place of being a prolific freelance contributor.

This too is ill-received by some of those listening to Robert. Peter has had a long association with the paper, and was full-time on staff once before, but for years now has done all his work from home, in private consultation with Denis, and is regarded as having no first hand familiarity with the interior history and aims of the newspaper.

Robert has been on the paper for only a year, and has had comparatively little contact with the principal production and editorial operations, issue by issue.

Two flatly contradictory interpretations of what is now declared to be going on are floating in the atmosphere, though they aren't outspokenly defined or debated.

There is Denis's interpretation: so far as he is concerned, he has made sure that the paper will be under good management (Robert) and competent journalistic direction (Andrew) and be sure of the services of an expert on the gay entertainment area (Peter).

The fact that Peter and Andrew are friends of his is the guarantee that he knows what they are like, and that they will not take *Gay News* off into some inappropriate editorial departure.

The other interpretation, freely discussed among themselves in the days that follow, by those who share it, is that a clique of Denis's has been foisted on to *Gay News* by Denis so that even in the act of leaving he makes sure that his hand will rest on the paper's affairs and future for years to come. For some, it appears that he will go on 'ruling from the grave'. There is no possibility of challenge.

However, beaming at *Gay News* staff, Robert has talked in terms of 'getting rid of' Denis – and he adds that it will be his intention in course of time, whenever feasible, to offer shares in Gay News Ltd to members of staff. From the standpoint of those who have found so much in Denis to disapprove of, Robert is placing himself on the side of the angels.

Perhaps better the saint they don't particularly know, seems to be the overall consensus, than the devil they do, despite the fact that many are suspicious of Robert and wonder why it should be he. 'Why weren't *we* asked to buy the paper?' some mutter.

Later, upstairs in the news room, Andrew sits stiffly, with a rare look of anger on his face. When Gill asks him what the matter is, he replies tersely 'I am the only person here – the *only* person – who feels sad'. He means that only he feels no joy at Denis's departure. And yet Gill is by no means the only person on the staff who secretly wonders how Andrew, widely regarded as courteous and fair minded, can possibly be a friend of Denis Lemon.

PENNIES IN THE POUND

Robert has bought a business.

It is a single product publishing house, turning out the newspaper every fortnight, and nothing else; printing perhaps 1,500,000 words and 1,250 illustrations a year on the single topic of homosexuality. The British Museum, to which a copy must be sent free under statute law, keeps the entire output of the past nine and a half years in the North Library in Bloomsbury in the obscene section, despite the fact that the paper is freely sold on the streets.

Were *Gay News* a book publishing business, rather than publishing a newspaper, the annual output would equal some fifteen substantial and lavishly illustrated books. *Gay News* has no public funding; never had any start up grants, gets no subsidies from the many institutions which sometimes help 'minority' ventures (not even from the CIA); has no background Trust to pick up the bills should there be a loss; and does not, unless Robert turns out to be one, have a rich owner.

The printer's bill, office costs, the payroll, distribution costs, all must be paid for out of the money the paper earns.

Neither those who bring out a paper nor its readers, enjoy any jolting reminders that there are always lurking commercial urgencies. Indeed, everyone and everything conspires to provoke the illusion that an admirable newspaper will see to its money needs as if to its natural functions; discreetly, without drawing attention, hoping not to attract comment.

But there is a minority – as always on a newspaper's staff – which wants to be fully informed about the paper's finances. And, too, there are readers – particularly those who expect the paper to have a campaigning obligation – who see no good reason why the commercial structure, targets and performance should not be regularly publicised.

In its tenth year , *Gay News* is most reticent about these matters; most, most reticent. In Victorian terms, it would seem that while its subject matter of homosexuality is treated with a lack of sexual reticence, its treatment of money matters is positively prudish. About money, *Gay News* remains most definitely in the closet.

A lot of newspaper readers understandably suppose that the money they part with at the news-stall provides the paper's main source of income. It can be true of mass circulation popular dailies, but not of most papers, and not of *Gay News* in its tenth year.

Advertising provides the bulk.

There is display advertising, concentrated on the news and entertainment pages, running from a small 'box' to a whole page; and classified advertising, set aside on five special pages at the back of the paper.

The display ads are placed by businesses that want to promote their services and wares to homosexuals – gay clubs and pubs, gay travel agencies, gay hotels and boarding houses, and other consumer and even financial companies (a mortgage broker, Hometown, has recouped the cost of its advertising in *Gay News* many times over, through the response of readers).

Seventy-five per cent of the display advertising, perhaps as high as ninety per cent (no-one has ever done the exact statistics, or needed to, the broad position is so obvious) is placed by gay men in control of gay businesses, and aimed explicitly at the spending power of gay men, rather than that of gay women or of gay men and women together.

The classified advertising includes a commercial section where, in a few lines, gays offer consumer services ranging from house-conversion to massage, but the greater part of it is 'Men's Personals'. Issue 235 will carry 170 of them, from all round the country: 'Asian thirty invites correspondence with young guy over twenty-one interested in accompanying him on vacation this June/July to his holiday home in Florida, all expenses paid . . .'. There will even be a men's personal completely in Welsh.

There'll be 'Women's Personals' too, but only ten of them: 'Chelsea. Gay lady thirty-eight quiet homely type seeks same for sincere loving relationship aged twenty to forty. Photo please . . .'. And 'Mixed Personals': 'London. British gay man seeks American lady for mutual friendship and possible marriage . . .'.

The incoming responses, the 'box replies', will be sorted and forwarded to classified advertisers by Mike – a tedious job, unless you have a fancy for that sort of monotony, and a dead-end one which nevertheless must be conscientiously done; hell having no fury like a 'personals' classified advertiser who gets someone else's answers.

As in display, so in classifieds, the greater part of the revenue by far is from gay men rather than gay women. Yet, as it happens, with a woman soon to be appointed display advertising manager in succession to Sandy Murdoch, and with Amanda already handling applications for classifieds, this highest revenue-earning sector of the paper is to be supervised by gay women as 1982 gets under way.

Robert, still marketing and business director in addition to owner, of course controls policy.

The rest of Gay News Ltd's income is from net newspaper sales or the purchase price of copies of the paper less between fifty and sixty per cent taken by the distributors; from subscriptions (renewals and new ones); and from mail-order. (Every spare inch, and many which shouldn't be to spare, of the West Kensington premises seem to be stacked with the books, bought wholesale and sold for a profit through the pages of the paper itself. American gay fiction for men provides most of the income.)

Incoming money, which can be cheques, postal orders, international money orders, cash, or postage stamps, is extracted from each day's post by one or other of the Peters from accounts, logged, and either placed in the safe or banked.

Total income to Gay News Ltd from its single product, the newspaper, is about £20,000 per issue this February of 1982, or some £40,000 a month. On an annual basis, this newspaper by homosexuals for homosexuals is a half-million pound turn-over business (roughly $1 million), which, had they known it, would be a great surprise to most readers who haven't forgotten its shoe-string days.

The income doesn't by any means all come at once with each issue. Classified, mail-order and subscription income all arrive in advance of the service required; display advertising is mostly paid in arrears of up to three months; net income from the cover price can take up to six months, depending on how rapidly the distributors close their accounts on each issue, which can go on selling for weeks and even months, before 'returns' (unsold copies) come back to the office.

Here, for those who like bare facts, are the five revenues of the paper during the February, 1982, fortnight in which issue 235 is being prepared for press:

Last fortnight of February 1982

Advertising income	£10,000	53% of total
(of which, Display	£6,500	33% of total)
(of which, Classified	£4,000	20% of total)
Net newspaper sale income	£4,000	20% of total
Subscription income	£3,800	19% of total
Mail Order income	£1,500	8% of total
TOTAL	£20,000	100%

(Figures averaged, and rounded up)

All very impressive. However, *Gay News* is making a loss – the £20,000 or so that flows in during that production fortnight in the midst of which Robert announces he has bought the paper is some £700 too little to cover expenses.

Not a frightening deficit, but it is adding its mite to what will turn out, when a full year's accounts are made up to the end of March 1982, to be an accumulated loss over twelve months of some £17,000.

In the language of Mr Micawber, *Gay News* is spending 3p more than every £1 it earns. It is the third loss-making year in succession. The paper spent 1½p more than every £1 it earned in twelve months ended March 1980, and 4½p in the £1 more in twelve months ended April 3, 1981.

Things could be said to be improving (3p over-spending in the £1 these days against 4½p the year before) but the aggregate loss for three years from April 1, 1979, to the end of this March, 1982, is going to be some £40,000. The last year in which the paper made a profit was 1978–79, when it made just over £14,000 – on the right side of Mr Micawber's ledger, it spent 6p less than every £1 earned.

The record makes clear why by the end of 1980 Denis thought he needed a business manager, and brought in Robert in January 1981. The reduction in the deficit from 4½p in the £1 to 3p in the £1 in the first full twelve month financial year since Robert's arrival suggests some benefit from his management.

But the fact of the matter is, *Gay News* at the moment of sale is making a loss for the fifth month in succession, without a single intervening profitable one to help out.

The ways in which money is spent are far more complicated and various than the ways in which it is earned. Simplified, here is the spending as the paper changes hands:

Last fortnight of February 1982

Wages	£7,250	35% of total
Printer	£3,250	15% of total
Production & distribution	£1,250	6% of total
Postage	£1,250	6% of total
Mail order	£850	4% of total
Phones, electricity	£380	2% of total
Rates	£150	1% of total
Other	£6,300	31% of total
TOTAL	£20,680	100%

(Figures averaged, and rounded up)

By any ordinary standards (and particularly by the lax standards of most newspapers or magazines) there isn't much extravagance here. Wages haven't been raised for a year and range from £12,000 a year each to Robert and Andrew, at the top of the scale, to £5,500 at the bottom of the scale – eg for Mike doing reception and 'box-replies'.

The top wage, to the new owner and the new editor, may well be unique in the gay publishing world in Europe, with the possible exceptions of the editor–owner of *Spartacus,* an international gay guide, and Alex McKenna, publisher in London of a range of gay magazines for men only with titles such as *Mister* and *Zipper*; and in America would only be exceeded at *The Advocate,* and on the leading American gay magazines for men-only. However, they are not high by conventional commercial standards.

There are gay businesses in the UK, providing non-publishing services to gay men or gay men and women, where higher salaries, or salaries/profits, than £12,000 a year are certainly made. Against the yardstick of conventional newspaper publishing, the £12,000 a year now being paid to Andrew as editor of a national fortnightly selling 19,000 copies is very low. The gardening correspondent of a popular daily, *The Star,* makes – so a newspaper story happens to mention at this time – the same. And Andrew doubles up as news-editor.

'Fringe benefits' at the top, following the departure of Denis, are slight. Robert is using the £7,000 TR7 company car bought for Denis, pending its sale; and Andrew, who hasn't asked for a company car or been offered one, is using the company Metro allotted by Denis to Robert, until the day comes when Robert has disposed of the TR7 and will again want the use of the Metro.

Expense accounts, other than an allowance made to Peter Burton for taxis and drinks in his coverage of the London clubs, are negligible by the standards of experienced journalists. Peter and Alison, respectively with homes fifty miles out of London in Brighton and Cambridge, get two rail-fares a week refunded by long custom. When Inland Revenue queries the travel allowance their salaries are raised accordingly from £9,000 to £10,000 pa – again nothing out of the way by external standards for their expertise. Peter Coell as head of accounts also gets about £10,000 pa when his long hours of over-time on computerising are added in.

If the findings of the Survey of *Gay News* readers undertaken early in 1981 are to be trusted, about a third of the paper's readership earns more, at £13,000 plus, than anyone on the staff, including the new owner.

There isn't much fat to be cut, even from the most obvious place, the payroll, if it should be decided that economies are the route to balancing the books for the first time since 1978; unless it just takes the shape of a reduction in people's earnings.

There are some who have felt, from the moment it was announced on January 14, 1982, that Robert's invitation to Peter Burton to come on staff full-time is an extravagance, and will at the least make it difficult to obtain a pay-rise this spring.

But even if this is so, the tradition of the paper would make it extremely difficult in practice (as opposed to on paper) to decide to save money by a drop in the numbers employed. It isn't only that gay men and women who as individuals have been through so much to be 'out' and working on a gay paper would be appalled – in a time of still-rising UK unemployment – by the task of deciding who is to go.

More than that, it has been the aim for years to make the newspaper as self-sufficient as possible, short of owning its own printing presses and distribution network. A perceptible reduction in numbers employed would apparently mean scrapping one or another of the 'in-house' activities: typesetting, lay-out, space-selling, news-gathering.

If the total wages-bill were to be cut, but everyone involved stay on in employment, then £7,000 a year each to everyone would wipe out the deficit at its levels of the year ending this March.

This would be best, of course, for the lowest-paid on the staff, who receive less than £6,000 per year. It is becoming obvious that in the London of 1982, £7,000 per year is about the minimum that anyone can hope to get by on without having to live with permanent money trouble. Gill and Wendy, both earning under £8,000, are finding it hard to support their children and themselves. Yet Andrew, Alison and Glen, among the highest-paid, believe that they would eventually have to sell their homes if they had to take £7,000 in salary.

Gay News is a small business, never employing more than twenty-three people. Yet there are nearly as many different salary levels as there are employees and neither the nature of the differentials nor their amounts are seriously questioned by the staff as a whole. Everyone works long hours under grotesque conditions and everyone's work is essential to the style and standard of the paper as it is conceived and produced. Yet some are paid twice as much as others; some may draw overtime and others not; some – Alison and Jo, for example, whose departments are run single-handed – may never take more than one week's holiday at a time without seeming to cause disruption. *Gay News*'s closetry about money is infectious, since, internally, the staff themselves feel guilty and selfish if they wish their livelihoods to be openly and objectively discussed. Wendy suggests rationalisation and refrains from going privately to Robert and plead her individual case, but not all follow her example. 'Adjustments' for some are made upwards.

The staff do not agree to £7,000 for everyone. Yet any accountant might suggest that the business is either plainly over-staffed or is plainly paying too high a wages bill – unless, from the work they are paid to do, the staff can generate more revenue fairly soon. The women propose – and go on proposing – that new revenue could be solicited from women's advertising. Robert does not take up the suggestion. Andrew proposes – and goes on proposing – that a promotion drive, particularly in women's venues where no serious effort has been made to sell *Gay News*, can be efficiently planned with the aid of posters. Robert does not take up the suggestion.

In the early months of 1982, as Robert takes over his new responsibility as owner, he says explicitly that there must be a careful watch on spending and – when talk gets round to pay-rise discussions set for April – says not to expect too much.

In the event, a modest pay-rise does occur in April 1982. Six successive months of trading losses – a cumulative £29,000 – turn into a trading profit in that month of £2,700. This, seemingly, gives Robert the confidence to approve the rise. Some members of staff do not press claims which might well have been justified, including Jo who – a year later – confesses that she had found it hard going to survive on her £6,750 but who thought the younger lower-paid people should come first. The two parents – Wendy and Gill – also hold back and it is Wendy who suggests the rise which Robert agrees: a flat £500 per year increase for everyone except Andrew and Robert. This is the first attempt to try to reduce the existing differentials.

Robert's manner belies any anxiety. He is bustlingly cheerful, which is a relief to many, after the gloom and general awfulness they associated with late-period Denis. Robert's air of energetic optimism runs counter to any notion that severe stringencies might be on the way, or should be on the way.

Anyway, he is seen to be spending money. Already, to ease the congestion in the office, he has rented a vacant private house next door, pending its sale. And he takes on a personal adviser – at some £300 per month – called Brian Homan, who is rarely seen and generally presumed to be 'straight', but who is a distribution expert.

Other than the two Peters in accounts, people on the staff are unused to having any information about the newspaper as a business, and completely unused to sharing in setting financial policy. Denis didn't permit it, other than to the directors of the holding company, Gay News Ltd, on the dual grounds of a right to be secret and a need to be secret. The right of secrecy was his as controlling shareholder; the need alleged was the conventional one of commercial secrecy, lest the competition – not that *Gay News* had much competition – be able to take advantage of what Denis invariably called 'the leaky sieve' of *Gay News*.

An uninformed staff, but equally an ineffectual board of directors. Art-room's JC, a director of the holding company for years, considered himself 'a rubber stamp', neither learning to comprehend all the financial workings of the newspaper nor having any real say, he felt, in decisions arrived at.

A mood of good fellowship, and of an end to all that, has swept through financial control in the wake of Robert buying the paper. He widens the board of directors taking onto it in addition to himself, Peter Coell, JC, and Andrew, five extra members of staff: the two features editors (Peter Burton and Alison), Jo, Wendy, and Amanda.

The theory is that each working department should have representation, plus some *ex officio* directors, such as Andrew as editor. Directors are asked to preserve commercial secrecy, but are welcome, inside the monthly meetings, to raise any matter they like.

So cramped are the offices that the early meetings of this democratised and enlarged board are held in the sitting room of JC's flat a few streets away, giving them a remarkable resemblance to the kind of meetings in sitting rooms which had occurred incessantly, years before, when *Gay News* was only being planned, and had not yet been published.

Democracy, answerability, a running debate on the commercial objectives and 'personality' of the paper – at last, after the dead years, they have arrived at, or returned to, *Gay News*. Or have they?

Jo becomes distressed, feeling she doesn't understand what's going on; Wendy feels that this form of participation in the 'secrets' of management is a mistake, when her political principles commit her to wholly 'collective' decision taking, without 'hierarchies'; JC continues to find it tiresome; everyone feels that they can't really attend to business in directors' meetings which on every occasion interrupt work urgently needing to be done on producing the newspaper itself.

It is perhaps democracy in one of its inefficient forms after all, so inefficient as to be upsetting – participation, so long dreamt of by those who found the previous owner–editorship so dictatorial, turning out to be a bubble and an illusion.

Peter Burton looks very bored with it all. The one person on the staff who would be positively delighted to take part and be as fully informed as she can manage on financial, as on other affairs, is Gill Hanscombe. But since Andrew is news editor as well as editor, the news room is regarded as having no need for separate representation on the board; so neither she (nor Chris) is invited.

No-one receives a fee to be a director; no-one feels impelled to study company law and discover what the powers or obligations of a company director might be. Between the annoyance of the mid-day timing of meetings, the inefficiency of the proceedings, so many not knowing quite what they're expected to do, and the sense of unreality that many have in the face of the very title 'director of Gay News Ltd', the new broadly-based board of directors is soon felt to be a sham.

A sham because a shambles? Something that can be rectified as systems and people sort themselves out in an unfamiliar climate of open management? Or a shambles because a sham?

Or perhaps a sham for less reputable reasons? Perhaps people can't shake off the psychological comforts of being permanently adversarial, of hating and blaming 'management'; and so can't endure the reality of being asked to consider alternatives and put themselves personally on the line with a decision.

Gill is one onlooker (kept off the board as she is) who sees, indeed, some signs at *Gay News* of an 'English disease' of workforce passivity, of a dependence on being led, and then crossly blaming all ills on the leader. With her Australian background, she is particularly startled by how resigned to almost anything the gay men seem to be.

She is astonished by how quickly people are mollified and give up, when even for a moment they looked like creating a fuss.

Which leads to the second possibility, that the new freedoms of information and policy participation enshrined in the 'representative' board of directors disguise, with rapidly decreasing persuasiveness, ownership aims no less secretive than they had been under Denis.

It's all very well for Robert to hold a 'teach-in' for the entire staff on the company 'cash-flow' (revenues and outgoings), as he does at an away-weekend in Gloucestershire, on January 29–31. So far, so good – so very much better, to be sure, than for years. But February 22, 1982, and the completion of the transfer of shares in Gay News Ltd from Denis to Robert, goes by without information about how much Robert has paid; what obligations he or *Gay News* has taken on; what necessities are felt by Robert; or what personal ambitions.

There is enough light to induce a consensus that the worst of the secretiveness about Gay News Ltd is over; enough shadow to make it compulsory that staff and readers and that loose network 'the gay community', take it on trust that Robert will be a wiser owner than Denis had become, and that he has made wise arrangements for the newspaper as a business.

If it had been hoped that the reticence asked of staff between January 14 to February 22 – while the deal was not yet legally complete and staff were threatened with a change of mind by Denis – would be followed by complete disclosure of the terms on which the paper has changed hands, the hope is dashed.

Robert can't, he says, spell out to those who produce *Gay News* (let alone to readers in the columns of the paper) the contents of the documents of sale. He is absolutely bound by conditions of continuing secrecy exacted by Denis.

He will be bound by these conditions of confidentiality for years to come. He can't disclose the price for the shares, but it is to be met – this he can reveal – over some five years. He will not be allowed to dispose of shares to staff or anyone else over that period but would certainly then hope to bring individual members of staff, or staff as a whole, or interested members of the 'gay community', into a share of ownership.

A 1,500 word article about Robert has been sketched in for an issue not yet in production : No 236, due out in mid-March. It will say with his approval:

'He isn't a rich man. The price he's paid for Denis's shares hasn't been made public, but he's borrowed in order to do it. He plans that, in time, when the financing burden eases, a share–ownership scheme for employees should be devised so that ultimately ownership may well be vested solely in those who bring out the paper.'

Robert poses for a photograph by staff photographer Bob. In suit and tie he stands by one of the canals near his home in Little Venice, looking responsible and serious. For inset in the article there's also to be a laughing head and shoulders snap of his lover Alan Clark.

Despite Robert's outright statement that he isn't rich, Bob is one of many, not seeing how else it could be done, who suppose that Robert must be very well-off to have bought *Gay News*, whatever the terms of payment.

BIG MONEY

Two floors up a rambling old building in Mount Pleasant in the commercial district of the City of London, the small staff of London's free newspaper for homosexuals, *Capital Gay*, are working frantically to get another issue ready for press.

A twelve page weekly distributed only in the London area and South of England, and the sole alternative newspaper to *Gay News* in this part of the country, *Capital Gay* is still, in February 1982, fighting for its financial life.

Printing 6,000 copies, launched in June 1981, it was priced at 20p but by Christmas was foundering. Too few were buying it, too little advertising was coming in.

In a desperate decision, owners Michael Mason and Graham McKerrow have taken the price off and are trying, by proving that thousands of gays happily pick it up and read it in the gay clubs and pubs when it costs them nothing, to show advertisers that it's worth their while to place ads.

A commonplace of the smaller end of newspaper publishing for many years now, the 'free paper' method has never been applied to newspaper or periodical publishing for gays in the UK. Things are still perilous, but it looks as if the risk will come off.

The *Capital Gay* staff have the closest possible associations with the 'big brother' *Gay News*. It makes it hard for either of the two working journalists, Michael and Graham, to do properly impartial news stories on the other paper if something is up.

Just now they have to work out what to put into *Capital Gay* about the sale of *Gay News* to Robert. The problem isn't that they have to restrain themselves from being unpleasant about the competition, or stirring it up; the impediment is the feeling of friendship, and a helpless instinct to refrain from criticism.

They neither of them have a good opinion of Denis, and are delighted that he's going. Yet they've no wish to use their own paper to publicise knowledge they acquired as insiders, either working for *Gay News*, or close to its inner goings-on. They are in a common state for journalists: they have information given in confidence and 'embargoed' and some information which would risk libel action.

Michael, for example. The thirty-five year old son of a publisher, he news-edited *Gay News* between 1974–80 and was a director of the holding company Gay News Ltd between 1973–80. Other than Denis and Alison, he was the best-known personality to emerge on the paper, and spent the most impressionable years of his life on it.

He left in 1980, relations with Denis strained beyond endurance, but came back for a few months – only, he explicitly said, to help the paper – when *Gay News* was in danger, after the firing of Harry Coen, of having an empty news-room. During this time, over lunches with Graham, when the two discussed the lead-time and outside London limitations on the news section, they 'invented' the ideal gay newspaper. Later in March 1981, the idea began to take on a life of its own and they decided to investigate the possibilities of turning the idea into reality: *Capital Gay*.

If he was to work in news journalism for homosexuals in the UK without working on *Gay News*, Michael had no option but to found a paper of his own. The only other publications, other than local ones in Manchester and one or two other localities, were the men-only monthly magazines such as *Him* and *Zipper* with their lack of interest in 'serious' coverage.

Co-opted to help Michael and twenty-six year old Graham are two more with *Gay News* connections of one sort or another – David, lover of the self-same Harry Coen who was at the centre of the sacking row of 1980, and himself an ex-*Gay News* worker; and Eric Presland, entertainer on the British gay club, pub, and conference circuit, who wrote and performed the song accusing Denis of having abandoned all belief in the causes still fought for by homosexuals.

Seasoned in the politics and inner friendships and feudings of the 'gay movement' in Britain – even their love lives would help to plot a graph of who, over the years, has contrived to land in the news – they say that when called on to write a news story about *Gay*

News 'it's like having your face pressed up against a plate-glass window'.

They give a front page 'splash' to the sale of *Gay News*. They have more inside knowledge of the terms and size of the deal between Denis and Robert than anyone else since friends of Denis and Robert have 'leaked'. Michael has also had the advantage both of costing and running a paper – *Capital Gay* – and of having been a director of Gay News Ltd between 1973-80. He can make a stab at putting a price into *Capital Gay's* headline.

This February 1982 he speculates that Denis has sold out from *Gay News* for about £100,000.

In fact the figure is £121,000 – down from some £200,000 (Robert is later to say) initially demanded by Denis as his price for relinquishing control of the newspaper.

It's scarcely surprising that Denis should want to keep such a sum as £121,000 (let alone the higher one) unconfirmed and therefore as little publicised as possible, until it has one day become too historic to upset anyone.

Readers who had spent £5 or £10, or more, to help both himself and the newspaper when it was threatened with financial extinction during the 'Blasphemous Libel' trial of only five years before (1977) would for the most part be shocked to think that such private wealth could be or was going to be, extracted from *Gay News*.

So scanty has been the financial information published inside the paper or anywhere else that there are many who suppose that the newspaper is non-profit-making by design, in the manner of a charitable trust, or that it's collectively owned by staff; or that in view of the public appeals for money only five years before, it is inherently incapable of declaring profits for any private shareholder; in which latter case it would be of no practical consequence who happened to be nominated as the shareholder or shareholders.

At times over the nine and a half years since the first issue in June 1972 (and throughout all the months before then, when people were trying to get the newspaper launched), *Gay News* has happily accepted the services of 'voluntary' workers – homosexuals who, in admiration for the paper, came into the offices to give hours of their work free.

There is still one at work every fortnight at *Gay News*: John

Wilmott, the enormously tall (6ft 7in) retired man with a shock of white hair and leg trouble who prepares the copies of *Gay News* that go out to overseas subscribers.

Freelance workers (writers or illustrators or cartoonists) have taken low rates on the understanding that this is a brave newspaper which should not be dunned for the sort of money obtainable in the usual 'straight' world of newspaper and magazine publishing.

For the most part the staff are unionised. Editorial staff belong to the National Union of Journalists (NUJ) and production staff to the National Graphical Association (NGA). Administration staff are in the process of joining the Association of Scientific, Technical and Managerial Staff (ASTMS), but by the summer, the NUJ recommends – after enquiries were made to them – that administration staff would do better to join the Society of Graphic and Administrative Trades (SOGAT).

Despite unionisation, staff have never regarded *Gay News* as the sort of paper against which strike action, or a go-slow, or wages-and-conditions bargaining in the full industrial sense, would be an appropriate reaction, even when the actions of the owner-editor-manager might more than justify taking such decisions.

Long-term readers regard *Gay News* as 'their' newspaper; staff regard *Gay News* as a 'community paper'; the gay population of the country, whether approving of *Gay News* or not, regards it as a remarkable achievement against odds only fully perceptible to homosexuals themselves; the 'gay movement' considers it an institution, like CHE, or London Gay Switchboard; those who run newspapers for homosexuals in other countries round the world think it as one of the finest three or four such papers in existence.

Very few would be pleased to learn that one man, however long he had worked and however great his contribution, had managed to dispose of it for what, to most, would be an unimaginable sum.

The discretion of the departing owner does indeed seem to be the better part of cautious good sense, if he is to avoid vilification in the minds and hearts of many who had thought him the complete hero. If it is true that Denis has become much concerned with respectability, now that he is rising thirty-five, then the less comment, and the fewer publicly raised eyebrows, the better.

Asked on the phone by *Capital Gay* whether he will confirm or deny that he has sold *Gay News* for 'around £100,000', Denis says the matter is a private one, and of no concern to anyone other than himself and the purchaser Robert.

Of course, distaste for the idea that such a newspaper as *Gay News* could be made the vehicle for the creation of £121,000 of private wealth might be regarded as merely envious – a sectarian 'Socialist' reaction, showing a knee-jerk antagonism to success on its conventional measurement of money-making.

This would not be full description of the reasons for dismay that many homosexuals would feel in early 1982 if they were provided with the full facts, but there are wealthy gay men among the readers of the newspaper, and thousands who undoubtedly voted for Mrs Thatcher's Conservative Party in 1979, and are to vote again for it in 1983, who would feel no great unease that Denis had done well.

They might be taken aback, having shared the widespread assumption that *Gay News* wasn't founded on ordinary lines of private enterprise. But after the initial surprise, they might confine themselves to enquiring whether he asked, and whether Robert paid, a fair price. The entrepreneur, they might say, is worthy of his reward.

In a newspaper conducted for free enterprise purposes, a share-holding properly acquired is property. The owner of such a form of property is as entitled by law to dispose of it where he wills, and for as much as he can get, as any reader of the paper, or individual on staff, is to dispose of property in the form of a flat or house or inheritance.

The first question such a mildly surprised, but by no means automatically antagonistic, *Gay News* reader might ask at this moment of transfer in ownership of the paper (if anyone would answer questions) would accordingly be: how did Denis come by the shares he has now privately sold, if nearly everyone off staff supposed the paper either to be 'collectively' owned by those who work on it, or in some sense held in trust?

The answer is a source of deep unease to those who have been longest on the paper and some, such as Michael, who have left it. They have only themselves to blame, they sometimes think, for the monopoly control over *Gay News* that Denis built up. He came by his shareholding legally, and with the consent, over the years, of the leading personalities in the newspaper.

When the newspaper was first conceived, in the winter of 1971/72, at the high tide of that era's gay liberation movements, it was announced – and was stated in the Editorial of the first issue in June 1972 – that the paper would be collectively run. Further, pre-launch advertising stated 'This is a non commercial venture.'

From this moment came the presumption, handed down intact (for many readers) to February 1982, that the paper had never ceased to be a 'collective', and that its finances were under group control, and would never yield any further profit to those who took part in producing the paper than payment of their wages.

A limited liability company had been formed on April 19, 1972 with the intention of compelling (through the requirements of Company Law) proper auditing, and of providing the necessary trading vehicle. It had 100 shares, which were almost entirely left unissued. Thoughts of private profit were in no-one's mind.

In practice the paper ceased to be a 'collective' (no workers excluded from policy decisions) within months of publication. In August 1972, exasperated beyond endurance by what he saw as the inefficiency of the 'collective', Denis withdrew from the paper, and said he'd only return if given the title and final say-so of an editor.

Few believed, and they may well have been right, that the newspaper would survive without the energy of the young man who had been embroiled in it from the very start, earlier than anyone else on the 'collective'. The title and authority were conceded, he was asked back. *Gay News* began its shaky climb up to the relative security of a net fortnightly sale of some 15,000 copies (eventually, 19,000).

There were some at the time who denounced the rapid compromise with the ideals of 'collectivism'. A handful of highly informed people doubted whether Denis had ever understood the notion of collective working and therefore felt that there was a vicious circle, by which Denis's incomprehension made the 'collective' inefficient.

Some looked to the example of Britain's most successful women's liberation periodical, *Spare Rib*, *Gay News'* almost exact contemporary, where no single editor had been allowed to emerge, and claimed that the women's paper showed how good a 'collective' and its product could be. And also to *Gay News*' contemporary in Toronto, *Body Politic*, which homosexuals seemed capable of running without electing, as it were, one leader.

But there it was. Denis had made editorship and the attached authority his price for giving his best to the newspaper, and the price had been conceded. 'Collective' policy formulation had been eroded to that degree, but 'collective' ownership effectively continued, and Denis was not yet owner as well as editor *de jure*.

There was no reason for self-reproach by anyone as yet, unless their 'sexual politics', or other politics, told them that a man should not have the unique say-so over a paper designed for both men and women: or told them, too, that an editorial 'collective' isn't only a variant way of running an enterprise, but the proper way to do it, an essential ingredient in the project of creating a national newspaper by gays for gays.

The paper was popular. More homosexuals were soon buying it than had ever bought a British publication for gays before. The 'political' mood around the western world had drawn back from the extremes of the zestful anarchy of the early 1970s – in the homosexual 'movement' as much as in any other. Consolidation and defence of libertarian achievement was beginning to be the catchword of most in Britain, as in America and elsewhere.

A little compromise (authority vested in one person; in the case of *Gay News*, in Denis) might have seemed not to be so very retrograde, given that even the most anti-authoritarian of recent Western movements – Black Power, Women's Liberation, Consumerism, Nuclear Disarmament – had encountered serious problems of aimlessness and divisiveness when individuals felt crushed or rendered incompetent by the 'endless' discussion of every option. A so-called 'tyranny of structurelessness' had been much discussed by those people who had most enthusiastically exposed themselves to prohibitions on 'leadership'.

Denis had become a fact of life. There at *Gay News*, seemingly immovable. Paid little, like everyone else. Turning out a newspaper on the dot, every fortnight (except at Christmas time, when everyone on staff took a two-week break).

And then in 1973 the finances failed to work. The paper had always been a breadline operation, the budget a moveable wake, but the paper had staggered by.

Now its own pages told readers that the situation was a frightening one. Closure was really a possibility: contributions, please, donations, please, money of all and every kind, please:

A solicitor by the name of Richard Creed stepped forward: if you'll let me have shares in Gay News Ltd, said he, I'll help out. The overt principle of ownership by an individual or individuals now came before staff, a year after the demand for the principle of editorship by an individual.

The lawyer Creed was allotted shares at a *Gay News* board meeting on July 23, 1973 and appointed a director with effect from March 30, 1974. He said he would lend £3,150 to solve the cash crisis if he could have forty-nine shares out of Gay News Ltd's share capital of 100 shares (forty-nine per cent of the equity). This was not control, outright control, as fifty-one per cent would have been, but unless some person or a group of persons were allotted at least as much (forty-nine per cent), Creed would be effective outright owner as holder of the largest single block of shares.

Michael Mason recalls that when he joined the paper in December 1972, he was told that a number of people had single-share holdings and that after a year or so he would similarly qualify for a single-share holding. He doesn't know if others were given the same promise on appointment. When he mentioned this he was told that the shares were simply being 'locked-up' to protect Richard's interests while his loan remained outstanding, with the implication – Michael suggests – that staff would qualify for single shares again after repayment of the loan.

A fifty-one per cent shareholding in Gay News Ltd (fifty-one shares) could have been allotted to the staff as a whole, to be held, perhaps through a staff company. (A complicated system of this sort was evolved, some years later, for the French homosexual paper *Gai Pied*.) Or such a holding, or any holding down to forty-nine per cent, could have been placed into some variety of trust.

Another route was followed, and certainly the simplest of the ones available. Denis was allotted forty-nine shares (forty-nine per cent of the equity) as a counterweight to the forty-nine shares allowed to Richard Creed. This seemed a very proper and unfussy means by which the 'conscience' of the newspaper, voiced through its staff and its editor, could always stall any inappropriate initiatives, should he suggest them, by Richard Creed.

There was a precaution. Denis was not established as personal co-owner of the company with freedom to do anything he pleased with his shareholding: he was allowed to have thirteen shares personally (thirteen per cent of the equity), but was to hold the remaining thirty-three shares (thirty-three per cent) only so long as he remained an employee of Gay News Ltd. Should he depart, or wish to sell to anyone else, he would be unable to make anyone into a stock-holder on the same scale.

He had already, in 1972, been issued with three shares in Gay News Ltd, making his personally disposable stake in the newspaper sixteen shares (sixteen per cent). And so long as he remained on staff, he voted these plus the conditional thirty-three shares (a forty-nine per cent vote in all).

The fact of the matter now, two years after the formation of *Gay News* with an intention of collective policy-making and collective financial control, was that if two men chose to vote together, there was no-one to gainsay them in law. But if they differed from one another, Jean-Claude in the art-room, who was issued with one share precisely (one per cent), would in theory have a casting vote – and might exercise it in conformity with the views of the rest of the staff, though only to opt for one or other of policies advocated by Denis or Richard Creed. He would not be able to initiate policy himself.

Necessity being a hard task-master, this abrogation of the old hopes that those who brought out the paper would be the best-fitted to supervise all aspects of its policy, financial and editorial, was perhaps not too dreadful. A pity, like the deterioration of any dream, but far preferable, that 1973, to bankruptcy of the paper and an end to publication.

Necessity also making strange bedfellows, Richard Creed was an unexpected addition to the newspaper (he remained in practice as a solicitor, but took on the running of the finances). A conservative sort of man with a middle-class career, untutored in the political debates of homosexuals, though himself homosexual, the best that could be hoped was that he would bring 'sound money' to *Gay News*.

He set to work energetically, his investment saved the paper, and by 1977-78 it was modestly profitable, making £8,821. The following year, 1978-79, before the three year run of losses, it made just over £14,000. The 'blasphemous libel' trial had come and gone with all its attendant publicity and given the difficulty most British periodicals experience in keeping out of the red, the combination of Denis as editor and Richard Creed as financial controller would seem to have turned out a credit to both and to everyone else at *Gay News* even though they had abandoned wished for, not to mention declared, principles and allowed it to happen.

Then came shame.

Anyone might have thought that the next development in the affairs of *Gay News* as a commercial undertaking would so have destroyed the 1974-78 experiment with large private share-holdings that the paper would have closed on the spot rather than have perpetuated it.

Instead, the wheels began to turn by which two substantial holdings were merged into one; and so far from the base of *Gay News*'s ownership and answerability being widened, it contracted into the hands of one. Denis became lawful sole owner of every-thing, free, as later emerged, to dispose of the newpaper as he willed.

Open government was not a feature of *Gay News*' affairs under the allied management of Denis and Richard Creed. By 1978 the board comprised the two major shareholders, plus Michael Mason, news editor, and Jean-Claude, art-room. But neither of the last two felt that his views were of much use or interest.

On the contrary, they felt initiative was discouraged: that *Gay News* as controlled six years after its foundation was a timorous small business of the kind which since the 1960s had been most rebuked at management schools, most harangued by government departments calling for efficiency and growth.

It was under-capitalised, because no-one else was encouraged to come in. It suffered from lack of investment or re-investment – very poor office equipment, or simply too little of it, and continuingly cramped and unappetising working conditions. (*Gai Pied*, across the Channel, took only three years to move to spacious premises high on the Parisian roofline.)

It undertook no diversifications, unless mail-order sales are to be counted as such, but remained a single-product enterprise in one of the most notoriously insecure British industries, publishing. Yet Michael, for one, pressed for paperback, or calendar, or greetings card, ventures – all of which were scarcely provided for homosexuals in the UK in the 1970s by anyone except through American imports. No action was taken.

In short, it gave every appearance, to the handful of men and women in close touch with its affairs, of being the most anathematised of small businesses in any economy – the 'peasant company', run in a mood of fear that its workings will be understood or its purposes criticised. Run, in the end, for the convenience of shareholders of a timid vision, who can't be dislodged and won't open themselves to advice from those over whom they have the power of an employer.

Such businesses have a strange way of going on forever. Perhaps their very refusal to seek extra advice or capital, their reliance on one proven product, the state of catatonic hypnosis to which they reduce any workforce which will stay with them, saves them from all the potential disasters of initiative and expansion.

The controlling shareholders of Gay News Ltd were not quite so fortunate. Late in 1978 they came unstuck. They were detected in practices which Richard Creed, very possibly accurately, was to call very common in small businesses; but which resulted nonetheless in his departure from Gay News Ltd.

Money sent into the newspaper, by readers, to take out a classified ad, or to order a book from mail-order, seemed not to be as much as it should be. Arrangements for handling incoming uncrossed cheques or postal orders or plain cash had always been a worry to auditors, but only because the book-keeping by a small and hard-pressed staff could be erratic, not because of any suggestion of 'improprieties'.

Michael was approached by some staff members – and by Peter Coell as a director – with information that improprieties were occurring. In the best traditions of investigative journalism, Michael sent *Gay News* three uncrossed postal orders under pseudonyms, to see what would happen to them. He asked the Post Office to 'trace' one of them. The Post Office replied that they had not been encashed (it was only by the following spring that it was learnt that they had been: that's how fast the Post Office worked!), but feeling was running so high, Michael recalls, that it was decided Michael would phone Richard and put the general suspicions to him. During this telephone conversation, Richard admitted cashing some of the money.

The mother and father of office rows broke out. Michael told staff that when questioned about the postal orders, Richard answered that, as the person who opened the incoming *Gay News* post, he had been in the habit of removing a proportion of the money and dividing it with Denis.

Richard wrote Michael a letter in which he said 'I have been a Director and a share holder of *Gay News* for over five years and if anyone takes the trouble to look through the petty cash details throughout the history of the Company, they will find that my claims for expenses are conspicuous by their absence.

'Some people feel that this is as it should be because they feel that I have never incurred expenses on behalf of the Company. This however is not so. I have incurred the expenses, but until last year or so have not felt that the Company was sufficiently financially strong to reimburse me expenses and also to provide Denis with the sort of expenses to which I consider him to be entitled.

'Only in the middle of last year did I start on an informal basis to arrange for the reimbursement of the expenses incurred during the last five years. If I was at fault in dealing with this on an informal basis, I owe you an apology. The view I took on behalf of Denis and myself was that if the amounts involved were reasonable and fair it was a mere technicality how the matter was dealt with in the case of a company of which Denis and I are the sole share holders.

'I have not kept detailed accurate accounts of the amounts involved and therefore am not able to confirm to the nearest penny how much has been received during which period. I can however confirm that these payments only started in the middle of last year and as an estimate I would guess that Denis and I each received on average £50 per month for the period from the middle of last year to the 31st March, 1978. In other words, the amount involved for that period in my estimation would be approximately £500 each . . . .

'Again I have no entirely accurate figures, but my estimate is that the average monthly amount that we have each received for the period from 1st April, 1978 to the end of October, was between £100 and £200, ie making a total of approximately £800. What this really means is that over a period of five to six years we have each received £1300 by way of reimbursement for those expenses which proprietors of a company are reasonably entitled to expect.'

Michael asked Peter Coell and Jeff Grace (another employee) to record the discrepancies between order values received and money banked (in cases where the person ordering had said they enclosed postal orders or cash) over a period of a fortnight in October 1978. The results showed that in ten working days there was a shortage of £186.29.

There was no suggestion that readers in their capacity as customers of Gay News Ltd had failed to get the classified ad, or the book, that they'd ordered. However, it was never clear how much money had been involved over time – not much, compared to the total amount of money coming in, but several hundreds, people thought, without any possibility of confirmation – and the habit was not one which would be well received in the better class of accounting circles.

Staff met to discuss the revelations. Alison had only just joined *Gay News*, as assistant features editor, and was stunned at the eruption of so shaming a scene only a year after the 'blasphemous libel' trial, when the paper and its editor had been so admired. She recalls Denis weeping as he apologised for his own participation in the eccentric handling of incoming money and as he promised never to let such a thing happen again.

Richard Creed must take himself off, was the unanimous view of the staff.

Perhaps the incident would not have been thought so very shocking had Richard Creed, the solicitor who came to the rescue in 1974, ever been felt to be truly 'one of us' by the men and women who brought out *Gay News*. There had come to be something parasitical in his connection with the paper, in the view of many – Grace Darling, having rescued the shipwrecked, had stayed to live with them, though, in truth, rescuer and rescued had too little in common.

Apparently immovable if he chose to stay, he had unexpectedly provided the leverage with which, if people chose, he could probably be made to go. He put up a strenuous defence, emphasising the benefits he felt he had conferred by good overall financial direction – far outweighing any trifling inadequacies in the cash-handling that people might choose to allege – but consented, in the end, to depart.

The question then arose of what was to become of his forty-nine per cent shareholding.

The wise course at this juncture, early in 1979, is so easy in hindsight that even three years later, in February 1982, those who were on the paper at the time and had since moved on – like Michael – or stayed – like Alison – have a feeling of failure; as if their wits had strayed.

In retrospect, they feel themselves to have been paralysed by a misguided though overwhelming urge, shared by most at *Gay News*, not to sully the hard achieved reputation of the paper or its celebrity editor by mentioning any of the story in the paper, or even publicising the opportunity for a complete alteration in the owner-ship-structure.

Finance could have been raised to buy out Richard Creed on behalf of the staff, or – if preferred – a consortium of well-wishers within the 'gay movement' could have taken on an ownership participation resembling that of trustees. A 'co-operative' might have been established, whereby anyone at work on the newspaper would have had (or regained) an equal voice in its affairs.

There would have been no difficulty in obtaining the technical information for any of these courses, and it would have been perfectly feasible to have raised adequate money for any of them. On the other hand, it would have been a burdensome undertaking while continuing to bring out a newspaper: very time-consuming as options were analysed, agreements reached, fund-raising approaches made.

Habituated, maybe, by four years of most decidedly non-'collective' ownership and management which had brought the company to profitability and achieved the back-handed compli-ment, editorially, of the spectacular 'blasphemous libel' trial, people's minds remained in a rut of supposing that at the end of the day one private shareholding can only be replaced by another.

Richard Creed, most forgiving, it appears, of the detective tech-nique by which Michael had unearthed evidence of the peculiar handling of money, made it plain that if he must go he would like to sell his shares to the news-editor. The binary ownership, with Michael to partner Denis rather than Creed, would be repeated.

Michael had access to the necessary funds, through his publisher father, but had already decided that despite spending five years of his life already on the paper – or perhaps because of it – he couldn't face the prospect of being co-owner with Denis. He foresaw nothing but battles for control; a feud rather than a partnership.

The suggestion then emerged that Denis buy Creed's shares, and add them to his own. The simplest of all solutions on paper. In April 1979 the board of directors of Gay News Ltd (Denis, Michael, and Jean-Claude) agreed to cancel Denis's obligation to surrender thirty-three shares should he cease to be employed by the company; to let him buy the forty-nine shares owned by Richard Creed; and to let him have a substantial pay rise so that he could finance purchase of Creed's shares.

The intention was to maintain the position whereby Denis held his shares for only so long as he was an employee of *Gay News*. At the time, however, the only way for Richard to be bought out was for borrowing to be made against the shares Denis held and the bank would only advance cash if Denis owned the shares outright rather than conditionally, so that they could be lodged as security.

The decision to follow this course was taken – reluctantly – by a full staff meeting and then ratified by the board of directors.

The upshot, at the opening of the new financial year in 1979 was that ninety-eight shares out of 100 in *Gay News* became the personal property of the editor. From gaining one variety of title, that of editor, in 1972, that idealistically wasn't supposed to exist, he had gained another by 1979 that also wasn't supposed to exist: title to the entire 'property' constituted by the newspaper *Gay News*.

Good luck to him perhaps. It was done in proper form. If there seemed a strange discrepancy between the expulsion, if that was what it amounted to, of Richard Creed, and the elevation of Denis to a yet more responsible position, perhaps that had something to do with Denis very much being 'one of us' in the eyes of *Gay News* staff, however great the animosity or controversy he might arouse.

It was all in the family.

The inquisitive reader of *Gay News* in 1979 (and particularly one who, two years before, had sent a donation towards the legal costs of defending the paper in the blasphemy trial) might have wished to know on what terms Richard Creed ended his association with the paper.

He would have been at as much of a loss for information in 1979 as he is now in February 1982; she too, for besides women readers women also contributed to the fund-raising of 1976/77.

It was at this moment perhaps that the iron of complete resistance to the release of information about inner finances entered *Gay News*'s soul. Neither Denis nor Richard Creed were prepared to allow full disclosure of the terms on which Denis took over Richard Creed's forty-nine shares. As ownership changes again, in February 1982, that information is still declared by Denis (and by Robert, if he is asked) to be 'private'.

Word is, however, that Denis acquired Creed's shares for £12,500 down, and the guarantee of a consultancy fee of £5,000 a year, payable by *Gay News*, for the next four years. That there is a consultancy fee is definite, for quarterly payments begin to appear in the books now being handled by Peter Coell, who has joined *Gay News* just as the departure of Creed is being arranged.

As to the £12,500, who knows? If it is correct, then the simple calculation of four years at £5,000 a year plus £12,500 suggests that Richard Creed, who had loaned *Gay News* £3,150 in 1974 and been given forty-nine per cent of the company in exchange, wanted £32,500 to go away five years later.

Such a figure, if the true one, would not be considered excessive by ordinary yardsticks used in the valuation of companies: it would have been five years 'purchase' of a half-share in trading profits that by 1978-79 were running at some £14,000. It would have been no responsibility of the outgoing shareholder's to guess that such profits would not re-appear in the following three financial years.

People too unsophisticated to accept such yardsticks as applying to 'their' newspaper, *Gay News* (or too sophisticated to accept them) might feel very angry indeed if they knew of such a transaction, and knew for certain that the reported detail of it was true.

What kind of precedent was this, that people who worked in unsuitable conditions, at all hours, for no very impressive rates of pay, should be bound to provide £5,000 a year to a man whose usefulness was declared to be over, and in no expectation that any work would be done for the income? And all so that for the first time there should be one man – Denis – with total control over both finances and editorial content at a newspaper launched out of social rebellion, and widely thought to be charitable in intent?

The commercial life of even the best-intentioned papers is tough. Times change. People change. And compromise is the very stuff of survival for almost everyone and everything as years go by. There are many to whom the events of early 1979, and the settlement that emerged from them, would be no more than evidence that *Gay News* was adapting to necessities as they arose and refusing to be stuck in an outmoded past.

BIGGER MONEY

While the exhausted workers at *Capital Gay* contemplate their headline '*Gay News* sold for £100,000', the 19,000 people round the country who buy *Gay News* are going to have to wait in vain for any information on the new financial deal.

The issue of *Gay News* due out March 4, 1982, will dismiss it all in one sentence:

'With effect from February 22 our marketing director, Robert Palmer, has become sole shareholder in and publisher of *Gay News*, taking over from Denis Lemon.'

Neither in the pages of the paper, nor in any answer to outside enquirers, is there any official comment on *Capital Gay's* speculative estimate. Apart from the one sentence from which any figure is conspicuously absent, *Gay News*' own coverage of the change of ownership is effectively nil.

There has been a printed tribute, early in February, to Denis's nine and a half years as editor – but it asked no searching questions, and nothing was said of the financial present or past. And there will be a profile of Robert as new owner in the mid-March issue, showing him in his suit and tie beside a canal in Little Venice; but again, no financial data, and no mention of the unease felt by many that the paper can be bought and sold so privately.

Neither *Gay News* nor *Capital Gay* say anything about the unhappy fashion in which in 1979 Richard Creed departed and Denis came by his legal title to sell the shares however he pleased – both staffs too solicitous of the paper's reputation to want to dredge up old history.

All very responsible, everything done with decency and reticence. Foreign readers would probably say (if they knew the extent of the reticence) 'how typically British'. Labour Party supporters would probably say 'how typically capitalist'; informed 'gay movement' people, 'how typical of *Gay News* – the closet enterprise for the 'out gay'.

Feminists might be tempted to say 'how male' – except that there have lately been some glaring suppressions in their own papers, most notably about the contribution made by lesbians, who are allowed very little open acknowledgement in the pages of women's papers, or magazines, such as the best-known of them in the UK, *Spare Rib*.

But newspaperpeople in the general media would say that of course you don't print in a paper any information that might be picked up and reprinted or broadcast to your disadvantage elsewhere. And those who regard themselves as having sensible commercial attitudes would add 'dead right – never ruffle readers or advertisers with tales out of school'.

Prime responsibility for the early 1982 embargo in *Gay News's* own pages on information about the deal is Robert's, for consenting (he has said) to Denis's insistence on it. The editorial responsibility is Andrew's, for consenting to Robert's claim that in no way can the price or payment terms for *Gay News* be revealed.

The ex Fleet Street journalist who is now the *Gay News* editor is a lackadaisical individual in appearance, not one of your well-groomed gay men (very different, in this, from his predecessor) – grey hair uncombed, sweater torn, jeans unpressed, gym-shoes scuffed, a male journalist in a mess. Reared in jacket, tie, flannels, lace-up shoes, he's of that generation to whom a suit and a tie are the shades of the prison house and the very emblem of careerism and 'straight' values.

On the other hand, just now, he's conforming to the gay male trademark throughout the Western world of wearing his keys in a bunch at the hip, clanking wherever he goes.

He has hazel eyes, so his passport says, a fact which led a Liberal MP, Clement Freud, borrowing the passport to look inside it, to ask whether 'hazel' was the Christian name entry. He has bad teeth, which he ought to get fixed.

As a result of living for a while in Los Angeles with his thirty year old American lover Craig, he has difficulty remembering English spelling from American, and is forever having to be put right by Wendy or Lesley, the typesetters.

The reason why he hasn't yet had cosmetic dentistry is that he's in as poor shape financially as orthodontically – despite £9,000 a year from spring 1981 as *Gay News* news editor, and the £12,000 a year he's just starting to get as editor.

He took the job as news editor for no more elevated reason than that having broken away from journalism in 1978 to try to earn a living as a water-colourist, he was broke and homeless by the end of 1980. He was disconsolately seeking interviews with 'straight' papers when Denis made the infinitely more tempting *Gay News* offer.

For 20 years, on and off, he has worked for newspapers and magazines, without ever accumulating any money – for the conservative *Daily Telegraph*, for the London *Times*, for the British Institute of Management's *Management Today*; always as a financial journalist, of all absurdities, given his own financial situation.

He has just bought a London flat on a mortgage, and is permanently overdrawn at the bank. He is determined that the years of being broke come to a halt, and hopes, as *Gay News* gets into a new rhythm under Robert as financial overseer and himself as editor, to have energy left over to get back to doing some drawing, and selling his drawings.

It doesn't look very likely yet that he'll have the spare time. He's remaining news editor, as well as editor, and isn't best pleased about it. The appointment of Peter Burton to a full-time job on the features side of club and entertainment coverage means there's no money in the budget with which to replace Andrew himself as third person in the news room.

And anyway, though he won't be stirring himself to press Robert for all that undisclosed information about the deal completed on February 22, he expects to be very busy for some months. He feels that Denis, in the last disaffected year or more at *Gay News*, let the paper slide into a rut, and is delighted at being given the chance, as he sees it, to raise both the standards and the morale of the paper.

Forty year old Andrew stands in one respect in a very odd relationship to the paper he now works for – an odder relationship probably than that of any other employed journalist to any other periodical in the UK. His was the idea for the paper, but he has returned to it in an employee capacity. ('Every journalist', he says to writers on other newspapers, in the 'straight' media, 'should found a paper, just in case he ever needs a job').

Nobody on staff except Denis himself knew of that very early connection when Andrew came through the West Kensington front door as news editor and deputy editor early in 1981 – not even Jean-Claude in the art-room, who had worked on issue No 2.

Andrew it was who at one of the packed meetings of the short-lived London Gay Liberation Front had proposed, in the winter of 1971, the newpaper that was to be *Gay News*. He had set the objectives; named it; insisted on a limited liability company to enforce audits; and recruited Denis.

Andrew was twenty-nine at the time, and a journalist full-time on the London *Times*. He was in debt, as named borrower on a house being bought on mortgage for his parents. It took him another year to get free of the obligation; by then, he had long since had to leave the *Gay News* project, and ceased to have anything to do with it.

It was some time, in 1981, before people at the now long-established paper, who had been startled by Andrew's appearance out of the blue, found out that he had invented the concept but departed before physical realisation – had 'fathered' it, in a manner of speaking, but left the 'mothering' to the collective and to Denis as its leading light.

Awareness that he had left the baby to others (no matter that it was family money pressures that had made him do so) gives him a very high tolerance of all those 'foibles' or worse of which he's now aware Denis has been accused. Not for him, he thinks, to throw stones, even if he should feel inclined to do so; and he isn't inclined to do so, for since approaching him with the job in 1981, Denis has behaved perfectly, both as editor to news editor, and as friend to friend.

It could have been awkward, the initiator of a newspaper return-ing to it as an employee – still more, the founder of *Gay News* taking employment as editor under a new owner, Robert, who had done nothing to originate or establish it, but had merely, by still mysterious means, found the cash to buy it.

He has given himself, and stuck to, a stern self prohibition: no nonsense about having some special founder's voice in the paper's affairs (others had built it up); no refusing to accept Denis's, and now Robert's, ultimate power of decision as owner; no envy or resentment that Denis has apparently made a remarkably good thing out of the *Gay News* idea financially, or resentment that perhaps Robert is about to do the same.

If he has a disagreement about the paper too profound for him to go along with the owner, then, he tells himself, he'll make a fight about it, and get sacked or resign, just as if *Gay News* were any other paper, and he an editor in dispute with the owner, just like any other editor in dispute with the owner.

Of course, pride in his role as the parent of a newspaper that has grown, that has had its moment of fame, that now employs so many and is valued by so many readers, taken with the fact that he is now one of the older members of staff, give Andrew the vague *pater familias* sensations of any parent who has walked off, and come back to find the infant full-grown: sentimental, rather astonished.

Age, class, background, early involvement, affection for Denis, all combine to make the new *Gay News* editor very reluctant to enquire into any sorry goings-on of the past or even of the immediate present.

Unknown to staff in early 1982, Andrew sees himself as a transitional editor. He tells his close friends off the paper that he'll hold the post for two years at the outside, and then, his own finances sorted out, and hopefully the newspaper as well, go back to his interrupted efforts to live from water-colour painting.

He looks out for a potential successor from the moment, during January, when he moves across the news-room to the chair and desk that had been occupied by Denis.

Very corrupting, secrecy.

People ask Robert if there's any chance that Denis will use money he's getting for *Gay News* to set up in competition with *Gay News*.

Free to hire a completely new work-force with which he has no historic quarrels, free to set objectives without any inherited commitment to that 'gay movement' of which he's taken to speaking so dismissively, free to be a sole owner without anyone saying there shouldn't be a personal private shareholder, might he not revel in showing up his critics of recent years by creating a second successful national gay paper? Might he not even enjoy trying to beat *Gay News* (and *Capital Gay*) into second place?

Categorically not, says Robert. The terms on which he's sold the paper include a clause forbidding him to engage in direct competition. Besides, says Robert, making plain that *Gay News'* revenues are due to provide at least some part of the purchase price (just as they are still doing in the case of Richard Creed, still on the books as a 'consultant'), he would be unwise to start anything that might undercut *Gay News's* circulation or income.

Categorically not, says Andrew. Speaking as a friend of Denis, though no longer seeing him, for Denis is distancing himself from everything and everyone to do with the paper, he can assure everyone that in private conversation Denis makes it very clear that he's had enough of publishing for the gay reader. If Denis turns his attention to anything in periodical form once again, it'll be, says Andrew, for the general market and the general reader.

The only publicly printed guidance to what Denis might do with his now freed time and his money in 1982 is contained in a statement Andrew obtains from him for publication on January 21, in the issue that announces his retirement as editor:

'After ten years with *Gay News* I feel it is time to move on, and allow myself the opportunity to explore other interests in the media. I would particularly like to say how delighted I am to pass on the editorship to Andrew Lumsden, and I want to welcome back Peter Burton in a full-time capacity. I'd like to thank the present and past staff for their contribution to all that *Gay News* is and represents'.

Other than that, it's known that he may be joining a certain Paul Oremland in producing an 'entertainment' by and for gays to be shown, if accepted, on TV's Channel 4 at the end of the year*, but then the news staff hear that he's dropped out of it.

Denis fades from *Gay News* like the Cheshire Cat from its branch in Alice in Wonderland, though at last it is only the scowl, most people feel, which remains; and then even that's gone.

He never comes into the office after the announcement of his retirement as editor; and because of the hepatitis and his convalescence hadn't been seen in the office for weeks before that. There's no leaving-party, though nearly everyone signs a card, which is sent on to him at his home by Scotty.

*This was broadcast as 'One in Five' on January 1, 1983

Ever anxious to heal the petty wounds and feuds of those who seem so young to her, Scotty also encourages everyone to club together to give him a leaving present. Andrew is commissioned to ring him up and ask him what he'd like: 'One of Andrew's water-colours', he says.

But he says to please wait till some later occasion to do anything about it, and it all comes to nothing . . . in the spring, Denis leaves for one of the favourite resorts of gay men in the USA, Key West in Florida (which is advertised every alternate issue in *Gay News*). In a call from America he tells Andrew that he may well settle down for good in the States.

The waters close over what should have seemed a huge vacancy, after Denis's ten years on the paper. Punctually, cyclically, the paper comes out. 'Nobody is indispensable', Denis had grown very fond of saying, and here it seemed was a proof of it.

The waters begin to close too over the deal. The first flurry of excitement suspicion and anger – for some – that Denis has apparently made a great deal of money out of the poor old paper, dies down.

Except on the detail of the sale, Robert seems to be offering so much more open and consultative a regime. A mood of optimism, of real cheerfulness sweeps the paper: and sweeps under the carpet, being of no consequence any longer, some stray scraps of information about the 1981 negotiations which Andrew on the one hand, and Gill and Alison on the other, by and large keep to themselves.

Andrew had been told of the existence of negotiations during the winter of 1981, first by Robert, then by Denis – Denis rather put out to discover that Robert had already spoken. He was asked to keep the knowledge confidential: negotiations might not succeed, and it was vital that commercial confidence in the paper shouldn't be damaged by talk of uncertainty about its immediate future.

Aware that Denis wanted to leave the paper, aware that there was some force to the point about commercial secrecy, and bound by his own private ordinance not to become involved with any of the financial results of all the years when he had nothing to do with *Gay News*, Andrew kept the two men's confidence, and it didn't occur to him to consult with others on the staff, or to demand that he have complete information.

74

Both Robert and Denis separately asked whether Andrew would agree to edit, if negotiations did succeed, apparently finding it a necessary contingent arrangement to the deal.

Denis never had very much to say about the course of the negotiations, but he let fall some opinions, as distinct from facts and figures.

For instance, on his motive for going: he would be thirty-five in August 1982. It would be the beginning of middle age. If he didn't go now, he'd stay for ever. Soon he wouldn't have the drive to try any new ventures.

On the deal: his accountants advised him that he'd have a higher standard of living if he remained editor-owner of *Gay News* than if he lived off the proceeds of selling it.

On Robert: 'We're both presidential in style. There isn't room at *Gay News* for both of us. If I turn down the deal, Robert'll have to go – he'll take himself off, I shan't have to do it'.

(Andrew was amazed by this. While he thought Denis troubled by shyness, and acting arrogant in consequence, there was no doubt that the 1977 year of fame, and the success of the paper, had made Denis a forceful personality. Robert had so far impressed Andrew, after about nine months acquaintance in the office, as energetic and friendly, a man of good intentions; but lacking in forcefulness. Apparently months of negotiating with him had given Denis another opinion).

On the problem of selling the paper: nothing would induce Denis to part with control to the staff as a whole, or to any members of it other than the relative newcomer Robert. (He probably would have parted with it to Andrew, had Andrew had the money personally, and/or formed a consortium of financial backing).

He had thought of closing *Gay News* down, if that was the only way he could get free of it and get some money out. It was a very difficult 'property' to sell. 'Straight' publishing enterprises might well be chary of taking on a newspaper flagrantly by and for homosexuals.

All the same, Denis gave the impression that some 'straight' companies, or entertainment complexes, or very highly commercialised gay enterprises, might be interested if he allowed it. He couldn't dispose of *Gay News* in any way that would betray its reputation.

If he didn't sell: he might become absentee owner, perhaps calling himself editor-in-chief, get on with projects unrelated to *Gay News*, and ask Andrew to be editor.

(Andrew consciously made no attempt to influence Denis's decision. His hope, though, was that Denis would take this last course. Easy with Denis's faults and virtues, going 'way back' with him, he liked the idea of a continuing working relationship with Denis rather than with the comparative stranger Robert. But perhaps that was sentimental . . . .)

On members of staff: so far as Andrew understood him (and he didn't much want to understand him, on these old dissensions) Denis thought the two Bobs (photography and distribution) and Alison, and Michael (now at *Capital Gay*), as a coterie who if he'd ever given or were to give an inch would destroy the paper.

Bob in distribution, apparently, was a 'Leftie'; photographer Bob had no manners, and was getting worse and worse at his job (like Robert, he'd have to go if Denis stayed); Alison was so 'academic' in her handling of each issue's Literary Supplement that she was alienating the bulk of the readers; Michael, mercifully now gone, was slipshod and generally insufferable.

Again on the deal: if Robert's forecasts of what could be done with *Gay News*' profitability over the 1980s turned out to be accurate, Denis would 'kick himself' for selling out at the price offered.

Robert had given Andrew a hazy idea of what those profits might be, if all went according to Robert's expectations, during late 1981.

Very privately, one day, he had let Andrew in on the secret that he had started negotiating to buy *Gay News* from Denis. There were still many difficulties, it might not come off, but a great deal of work had been done.

He explained that he was breaking the news, before others could be allowed to know, because he was organizing bank finance; and would like to be free to tell the bankers that the present news editor and deputy editor of the paper had consented to become editor under Robert's ownership.

The door closed, greatly excited at being able to show someone, Robert produced a mass of figuring. A 'prospectus'. With 'upper' and 'lower' case estimates, it showed *Gay News*' potential profitability over approximately 1982-87.

Andrew was not too keen to pay close attention, partly from a former financial journalist's assumption that such long-range forecasts are 'window dressing' of the kind that financiers are always offering one another and outsiders; rather more, from unwillingness to attend closely to anything that might stir up annoyance that *Gay News* should have become such a possible source of profit to Robert, who after all had nothing to do with the paper's early struggles.

But he was impressed by the magnitude of Robert's expectations, remembering vaguely that trading profits of £50,000 or so were being looked to in a few years. Not much, perhaps, on conventional measures for a turn-over set to rise and rise from £500,000 – but stunning, if they could be realised, for a British fortnightly periodical in the midst of an economic recession catering to so complex a 'market' as the homosexual population.

The scrap of information about the 1981 negotiations possessed by Alison and Gill remains unknown to Andrew for a long time, and to most others on staff. (When deciding to edit the paper Andrew had made clear that he wouldn't socialise unduly with staff. It will be some time, therefore, before he learns of attitudes and activities which are not directly relevant to people's job descriptions).

During the winter of 1981 Gill and Alison decided to approach Robert privately and ask him whether he thought Denis might be receptive to a bid for the paper. Alison had already introduced Gill to Michael Mason, whom Gill had asked whether he thought Denis would sell *Gay News*, and for how much. Michael was convinced that Denis would never sell. 'He would be nobody without *Gay News*', Michael said. 'What else could he do?'

In spite of Michael's assessment, Alison and Gill approached Robert. They explained that, because of family money, Gill would be able to borrow up to £35,000 towards a purchase price. Robert neither told them that he was negotiating with Denis already, nor did he come back to them for information. When he told the assembled staff on January 14, 1982, that he had succeeded in principle in buying the paper, Alison and Gill were left feeling rather astonished by the ease with which – apparently – he had raised the money, since he clearly had felt no need of pursuing

Gill's offer. They were also – Gill in particular – sceptical from the very moment of the announcement about Robert's declared intentions of passing over shares in the paper to the staff. Why, they wondered, had Robert Palmer bought the paper on his own? He never said.

Andrew, too, told Robert that if he and Denis seemed to be coming unstuck for lack of some funds, he might be able to direct them towards one or two wealthy gay men. And Robert knew many affluent people from his time involved in the fund-raisings of CHE. A gay man who is a professional fund-raiser told Robert that for such a purpose as the buying and financial stabilisation of *Gay News*, he might well be able to drum up investors to the tune of perhaps £70,000.

These random background proposals received by Robert during the most covert period of negotations were of course known, as a whole, only to Robert, and they remained unknown to all but a very few different people early in 1982.

He wasn't, on his own say-so, a rich man, yet he'd found no need to pursue the very substantial proposal outlined to him by Gill and Alison; nor any of the other, perhaps less certain, proposals. It is all too likely that he thought Denis would be resistant to any financing proposal in which Alison, or rather Alison with Gill, had a part. But how had he managed without any of the stray financial offers?

The means by which he had done it entailed mortgaging the freehold premises and future profits, constructing an agreement that within five years would leave him with free title to the paper, and complete control of Gay News Ltd's shares, without personally investing one penny of his own.

In the interim, indeed, while *Gay News* bought Denis out and provided Robert with eventual outright personal ownership, he would be on the highest salary level. It was a deal which would not have been legally feasible until the year in which he started negotiations.

That it became possible at all was the result of a change in UK Company Law, contained in the 1981 Finance Act, under which Thatcher's administration considered it was trying to ease the difficulties of the small entrepreneurs who want to realise their holdings in companies which, for whatever reason, are difficult to sell.

The alteration to Company Law made the new provision that employees of such a company could borrow against the company's own assets and prospects in order to pay off the existing shareholder or shareholders; who might otherwise decide that if there was no other way to realise shareholders' 'locked-in' funds, they'd close the operation down, and sell up the bits and pieces.

On the face of it, legislation of equal potential benefit to entrepreneurs wishing to retire after their labours; and to work forces in danger of being put out of work if their employer felt compelled to close down.

Whether it was meant to apply to the whole of a work force rather than to any single individual or group on staff, the drafting of the new law didn't specify. The effect was that a company could be 'stripped', and no extra working capital brought in, merely in order to produce a change of shareholders.

It wasn't the illegal company operation of 'asset-stripping', yet, to the untrained eye, had there been any such to study the method Robert found for purchasing *Gay News*, it would have borne an eerie resemblance. As it was, the newly feasible method of acquisition was passed by solicitors and by an international firm of accountants.

Robert was not a lawyer, nor was he formally trained in accountancy. He was a graduate in philosophy and chemistry. How he came by the information which allowed him to pursue this course – or who might have suggested he do so – was never to be disclosed. Nor did anyone at the time ask him, since the details of the deal were not disclosed. Such questions depended on the more basic one, also not pursued by anyone on the staff at the time: why had Robert wanted to buy the paper without, himself, paying for it?

Robert promises £121,000 in all for a loss-making newspaper, into which he will be putting no new working capital and for whose shares he will personally be paying nothing. The untrained observer would find this one of those improbable coups which apparently can arise in the business world and defy the lay person's notions on the laws of financial gravity.

Yet, maybe, all praise to Robert for having the wit and determination to discover that it was possible, and for succeeding in carrying it through. Anyone else besides himself on staff could have worried away at the problem of lacking personal realisable wealth, and yet wished to buy the paper. To the victor the spoils: in commercial life, getting away with the unexpected, just once, is often the foundation of the most respectable fortunes. It may have been technically legal; but to many, much later – when the terms of the deal were known – it seemed deeply immoral.

And how is it for Denis? Setting aside the objections that many would have, if they knew the whole, to his requiring £121,000 as his price for walking away from *Gay News*, how do the arrangements shape up by the standards of those who would consent that *Gay News* was a business, whatever its other pretensions, and could be traded to and fro like any other business?

Richard Creed retired as forty-nine per cent shareholder of Gay News Ltd in 1979 for some £32,500, so it seems: £12,500 payable 'up-front' by Denis, who had to borrow for the purpose, and £20,000 by way of a £5,000 a year 'consultancy' (which in 1982 is still being paid out, and will continue to be so into 1983).

At first glance, Denis is asking, and Robert is agreeing, an exorbitant price. If forty-nine per cent of *Gay News* shares were worth £32,500 or so in early 1979 when the year's trading profits were about to run out at about £14,000, how come double the number of shares fetches nearly four times the sum early in 1982 – when a loss of about £17,000 is about to be turned in on top of two previous years of losses?

Even in a time of inflation (which during Thatcher's government is reducing rapidly), it looks generous.

But the figuring is complicated, and it includes a 'real estate' element, the freehold West Kensington offices: and it includes different modes of payment to create the eventual £121,000.

For one thing, early in 1982, Denis is to have £24,000 of the overall £121,000 in the form of 'compensation for loss of office' as a director or editor, a 'golden handshake'. An entirely legal tax-avoidance scheme, no doubt proposed by the lawyers and accountants, it doesn't affect the generalisation that Denis has put a £121,000 price on leaving all his rights over *Gay News*.

'Net equity', or realisable value, in the freehold of the offices by the time Denis and Robert are negotiating, is probably around £40,000 – £50,000, after repayment of any company borrowings already outstanding against them.

So, on the back of an envelope, £50,000 of the £121,000 required by Denis can be put down to the property that he owns as sole owner of *Gay News* – leaving £71,000 as the money he wants for other physical assets, for subscription and other lists, for profit potential (if any), and for the title '*Gay News*' itself, with all the commercial good will and general fame that may be thought to attach to it.

To assess whether £71,000 for the business as distinct from, say, £50,000 for the building alone, is a commercially fair price, it's necessary to do some more hypothetical scribbling on an envelope.

£8,000 at the very outside is enough to account for *Gay News* office equipment such as the 'copy camera' used by art room, the typesetting machinery, desks, chairs, typewriters, company van, etc. Subscription and other lists – upwards of 15,000 names and addresses of homosexuals of both sexes – have no resale value in real life, such are the risks of misuse.

This leaves £63,000 as the price put upon the title '*Gay News*' and its goodwill, and on what would have been Denis's entitlement to future profits, if any, as the shareholder. If he still owes any part of the £12,500 he paid to Richard Creed in 1979, or feels that it should be subtracted from any overall figure that he is asking, then that produces a sum of about £50,000 yet to be accounted for.

Gay News the title, with its commercial value of being comparatively famous, can notionally be priced at some £20,000.* It appears then that for premises, equipment, and title, Denis is asking about £78,000, and for the loss of his entitlement to any future profits, about £30,000.

Given that *Gay News* has been making a loss for three years, the implied assumption that trading profits will average £9,000 or so a year for the next five years is a bit cheeky; but then, by leaving the paper, Denis will be giving up earnings of perhaps £15,000 a year as editor, so commercially it isn't so unreasonable. And he may have some tax to pay on the whole transaction.

All in all, the £121,000 valuation on his ownership has wound up looking fairly reasonable on this analysis, however excessive on a simple comparison with the 1979 price for Richard Creed's shares. Such are the strange geometries of share transactions, proving that

---

* 'Zen' though it sounds, newspaper titles are worth nothing other than what someone is prepared to pay for them. This estimate is based on later events.

everything depends on the event – what happens next to the company – rather than on the past.

The 'golden handshake' is raised by a bank borrowing on the newspaper's freehold premises. So is a further £26,000, making for a £50,000 borrowing in all, from Barclays Bank, secured on the premises. Early in 1982 the £50,000 is paid over to Denis, meaning that £71,000 is left to be paid in instalments over the next five years.

There is also – of course– interest to be paid on the loan. The interest payments to the bank turn up in the books of Gay News Ltd, along with legal fees. Neither Robert Palmer himself, nor Robert Palmer Marketing Ltd, pays, it seems, these amounts. In effect, Gay News Ltd from the work of its staff is buying itself for Robert Palmer to receive as a gift. His work for the business is rewarded – like that of all the other members of staff – with his salary.

The deal means that Denis, for his part, has extracted the greater part of the value of the building he owned as controlling shareholder of Gay News Ltd; and that the newspaper, for its part, has lost the accumulated 'reserve' attributable to it after 10 years existence, and which might have been used instead for expansion and reinvestment, or kept as a cushion against bad times.

Payments on the outstanding £71,000 are set to begin with an initial £10,000 or so on December 31, 1982, and will continue with quarterly instalments of varying sizes thereafter, up to 1987/88. *Gay News* shares are taken into trust by Robert's solicitor, and he is forbidden, under the undisclosed terms of the contract, to dispose of them, or make any borrowings until Denis is completely paid off; or unless Denis gives his consent.

The 'vehicle' for these transactions is a company - with no trading history or assets – called Robert Palmer Marketing Ltd. Entertainingly, for so very up-to-date a deal as one dependent on a 1981 Company Law change, the board of directors of Robert Palmer Marketing Ltd has a distinctly Victorian air: directors are Robert himself and members of his family. 'Straights' are directors of the *Gay News* holding company.

Less entertainingly, though perhaps of no real consequence, the ultimate holding company of the newspaper is no longer Gay News Ltd – on which representative members of staff have been invited to sit – but Robert Palmer Marketing Ltd, through which Robert is making his purchase.

Though he has found a means to buy *Gay News* out of its own present and future resources, Robert lays himself personally on the line in one respect. He gives a personal guarantee that Denis will receive all his money. If there is any default, Denis, if he chooses, can sue Robert personally, and not only Robert Palmer Marketing Ltd.

Or, if there is a default, Denis Lemon can give notice that he intends to reclaim all the shares in Gay News Ltd from Robert's solicitor.

A fair enough price, £121,000, commercially speaking, would probably be the verdict of some – if people of all kinds of 'moral' and 'political' perspective were allowed, this early 1982, to give their various verdicts on the terms of sale of *Gay News*.

Not so, others would answer. A newspaper 'collectively' launched for gay liberation motives, to support a minority travestied or ignored by the greater part of the traditional media, should never be traded in as if it were a factory with a product-line of no social or community significance. Commercial 'standards' don't apply.

Back might reasonably come the rejoinder: gay folks who don't want 'their' national newspaper to be bought and sold at the discretion of one shareholder had better not let it belong to one shareholder in the first place.

Look at what £121,000 represents, the horrified might reply. London Gay Switchboard, for example, the most important help organisation for homosexuals in the country other than *Gay News* itself – ranking at least as *Gay News*' equal – could be run for fifteen years without any further recourse to public benefits and private donations on such a sum.

Or, most humanly, the longest-serving member of *Gay News* staff Jean-Claude, who has worked there almost as long as Denis, would need a century to pile up such a figure, even if he saved most carefully from his earnings (assuming that everything, himself included, could stay still for such a purpose).

The lawyers might say that Robert and Denis have full clearance for what they've arranged. But the cautious business-minded would look askance: to remove the major asset of the company, to pledge a large part of profits, when for three years there have been no profits, and all in a time of recession: 'Wheeler-dealer' stuff, these kind of optimists come unstuck.

A historian of *Gay News*, if such a person existed, would remark that a habit seems to be setting in: first *Gay News* buys out Richard Creed so that Denis Lemon can own the paper, now *Gay News* is to buy out Denis Lemon so that Robert Palmer can own the paper. Are any of these men so invaluable that year in, year out, from 1979 to 1987, revenues must be set aside for such a purpose?

A psychologist might hazard a guess that Robert's failure to find or to follow up any offers of fresh capital with which to buy the paper, and reliance on the one peculiar method that could make *Gay News* wholly his own, could cast some doubt on his statement that his whole motive has been to free the newspaper of its incubus, the previous owner. A self-serving solution perhaps, not a public-service one.

Anyone of the mildest political views might note that the *Gay News* sale arrangement of 1982 needed a willing seller and willing buyer who saw no rooted objection in principle to what the law allowed – and wonder whether buyer and seller are not dangerously removed, in their principles, from those principles likely to be held by people who bring out, and people who read, a community-service newspaper.

And as to the effects of the deal on *Gay News* as a newspaper (not just as a business) – wise heads used to the tensions between content and commerce might fear that by mortgaging the future profitability of the newspaper, Robert and Denis between them have locked it into an unadventurous, safety-first, mould for years to come.

As if both of them were only business people, and neither of them accustomed to the facts of journalism.

Never mind. None of this is yet known. Ignorant of the good and the bad, the staff, and the journalists among them, are full of the joys of the coming spring. At least they can modernise the paper, whose contents leave a lot to be desired.

WOMEN'S WORK

By private car, by company car, by company van, by motor-bike, they make their way to Mickleton in Gloucestershire. It's a *Gay News* works outing, nineteen homosexuals off to ruralise, so they can talk among themselves free of production deadlines.

Anyone would think it was a tradition.

But it isn't. The idea is Robert's. It's Friday to Sunday, January 29–31, the halfway point between the announcement that Robert is to take over the paper, and the February 22 legal completion of the deal. Everyone is on their best behaviour lest at the last second the previous owner refuse to sign.

The mood is exuberant. Not even Chris, sorry to see Denis retire, would do anything to shake the deal and disappoint his colleagues. Most of the staff are very anxious indeed for the new era to be sealed and delivered. And pleased enough with Robert's thought of a long weekend to get to know each other better.

For the fact is that life under Denis was so heads-down, so departmentalised, so 'machine', that there are people on the little staff, working in cheek-by-jowl premises, who have learnt virtually nothing of the opinions and lives of others.

You never saw a staff so well-disposed to give a new owner his chance.

Not that he hasn't suffered what he plainly regards as a defeat in the first instants of ownership.

He wanted to bring someone he calls a 'facilitator' – an outsider to chair meetings, take suggestions for changes in agenda, stroke the fur if hackles rise. Whatever for ? The political beliefs of Wendy in typesetters are particularly outraged. Do people need 'managing'? Can *Gay News* in country assembly not manage itself?

Robert kicks up most remarkably before giving in. He talks of the 'expertise' of his nominee in the running of group encounters. He says how he himself is desperate not to be seen in a role of authority and mustn't himself be expected to chair the occasion. He will not, he repeatedly says, with a most agonised fervour, be placed in the position of 'becoming Denis'.

There is every sympathy with that, but it seems to be missing the point. People who have felt manoeuvred from behind closed doors for years past – and, frankly, have just been manoeuvred with a new owner and new editor, and are having to lump it – don't want any gratuitous additional manoeuvring by industrial psychologists and the like.

And Andrew says to Robert that if anything about to be said in Gloucestershire precipitates a row, have the row, and don't smooth away from it. Those with a terror of 'rows' – club and entertainments editor Peter is one of them, financial manager Peter is another – say for goodness' sake let Robert have his 'facilitator', if that's what he wants.

But many of the women won't come if that's the way the new regime is going to begin. Robert cancels the 'facilitator', already booked. Andrew tries to buck him up by congratulating him on the 'moral courage' he's shown; but finds it all very awkward, because he's been telling Robert that an owner mustn't expect to avoid being unpopular from time to time, or an editor. Robert seems to have chosen the wrong issue on which to make a stand.

Gay News is paying for the accommodation and meals for this weekend in the country. Rightly seeking somewhere economical, Robert has used his clerical connections to find a rambling village hostel run by a religious sect of some unclear persuasion. To their credit, they don't turn down a London gang of committed transgressors.

Even so, the atmosphere is strange. Meals have an air of the refectory. The bar has to be unlocked every time anyone wants a drink. Staff behave terribly well, conscious of Robert's anxieties, but there's a suppressed hysteria, as of Divine balancing a cup of tea at the vicarage.

There is a converted barn for 'plenary sessions', a garden for taking a breather. Wendy has brought her fourteen year old 'skinhead' son Mark; Gill has left her son at home in London. Jean-Claude hasn't come at all. Weary of meetings after his ten years on the paper, shaken by the end of the long era under his former lover Denis, he has pleaded to be allowed to stay away, but has said as emphatically as he knows how that his warmest good wishes and hopes for a successful, 'New Dawn', weekend go with his colleagues.

Financial manager Peter, one of those who has felt most isolated from real human contact with colleagues, has been disappointed that the only suitable weekend clashed with the Sunday christening of his niece. He stays as long as he can. When he goes, his friend and colleague in accounts, the other Peter, goes too, dismaying those who had hopes that at least one member of accounts would be present to the end. 'Accounts' has always seemed a remote and unknowable end of the paper's operations, in terms of personalities as well as of figures.

Advertising's Roger Jay also leaves early, for a previous appointment, another disappointment – 'advertising' has never seemed remote, but he is the only representative of display . 'Sexism' in display advertising always comes up as a topic when any two or three are gathered together, and his views are needed.

Like Jean-Claude, Mike of reception and box-replies hasn't come at all, saying, in his case, that it'll all be 'above his head'. Unlike Jean-Claude, who considers that women on the staff need to have more of a voice in affairs, Mike, noisy and full of jokes, twenty years old, has shown clear signs of feeling put down by such articulate voices as Alison's and Wendy's and – when she chooses to make one of her abrupt comments – Lesley.

There's a newcomer, a part-timer longing to join the staff, twenty-four year old David Bird. Another who would like to write, he's been helping out on the frequent administrative backlog. Like Andrew and Peter Burton, he is somehow asked into his job. No position has been advertised, nor have interviews with competing applicants taken place. He has just most efficiently sorted out and refiled the thousands of news-room photographs, and Andrew is pressing, if the budget can take it, to have him on full-time staff to create a *Gay News* cuttings library. (No such thing exists after ten years).

On the 'plenary sesstions agenda' there is one in which each member of staff in turn tells the life-history of another member of staff; another in which, with the aid of charts on an easel, Robert spells out the basic economics of the paper – and claims that in the past year Denis had drawn £17,000 expenses. Just cancelling those, he says, will balance the *Gay News* books.

And another in which it is formally proposed that Alison become editor of the paper instead of Andrew. Or if that is not possible or acceptable, that she become joint-editor.

All the women come for the weekend – Scotty though hers is only a four-day a week commitment; Wendy though she has a son; Gill though she has a much younger son; Jo, who would normally be in Brighton with her lover, another Lesley; Lesley of typesetters, whose love-life is currently the most turbulent of anyone's in the office; Amanda, of 'classifieds'; Alison, who normally enjoys her weekends at home in Cambridge.

This weekend, as always, the women show a higher sense of the obligation to attend meetings, and of the need for meetings, though some grumble – Lesley of typesetters, who easily gets bored and shows it, Scotty who longs for efficiency and brevity. Amanda is usually the most silent. Jo, to whom, as to Scotty, most on staff seem very young, gets very distressed at any signs of animosity. The paper and its readers, men or women, are very dear to her, and she wants peace and quiet and good fellow-feeling, so the paper may be well made, and people have cause for gratitude at the chance to work on it. (There is a tendency amongst almost everyone to find her 'motherly'. Greatly disconcerting her, Robert has once or twice come to her for what he calls 'a cuddle', and has got it, against Jo's better judgement.) Nor is she taken behind his closed door only for cuddles. Several times he uses her as a 'go-between', trying to solicit her support for an action he intends to take, or wanting her to intervene on his behalf, or wanting to know from her the best way to approach one or other of his staff. Jo finds these sessions acutely annoying, or embarrassing, and – frequently – both.

Together with Wendy, Alison and Gill are the most indefatigable in attending and trying to make effective use of the fortnightly set-piece staff meeting for which most of the men have to be rounded up, and which some – the two Peters in 'accounts' almost always – say they're too busy to attend, protesting that meetings are a waste of time. Gill, appalled by the illiberal hierarchy she encountered on joining staff in 1981, sees them as the only avenue to breaking down entrenched divisions of every sort – class, economic, gender. And as a way, too, of breaking through the sheer conventionality of everything, the passive acquiescence in a 'them and us' relation between workforce and management.

Debarred from executive authority – never until now on the board of Gay News Ltd, kept out of features, though styled 'assistant (features) editor', siding with Michael during the long implicit rupture between Michael as news editor and Denis as editor – Alison has always seen staff and other meetings as the opportunity to fend off encroachments on what should be the rights of herself and others and invariably keeps extensive notes, in case proof of anything said or decided should be needed. She often produces these, to check an assertion.

And besides, she loves a good gossip.

To Alison, entering her fifth year at the paper, *Gay News* is another home. For Denis, it may have become a platform to higher things; for Andrew a two-year engagement; for Michael of *Capital Gay*, her great friend, an impossible situation, which he left – for Alison, it's her anchor, the London base from which her professional life now flows. She has never done another full-time paid job.

For her, as perhaps for everyone on the paper, but particularly for her (it is true of Jo also), *Gay News* is a 'caring' enterprise, whose threads run through the whole tapestry of self-help by homosexuals for homosexuals in the UK. Over and beyond 'news', about which she does not regard herself as an expert, it is *Gay News* as a cultural object that concerns her – a thing of social significance to the readership and beyond the readership.

Her place as literary editor is tailor-made for her. Two pages per issue when she joined in 1977, eight pages an issue at the peak, an alternating five pages and three pages now, the *Gay News* Literary Supplement, coming out fortnightly in the back half of the paper, is one the the most extensive literary sections available in any British periodical. Publishers, very pleased to send her books for review, are well aware of the fact.

For Denis, despite his 1981 complaints that the Supplement is 'academic' and alienating to less high-brow readers, it has been a mark of 'respectability' – something he couldn't himself have run, but which reflects credit on the paper. Truth to tell, his objections, before he left, probably had more to do with Alison's comparative fame, and her 'solidarity' with Michael, than with any desire to get rid of the serious book-reviewing.

For in the 'movement' she is very well known indeed. The reviewers she picks come mainly from one or another branch of the gay and/or feminist network, and the space she offers them is unique in British publishing – where else, twice a month, can they write as the 'out' lesbians and gay men they are, addressing themselves to other homosexuals without any fear that the editor will instruct them to remember that there are heterosexuals out there as well, who won't understand?

And, before *Gay News*, she was one of the national organisers of Friend, one of the country's befriending organisations for gays just 'coming out' or facing other kinds of trouble. There had indeed been a move to elect her Chair of the Campaign for Homosexual Equality in 1978 – she turned it down, preferring the move into literary journalism at *Gay News*. And Robert became Chair instead.

She has judged short-story competitions; she has recommended authors to publishers; she attends book-launches; she goes on literary platforms; she goes to lesbian and gay conferences. With her long dark hair, her ample figure – 'I'm getting fat', she would say herself – her flowered smocks, her sandals in summer-time, her astonishing recall for faces, names, and conversations, her articulacy (so stunning to Mike), she has been seen on the nation's screens, in the two late-night 'Gay Life' series of London Weekend TV, in 1979-80.

And behind all that, there is shyness. She says herself that it's an endlessly repeated fight not to recoil from all the activity and bury herself in her Cambridge house among her books and her garden. The shyness betrays itself in the labour she finds it to write, though she speaks so fluently; and in putting things off.

She admits herself that when Denis as editor 'quite rightly' wanted to expand coverage of paperback re-issues, she delayed so long that he had to get the section going himself – and kept it going until he left, since when Peter of clubs and entertainment has done it. Her own view is that her delay had as much to do with her suspicions of the criteria and standards which Denis had in mind.

She suspected he wanted 'trash coverage' for commercial Mail Order reasons, which she wasn't prepared to undertake. She says of herself that she's conservative; the 18th century, and the women who wrote then but whose memory was almost wholly obliterated by later publishers' 'masculinist' assumptions, has become one of her passions in literature.

For the *Gay News* on which production work will begin next week after the return from Gloucestershire (No 234, due out February 18, 1982) she has obtained a two-page article by Rosemary Manning, who in the 1960s had successfully published three novels, under her own name, and then in 1971 published an autobiography under a pseudonym.

It is a 'coming out'. The autobiography, *A Time and Time*, is being re-issued, this time under its author's true name. Rosemary Manning explains how in 1971 as the head of a girls' preparatory school, she dared not risk the parents' disapproval if she wrote of her lesbianism. Now, eleven years later, retired, she can at last be honest:

'. . . At last the built-in habit of concealment has crumbled. Liberation has come to me, but only in my sixties . . .'.

It is a moving account, one which will stir writers or artists of either gender who have ever had anything they felt compelled to conceal; and which will stir any gay woman, and any gay man whose feelings are not completely closed (as are those of some) to the experiences of all homosexuals, women or men.

Issue 234 is to be one of those in which Alison has five pages in all to fill. For the other three she has chosen an illustration from a 'gender-fuck' cartoon-book, and another from a collection of 1922–23 war drawings by Kathe Kollwitz, to represent latest arts/ graphics publications. The life of another artist, the 'violently anti-gay' Eric Gill, illustrated by a Gill woodcut, is reviewed by Simon Watney.

The 'lead' review is to be by Diarmaid MacCulloch, of *Treason against God: A History of the Offense of Blasphemy*, which needless to say pays attention to the 1977 trial of *Gay News* for publishing the 'blasphemous libel' poem. (The author, who gets rebuked for it by gays in America, where the book has been published, refers to *Gay News* as 'an obscure homosexual fortnightly').

A novel about 'blond and beautiful Peter Asbrand, seventeen-

and-a-half, neo-Nazi' is damned by Peter Burton. Another, by John Broderick, telling the tale of 'Willie Ryan', a homosexual in the most provincial districts of provincial Ireland, is praised by Peter Parker.

Two other members of staff are contributing reviews: Linda Semple, a part-timer who does *Gay News'* proof-reading, gives cautious praise to *Adult Education*, a novel – despite its title – about an unconsummated attraction between two woman; and Gill, co-author herself of *Rocking the Cradle* (about lesbian motherhood), will be praising the English translation of France's latest *succès de scandale*, *The Myth of Motherhood*:

'Every so often a book makes it out of the black hole of sexual politics into the vacant interstellar spaces of the general reading public. This is such a book . . .'

And Pam Johnson will be strongly recommending *Women on the Line*, the experiences of Ruth Cavendish, a sociology lecturer who in 1977 left her job in academic life to work for seven months on a car-components assembly-line. Pam Johnson will be describing to *Gay News* readers how:

'Women . . . were trapped at the bottom of the pile. They had virtually no opportunities for promotion, whereas male workers had a hierarchy of jobs through which they could progress'.

On the weekend of January 29, in Gloucestershire, the ad hoc 'plenary session' debate on the proposal that Alison be editor of *Gay News* in place of Andrew, or joint editor with him, comes up on the Sunday, when the two Peters of 'accounts' and Roger Jay of 'advertising' have already departed.

It is of course most uncomfortable for all, very much so for the principals, most of all for Alison. Bob, of distribution, says plainly that in his opinion Alison's is the seniority, and she should be sole editor; so does Bob the photographer; so does Chris from the news room. (Chris is rather muddled about the whole thing. He doesn't object in principle to solo editorship, but he objects in particular to Andrew. And he admires Alison. Still, he is aware that such decisions should not be taken on grounds of personal taste.)

It is a muted discussion, not at all 'organised' in the sense of caucus politics, and badly timed – had it been that sort of an initiative – for people are getting weary after the Friday and Saturday of discussion, on top of the long preceding working week.

It is also the case that there are awkward divisions of viewpoint, for some – Wendy, very much – are less interested in one editor rather than another than in one day restoring 'collective' editorship.

Andrew and Alison are asked to speak up for themselves, to tell how they see the job of editor, or of editing. Alison is deeply unhappy, and quite plainly would prefer not to be pushed into such a hand-to-hand contest. Her usual articulacy deserts her. She doesn't feel strong personal disapproval of Andrew, which might otherwise have inspired her. She has been 'drafted', and suffers all the embarrassment of the nominee put forward by others.

She talks of policy: the need to make *Gay News* far more responsive to the gay men and women who live far from London, the non-metropolitan gays; the need to reduce the paper's London 'chauvinism'. But she says, too, that she isn't herself prepared to journey round the country in pursuit of feature material. She must have her weekends of relaxation and literary preparation in Cambridge.

Never was anyone more wrong footed by distaste for the form that a struggle has taken. The call for something she isn't herself prepared to do makes a bad impression on listeners, in that Gloucestershire barn, who knows so well how many hours and how much energy those who undertake the editing of newspapers have got to put in. She makes herself sound as if she would accept the title, but not the labour.

She has been preceded by Andrew, who has in fact been editing the paper for some two months, thanks to the illness of his predecessor; and been news editor, an intensive enough job, for seven months before that (as he still is). Andrew largely confines himself to the principle – saying that he believes single editors, who can be removed if they're no good, are best for newspapers, and that he would be delighted to have the chance of editing this one, *Gay News*. He emphasises that – in his view – editing a paper is a 'craft' and, like other forms of craft, is best done by an individual. For some of the women that is, whatever else a familiar 'male' view: familiar both in its orthodoxy and in its appeal to notions of superior expertise. Most of the men probably lean to the single editor practice, but not all.

He concedes nothing. Amanda, puzzled that there should be any difficulty, has already smilingly said, as a person who rarely speaks at such times, that she can't understand the problem. The paper is for both sexes. Andrew, who has been urging the editorial cause of the woman reader, and who in 1981 brought Gill on staff as a news reporter, despite the reluctance of the existing news reporter Chris and the then editor Denis (who both thought a man necessary), can surely have no objection.

Yet Andrew makes no move to agree. It is perhaps his refusal to welcome Alison as partner editor – let alone step aside for her – which brings the discussion to an oddly formless end. Alison has thoroughly hated the 'editorial debate'. In turn she has felt embarrassed, angry, defeated and despairing. But mainly she has felt inhibited. It seems to her that what should have been a forthright discussion of issues and principles is perceived as a 'Personal Contest' between herself and Andrew. It is not what she wants. Nor, she believes, does Andrew. Nevertheless, as the session has just demonstrated, issues, principles and people cannot be kept neatly and painlessly separated.

It is true that Andrew has many more years' experience than she as a journalist. Nevertheless, in her view she has had far more years relevant experience than he – via work for the national counselling organisation Friend and via CHE – in present day gay politics and campaigning. She also believes she has a greater day-to-day awareness of what being gay is like for a significant majority of Britain's gay people – that is, all those who do *not* live in London. She's impatient with, and angered by, a metropolitan attitude which regards 'not-London' as either a lifeless desert or a quaint garden for Londoners to dally in before returning to the capital and 'The Real World'. Regretfully she has come to believe that even those of her colleagues who most self critically condemn their own London chauvinism often don't really recognise the half of it.

Her belief that London is actually just another – rather bigger – parish pump, has affected her attitude to the paper's contents. Her own concentration on books and authors (often, ironically, regarded as 'elitist' or 'minority') springs in part from her feeling that, for the literate gay man or woman outside London, information about books likely to interest or benefit them has a greater and longer lasting value than the detailed coverage of a London night-life they'll probably never enter, or of short-run London plays and films they'll probably never see.

For Alison, the whole editorial discussion which has just happened (or failed to happen) has been distressing and disturbing in a number of ways. The element of personal contest ('In the Red Corner we have . . . and in the Blue Corner . . .') is difficult because it is distorting. She doesn't see the issues in terms of Alison being overall better and Andrew being overall worse. She does think she is 'better' than Andrew in certain important respects.

She feels that the gladiatorial mode is completely alien and an inefficient way of resolving anything. She realises, too, that if it is the way most men like things done, it is also a way that most women find distasteful and unproductive. Almost immediately she realises that only by behaving in a way which she rejects, can she 'win'. She would have to list her own strengths (as she sees them), list Andrew's weaknesses (as she and others see them), make capital out of the friendship and loyalty which Andrew feels towards Denis Lemon and which is far and away the biggest single cause of the underlying suspicion with which she and others regard him at this stage. Finally, she would have to make a conscious decision to manipulate the complex emotions of loyalty, affection and confidence in her editorial ability which virtually all the production and editorial staff have been expressing for some months now.

She can do none of these things. Later, she realises – with a strong sense of irony – that according to one school of thought her very inability to do so makes her irredeemably 'not leadership material'. As she listens to Andrew 'put his case' she recognises, as so often, his statesmanlike ability to make personal points forcefully while seeming dispassionate; to give a technically neutral analysis which in fact leaves no-one in any doubt of his own preferences. It's a curious and distinctive blend of impartiality and egotism which she comes to call his 'F.O. manner' – an inextricable mixture of 'Foreign Office' and 'Fuck Off'. In later months she will often have cause to be grateful to that manner and what it can achieve. Sometimes she will envy it and wonder if it's too late to learn it. But mostly not. It is, she feels, the highly polished product of a very masculine world and one from which she is – inevitably and permanently – disbarred. Not least among the day's distressing events is the growing recognition that *Gay News* itself belongs firmly to that world.

There is an attempt at a straw poll to see if staff support Andrew as sole editor, but the discussion drifts between Andrew's position and Alison's position and whether or not there should be co-editorship in principle. No vote is taken. Robert – hedging in his familiar way – says that the issue is still open. People leave their chairs and drift towards the garden. A group photograph is to be taken. The outing is over.

It has been strangely like those sequences of 1972, 1973 and 1979, when significant allotments of authority were made (Denis made editor; Richard Creed given a shareholding; Denis made sole proprietor) without fully-organised debate or lobbying or voting. It is as if politics as understood in the larger political world are unknown at one of the world's rare journals of sexual politics.

Andrew had said, in the wake of the January 14, 1982, announcement that he is to succeed Denis as editor of *Gay News*, that although he has accepted so far as his own willingness is concerned, he will step down again if it becomes apparent that it would be without the consent of the staff. It had come to be understood that the question of whether he had consent would be resolved in Gloucestershire.

The ground was laid for any combination of factors. The *Gay News* lesbians, seven vital members of the paper without whom it couldn't come out, could have chosen to agree that they would walk out if Alison were not made editor on grounds of seniority – or at the least, made joint-editor in recognition of four years of highly-respected work and as a sign of commitment to a modernisation of the paper so that it take fully into account the requirements of the lesbian reader, which it has never in the past succeeded in doing.

Jean-Claude, the two Bobs, and perhaps Chris (whose attitude seems muddled), might have added their names to the threat.

Yet the move to 'draft' Alison peters out, seemingly for no stronger final reason than that Andrew doesn't add his name to it. Why? Alison's failure – if failure it can be called – to fight for the position with all her usual articulacy and perhaps with a stated determination to go if editorship or joint editorship is not granted her, may be due to many reasons, not the least of which is that any woman finds it difficult to say 'I'm best'. She is also, perhaps, not prepared to 'have a go' at Andrew in public, listing those personal and professional short-comings which she finds pertinent. She believes that this time *Gay News* needs a joint editorship in which both genders have representation.

Women on staff aren't unanimous in their attitude to the proposals on behalf of Alison. Wendy's heart isn't in making a fight to have anyone be sole or even joint editor of *Gay News*, as she continues to long for an end to overlords (or overladies). Each woman has her own opinion, whether it is about Alison's qualifications or Andrew's, and each woman, by the very fact of working in a 'mixed' (male and female) paper, is resistant to operating as 'the women', wheeling about, in closed ranks, to wrest advantage from 'the men', a confrontation that – once started – they all know they would indubitably lose.

Defeat for women, if defeat it was, was built into the situation of late January, 1982. Individual women who had done so much for the paper weren't going to make threats against its existence for the sake of a hierarchical gain; women who saw hierarchical position as itself inappropriate and the cause of past damage to the paper weren't going to fight to make a 'hierarch' of one of themselves. It was easier for those men who pressed the case for Alison. They could be good-hearted, and untroubled by the many impediments felt among the women.

But the outcome was built in for another reason, so plain to the uncollectivised unconscious that there was no call to refer to it. The legal transfer of the paper had not yet taken place. If Denis's evident satisfaction in the appointment of Andrew by Robert were flouted either by Andrew stepping down, or by Alison stepping up, or by an ultimatum from any group on staff, he would perhaps cancel the deal and come back.

That reason was very much in Andrew's mind. His own estimate was that if he retired from the fray in favour of Alison, Denis would come back, or at the very least would re-open negotiations with Robert with the intention of writing into the contract some power of veto over the editorship. His further estimate was that it could only be disastrous for morale, and for the paper, if Denis now returned in any fashion whatever.

He was on his own in the editorship debate. He neither lobbied on his own behalf before it (on the contrary, telling Chris, as a close working colleagues in the news room, that he would expect him to say what he pleased in Gloucestershire) nor looked to Robert to intervene. It seemed to him that people were foolish to press anyone's claims in opposition to the broad settlement between the incoming and outgoing owners of the paper and that fundamentally it was thoughtless – unkind in a minor way to himself, but the question was too significant for that to matter; unkind in a very considerable way to Alison, unless those who spoke for her were prepared to push the issue 'to the death'. Andrew was on his own, but backed, of course, by every circumstance if he chose to withold his own voice from those raised on behalf of the best-known woman ever to have worked for the paper. Though Robert would be silent – and was silent – during the January 31 discussion about the editing of *Gay News*, the new owner had held his ground on one matter, despite conceding it on the 'facilitator': the ultimate power of appointment.

Approached before the weekend with the request that he leave the choice of editorship, or method of editing, to staff assembled in the country, Robert had declined. He would listen to everyone, but his, he said, was now the financial responsibility for the newspaper, both as owner and as business director, and he could not give away his proprietorial right to state how the paper be edited, and by whom.

Nothing improper about that, if the principle of private ownership of a publishing medium is conceded in the first place. Admirable, indeed, if it meant that 'performance' would be the sole measure – quality of achieved newspaper product delivered to readers – rather than reward for long service, or extraneous political opinion of no essential relevance to sustaining production and paying bills.

If. Alternatively, Robert's reservation of his legal authority to decide was the assertion of moneyed (seemingly moneyed) power, and only too symptomatic of men's organisations' instinct to value the efforts of talented women but to see them as 'unfitted' to make policy. Symptomatic perhaps of another attribute held by many women to be typical of men's relationships with other men: was Robert, frankly, under orders from his predecessor in no circumstances to let any women get near to the levers of power over a paper the majority of whose readers, and overwhelming majority of whose advertising income, were male? Had he been given, and would he take, such orders?

The allocation of bedrooms at the so strangely inappropriate vaguely evangelical inn at Mickleton, contained a message unobserved by the men, but rapidly decoded by the women. Hosting the *Gay News* variant on the traditional English country-house party, Robert had done the sleeping arrangements. Very well done too.

Alison and Gill had been put together in the best and biggest bedroom of them all. He wasn't match-making. He was placating them. Or making it up to them. He knew of their 1981 efforts to organise a widely based new form of ownership for the paper, and on the uncharitable interpretation, had out-manouvered them in a take-over battle. He knew, or hoped, that Alison would not receive the title of editor that others were urging for her.

He had identified both Alison and Gill as potential trouble-makers for him. Or perhaps more exactly, human nature being too complicated for any one motive to stand alone, wanted his good and friendly intentions towards Gill and Alison to be plain, as towards any member of staff – yet had more catching up to do in this area than in others. The allocation of best bedroom to Alison and Gill had the covert appearance of a gesture of ceremony towards persons he saw as ambassadors from that hopefully allied but never wholly to be depended upon state, 'the women'. If you wished, it was touching; if you wished, it was clumsy; if you wished, it was that form of courtesy with which the powered pay forms of honour to the unempowered.   Or it just happened to be the only suitable bedroom available.

Alison's record covered years of work and a reputation gained both for herself and for the newspaper. There was no personal quarrel between herself and the newly-nominated editor, and yet no support from him, any more than from the new proprietor, on the question of her entitlement to move upward, to the top, at the start of the new years of *Gay News*. A declaration of non-confidence from the chief of the editorial side, as from the owners.

As to Andrew's thoughts, he shared them with no-one, before the discussion or after it. Had he done so, he might have been told that it scarcely mattered what he thought, since, in reality he was refusing to part with power, as men do refuse to part with power to women, and the rest can only be rationalisation.

Had he believed it right to step down for Alison, and done so, it is probably the case that Robert, whether of his own volition or under influence, would have refused to accept her. But had he chosen to agree that she should in all conscience be joint editor of *Gay News* with him, it is possible that he might have been able behind the scenes to cajole consent out of Robert and/or Denis.

He knew there was a chance he'd be able to at the moment on that Sunday morning January 31, 1982, when Amanda asked in such gentle puzzlement what possible objection there could be to Alison's promotion; when she pointed out what was so apparent to many, that for the nation's homosexual newspaper to enter the 'eighties with a lesbian and a gay man sharing the editorship would be the best of all declarations that indeed, as it had been founded to be, it was a paper for both sexes.

So far as he understood himself, he honestly believed that one, removable, editor is best for comparatively large-scale publishing and that of the candidates to hand for *Gay News*, he was himself the best. In a year or so, who knew? He believed that as things stood, Alison wasn't equipped to edit the paper alone; and if not alone, would infallibly become his deputy, as joint editor, though by title his equal.

He felt tempted by the 'public relations' advantages of the suggested arrangement, but felt that holding the opinions he did, it would be bad for the paper. It would be 'tokenism' (the appointment of someone for what they represent, rather than for what they're specifically suited to do) at the very moment when the newspaper, and he himself, very vocally, were trying to get away from that very thing with a new commitment to freedom of expression for women readers.

Rationalisation perhaps. Almost the worst of it for Andrew, who liked Alison and respected her place at the paper, and was most conscious that she had been working there longer than himself, was that he knew himself to be trading on the unlikelihood that she would promptly denounce *Gay News* and leave. As unattractively happens at such times, he wished there were some recompense he could make.

Edged out of any role in the acquisition of the paper during 1981, and now once again edged out, when she might have been the first woman in the paper's history to take a publicly acknowledged role at the very head of affairs, Alison shows no grudge.

The motorcade returned to London. A week later, Alison lunches with Peter, of clubs and entertainment, whose pages run alongside her own literary ones, and they come back saying that they'd like to have charge of general features under the style of 'joint features editors' – charged with procuring the four or five pages of wide-ranging features the paper will try to carry each issue.

Relieved that Alison has herself found means to restore her own dignity, and by association, the dignity of women's work at the paper, Andrew makes no objection. Robert, no doubt equally relieved, agrees to pay-rises they ask for, to reflect their newly stated responsibilities. Gender-parity in pay and rank has been installed at the second rung if not at the first. And – some note – 'hierarchy' has been reinforced, and so has *Gay News'* tradition of wide differentials in pay between the top and the bottom.

The conclusive yet inconclusive, fought and yet unfought, question of a woman's right to a place at the top has been the most painful jolt in the change of regime. Rough politics have shaken the darling buds of the new dawn.

Nothing is said of the Gloucestershire tensions either in the next issue or in subsequent issues. Not even in a page which, for the first time ever at *Gay News*, the women are to prepare without any intervention from the editor or any other man on staff; and on which work began in the very week that everyone packed their bags for Mickleton.

Part Two

THE FIGHT

March 1982 – Spring 1983

PART Two

THE YACHT

March 1982—Spring 1983

THE VISIBLE LESBIAN

Lavatories are mixed at *Gay News*, the most used one being next to the typesetting room on the upper floor.

So throughout the working day Wendy, with her recurrently re-dyed hair, and Lesley, who is still being trained in the use of the typesetting machines, can hear the tramp, tramp, tramp of feet going to and fro in the corridor outside, the flushing of the loo, the bang of the lid, and the splashing, from time to time, of Amanda or Alison washing their hair in the hand-basin.

Out of their one window Wendy and Lesley can see only the back and the back-yard, of a typical suburban London home, where every now and then a household mother can be heard yelling at her child.

Quite in the worst tradition of newspapers, Wendy and Lesley's office. The leased £6,500 typesetting machines with their valuable golf-ball fonts rest on tawdry working surfaces. The chairs they sit in, of burnished steel, are half broken – every so often Wendy lies on the floor to relieve the ache in her back.

Never-filed files from the news room lie in drifts in one corner of the room, the lava of those extinct volcanos, back-numbers of the paper. The 'copy' flows in to their wire baskets, they churn it out, they stay late for the days when everyone's running late, they 'set' 50,000 words a week.

Indispensable. If all the copy for an issue of *Gay News* were sent out to 'jobbing' typesetters, the cost would rocket, material would be late, and there would be no last-minute correction of inaccuracies. The engine-room of the enterprise, pounding away.

Just now, in March 1982, the engine-room is crowded. All seven lesbians on-staff, smokers contending with non-smokers, have squeezed themselves in for the regular weekly meeting to discuss what should go into the next fortnight's page for lesbians in *Gay News*, and – further ahead – what might be done with the two pages per issue that start up in April.

The machines are silent. Present are Alison, Amanda, Gill, Jane, Jo, Lesley, and Wendy, a third of the staff – which in total has gone up to twenty-two, with the addition of David Bird, who will spend half his hours sorting and filing (at last, at last!) editorial cuttings and photos, and half at the disposal of Robert in general office administration. Between them, the women on the newspaper cover, or take part in covering, general features, literary supplement, classified ads, display ads, news, diary of events, gay guide, editorial administration, and typesetting.

Scotty drops in, but she leaves soon, declaring she'd sooner get on with making out the contributors' invoices that have to be forwarded to accounts. Scotty has recently been deeply upset by being asked by Robert to change from personal dictation to 'audio-dictation', something she's not prepared to do 'at my time of life'.

(Forever lamenting his inarticulacy, in speech or writing, *Gay News*'s thirty-three year old new owner seems to find it difficult to do anything face to face. Or is that unfair? He likes to dictate answers to correspondence in the quiet of his home, away from the admitted racketings-around of a newspaper. Bizarrely enough, the inarticulacy except among closest confidantes is a characteristic that seems to have become hereditary at *Gay News*, 'the voice of the formerly silent'. The previous owner was just the same.)

Sandy Murdoch has been replaced as advertisement manager by Jane MacDonald, chosen from a number of applicants. Jane, very much the career woman, newly on the payroll, still in the usual state of new-appointment shock as she learns the advertising department routines and simultaneously under pressure to sell more space, has been protesting at being asked to spare two hours. She isn't let off so lightly. She's full-time, and any of the women present could say they ought to be 'getting on' – she's beginning in fact to see the point of this informal education in how editorial-style decisions can be made.

This morning they have issue 236 in mind, which will be published on March 18. The general news pages are going to include a tale about a Leeds gay club owner who, over the club microphone, gave a tirade against lesbians after two of them had a fight – local gay organisations are anxious that he might ban women from the club altogether which he has a legal right to do.*

There's to be more about Eliane Morissens, the Belgian lesbian teacher who went on hunger-strike after being 'suspended' for publicly revealing her sexuality – she's ending the strike. Alisdair is organising a full-page 'clearance' sale of mail-order gay women's books. But the bulk of the issue, as usual, is going to be 'mixed' (material hopefully of interest to both sexes) or of most direct interest to gay men.

Gill is doing an interview with a gay man thrown out of a London gym because he has nipple rings, for the news pages. Irish customs have seized issue 234 (February 18) and are thinking of banning the paper from the Republic of Ireland altogether – Chris is doing the story. John Russell Taylor, of the London *Times*, has written up the Berlin film festival's gay entries, and Alison has done a major interview with Julian Mitchell, the playright who wrote the hit *Another Country*.

The major feature of the issue, and cover-story, is going to be a four-page centre-spread on the lives led by gays in the North of England 'Manchester – the Muck and the Magic'. It's by Chris and Peter (Burton), who went north for three days to do the investigation.

Display ads, directed primarily at the 18,000 or so gay male readers who buy the paper every fortnight, are coming in apace, so apace that they're elbowing out some of the editorial material and dislocating the art-room through late delivery of ad-copy. 'The thing about *Gay News*', new editor Andrew is disreputably going around saying, as he surveys the resulting problems, 'is that when it isn't all come it's all go'.

Never mind about that for now. All this is context. What the women have gathered to consider, even though discussing the general contents of the newspaper en route, is what to put into the one page (out of fifty-six pages planned for issue 236) which the new editor has reserved as a 'women's space': nothing by or for gay men, though available, of course, to be read by the male reader.

It has an 'early position' – page seven. What the women decide

* In Washington DC, at the same time, club-owners (gay or 'straight') are pro-hibited by law from discriminating between women and men.

to do with it this time is to allot most of the space to an article in praise of the most famous single club for gay women in the world, London's 'The Gateways'. The 'Gates' used to allow a few gay men to be members, but doesn't any more, a cause of irritation to those gay men who would like women out of all 'their' gay clubs.

It's agreed that one of the women present, Jo, will do the article, because she's known the 'Gates' for twenty years, though the aim for the page is that it should be written as much as possible by outside contributors. 'Women coming from all over the country just to spend an evening at the Gateways, such was its magic', she writes. 'It was the only club of its kind – it was ours . . .' A photo of Jo with her lover Lesley and one of Lesley's children will illustrate it.

A satisfactory article in itself, but perhaps a bit 'timeless' for its high-profile location in an early part of the newspaper, and not going to do enough (236 will be the fourth fortnightly edition to carry the women's page) to justify its publication in the midst of thirteen vital pages of general news stories, with which the paper opens. Not enough to prove a case that Gill has increasingly been making, as a member of the general news team for the better part of a year.

She has been saying that while there are any number of news topics of equal interest to both sexes (regardless of whether the subject directly concerns only one sex), women will often receive as news what a man wouldn't think 'newsy'. Because men's activities, including gay men's, tend to be more public than women's, event and time-tied news reporting tends to swamp out developments of significance to the less extroverted world of women, and most particularly, gay women.

There's no question that it's true. No question, at least, in the editor's mind, given that far more homosexual women than men are debarred by economic disadvantages or by 'caring' involvements with children or relatives, or by a learned fear of men and even of public places, from doing the kind of things that can result in a news story good or bad, as traditionally conceived.

Gill believes that as the women's page develops it will offer a vantage-point on 'the news' that will be novel, and of equal interest to women and men. Andrew agrees, considering the initiative long overdue. 'It isn't pioneering', he says, mindful of all that has been done in the 'straight' media during the past decade to open out pages supposed to be of intellectual and emotional concern to women, 'it's just catching up'.

He has nerved himself for it to have an erratic start, and the women are self-consciously on their mettle to have it running fluently and impressively as soon as possible. Andrew itches to make suggestions about contents but has given a promise that he won't. The page will stand or fall on the use they make of it. They have his guarantee of twelve editions of *Gay News* in which to make the experiment, after which its success or failure, and its continuation, will be formally reviewed at the start of August.

(The promise given by Andrew is bent just once. He enquires whether the page might not be used in the near future to look into the recurrent rows – Leeds being just the latest example – about 'lesbian violence'. Owners of UK gay pubs open to both sexes make frequent complaints of fights between gay women, pointing out that pub fights among gay men, unlike 'straight' men, are rare.

Worried about dealing with a topic apparently so discreditable to gay women, when trying to get women readers' trust for the fortnightly 'space', the idea gets deferred.)

Run-of-the-mill stuff for newspapers, a new regular feature. A sufficient period for it to make its mark, or be scrapped. Run-of-the-mill, too, to make the experiment of a 'women's page'. In Britain, 'quality' papers have been trying it out in their various ways throughout the 'seventies – one daily newspaper, the profoundly conservative *Daily Mail*, has made its reputation and fortune by deliberately revising its treatment of everything, from news to features, to appeal to 'the women's market' – its sports pages virtually constitute a men's section.

Only one, however, the liberal daily *The Guardian*, has created a women's page which seeks deliberately to reflect the interests of people to whom such phrases as 'the women's movement' and 'feminism' aren't alarming; and to run cartoons in which awareness of 'feminist' hopes, and of what daily life does to them, are essential to the joke. By 1982, *The Guardian* is back-pedalling on its first fine flush of daring, but the effort has lent a new term to the language: 'a Guardian woman'.

Those who use it, with offensive intent, have a mental vision of 'trendy', humourless women, doctrinaire 'liberationists' whose men are condemned to faddy and inedible food, to pushing the 'unisex' baby in the stroller, to hostile analysis of their 'macho' habits. The mockery is the latest instalment in the long line whose predecessors have been 'bluestockings' and 'suffragettes' and 'the new woman'.

Many of the men on the staff of *The Guardian* don't care for the page, and wish that 'women's coverage' could be simply distributed through the paper wherever occasion justifies (as, within the traditional assumptions of a British national daily, it already is) and not have its own 'space' in addition in a prime spot, early on. Some women, on *The Guardian* staff and off it, wonder whether the page doesn't backfire by making women's issues appear 'singular' – divorced from the mainstream of life.

Whatever the truth, and whether in defiance of the women's page or partly because of it, *The Guardian* has been putting on sales steadily through the late 1970s and is at a peak circulation of some 400,000 copies daily. It has overtaken its main 'quality' competitor, the London *Times* and is in profit. There are those at Times Newspapers who think that if *The Times* doesn't soon climb down from the relentlessly 'masculine' assumptions of its latest editor and imitate *The Guardian* wholesale, it will never win sufficient advertising and a sufficiently wide readership to survive.

Very heterosexual, *The Guardian*'s page for women, and very heterosexual the mockery of it. But there's an overspill of mockery of lesbians, despite the scant attention paid to them in the women's 'space' in *The Guardian*. 'Lesbian mother' has been developing, in the right-wing press, as a subordinate clause of abuse, dropped without further explanation into onslaughts on 'Left-wing agitators, the GLC', and 'social undesirables' in general.

Women who put their heads above the parapet, and don't remain behind the lines where they ought to be, get sniped at. But it doesn't seem to follow that newspapers which encourage a new degree of visibility for women and women's interests are deserted by readers, men or women. Perhaps it's because newspapers reflect the innovations in society; or die.

In all its ten years' existence (up to the launch of this 1982 experiment for women readers) *Gay News* has always failed to win the trust of lesbians – of gay women. About 1,100 women buy the paper every fortnight, or one for every eighteen gay men. So the assertion is sweeping, and it has its exceptions. But it is a fact that though gay men in the UK (and indeed the general media) regard the paper as a very well known one indeed, it never occurs to many lesbians to buy or borrow so much as a single copy, and many of them have never heard of it.

From the very first issue, in June 1972, the paper's own pages have lamented the absence of material of interest to lesbians, and invited criticism and contributions. The four-page Diary of Events (listing everything that will be of interest to both sexes of gays in the coming fortnight) and the six-page Gay Guide (listing venues for both sexes of gays around the country) are referred to by more women than actually buy the paper, so they have always been to *Gay News'* credit.

The book reviewing, and attached feature interviews with writers, have for some years, and increasingly under Alison's editorship, paid close attention to writings for and by gay women, sufficiently so to be accused of 'feminist bias'; so they too have been to the paper's credit. Successive news editors, all of whom in the history of the paper have been men, have invariably tried to make sure that general news coverage fulfils the newspaper's commitment to be for all homosexuals.

But still, the paper has won the affection of very few lesbian women, compared to the large numbers of gay men in the UK who think of it as 'theirs'; and think of it too as a major achievement, fortnight by fortnight. The dismayingly widespread presumption is that it is a 'men's paper', which never has, and never will, break out of an obsession with matters really only of concern to gay men.

The presumption has become all the greater during the second half of the paper's life so far – from around 1978 onward – because its pages have been used by Peter's particular editorial territory, the 'gay scene', to promote the clubs, discos, pubs, and other service industries for male homosexuals which flowered on the American model in London and a few other British centres in the last years of the 1970s. AIDS had not yet been heard of. (First rumours of its seriousness are only beginning to percolate into England in 1982 itself).

As the only national regularly published newspaper for homosexuals, *Gay News* provides the indispensable medium in which the gay 'commercial scene' can advertise its wares. And those entre-preneurs' spending fuelled the late 1970s expansion in the number of published pages, and numbers on the payroll, of the paper – though not, strangely, profitability between 1979—early 1982.

The so-called 'commercial gay scene', patronised by gay women though primarily for gay men, isn't in the least unpopular under *Gay News*' new editorial direction – among women on the staff any more than among the men. The new editor, Andrew, calls it the bravest part of the gay world in the last few years, since its activities are on the front line of risk from police or local authority action.*

The paper's Diary of Events run by Jo continues to mention many of the 'commercial scene' events free every issue, the Guide lists every pub, club and disco around the country that she can get information on; again for free. The London van-run takes the first copies of every new issue to gay pubs and clubs all round the capital; owners of such clubs and pubs organised many of the 'benefits' that raised defence funds for *Gay News* as far back as 1977, for the 'blasphemy' trial.

There is no antagonism to the 'commercial scene' which most of the staff, male and female, make use of in their private life.

But there has been a drawback. Acres of male centred often crudely done display advertising with drawings or photographs of sexy young men, and pages of editorial matter serving to boost 'the scene', have exaggerated almost uncontrollably the impression *Gay News* has given of being a 'men's paper'. There's nothing 'hard core' in the paper, and yet to men and women sensitive to such things it is pervasively 'sexist' – its heart with daddy.

Even Peter, whose job it has been for many years, first on contract and now on full-time staff, to provide coverage of the club and pub scene, and whose interests lie very much in the leisure-life of the young gay man, shares the general opinion that *Gay News* in the late 1970s has become too entranced with the American gay male urban lifestyle as reflected in London.

It is a retreat to the 'ghetto', where the revenues of the paper are

* Early in 1982 he advocates the merits of 'the scene' to an Edinburgh meeting of Scots gays, who have been driven, by events in Glasgow, to seeing a hostile split between the 'scene' and 'the movement'.

safe, where a minority of young gay men – the town dwelling, the adequately affluent – are admittedly at their most 'gay' but also at their most divorced, for a few hours of an evening, from troubles that beset them at work and in the family; and most divorced from curiosity about the wide world beyond.

People point out that though no-one on an evening of pleasure wants to be troubled by all the rest of human life, it doesn't follow that they want 'their' newspaper to be equally uninquisitive. They don't read it, after all, in the club.

The solution to such economic and cultural predominance by the pockets and interests of men which is being increasingly attempted in Britain in 1981–82, as elsewhere in the Western world, is 'positive discrimination' – the highlighting of the work of people who come from the 'minorities', whether the minority is defined as coloured, or female, or – indeed – gay. The needs of homosexuals, male and female are at this very moment in early 1982 being advocated in some Socialist-controlled local authorities in the UK, above all at the County Hall headquarters of the Greater London Council, led by counsellor Ken Livingstone. Rate-payers' funds are being directed towards their enterprises, for the first time in local government history.

'Positive discrimination', a highlighting of the special interests of the woman reader, seems the obvious way of correcting *Gay News*' dedication to a limited set of gay male interests without dismantling what it does already for gay men.

Lesbians, other than those who separate themselves entirely from contact with any men, gay or straight (the 'lesbian separatists'), do constitute a 'minority' within that other 'minority', the homosexual population. It is a 'truth universally acknowledged'. They are next to invisible compared with the gay men.

The first working title for the women's page in *Gay News* now being planned for the fourth issue in succession, this March 1982, was 'Women's Forum'. Just before initial publication in February it changed to 'The Visible Lesbian'. The new editor had thought the draft title too bland. He wanted a title that 'told the story' and made as plain as possible the commitment the page and the paper were making.

'VisLes', as women on staff soon started calling it, had its origins in a serious blow suffered by lesbians in Britain in the autumn of 1981. *Sappho*, their ten years-old monthly magazine, with a circulation of about 700 on subscription, not news-stalls, collapsed financially and closed.

A petition arrived at *Gay News*, carrying the signatures of sixty women, among them some of the most prominent names in the lesbian/gay movement in the UK. Prompted by *Gay News'* own news room writer Gill, it asked that at this moment of crisis the national newspaper make a special effort to honour its commitment to lesbians. Another, and unprompted, petition arrived from another women's group based in London.

At the time, Denis was still editor, although secretly in the throes of his final negotiations to sell the paper, and not yet sick from the hepatitis that was soon to remove him from the premises. He, Andrew as news editor, Alison and Gill went to a *Sappho* meeting to discuss the petition. (*Sappho* was a lesbian group as well as the title of the former magazine.)

The outgoing editor consented to the idea that something ought to be done, and left it to his deputy, soon to be his successor, to work out the details in consultation with women on *Gay News* staff.

Accordingly, the fact of *Sappho*'s collapse and the existence of the petition (together with a separate one from gay women elsewhere) was recorded in the pages of the paper late in 1981, and in the last issue of *Gay News* to appear under Denis's name as editor – No 232, January 21, 1982 – Andrew wrote in an editorial that:

'The principle that *Gay News* can and should redress the balance between the lesbian viewpoint and the gay men's viewpoint is agreed . . . The working out of that agreement raises questions which are not so much difficult as fascinating – they go to the heart of the thing we wishfully call "the gay movement", and to the heart also of relations between the gay men and gay women on the writing staff and throughout the paper'.

The women were by no means sure at first that the situation required a separate page. The idea wasn't new. In the past, no-one had pressed for a page out of fear that it might shunt material for women into a restricted area, and result in there being still less attentiveness to the needs and feelings of women elsewhere in the paper. It had also been felt that the entire commitment of *Gay News* was that it was a newspaper for both sexes, and a separated page would amount to a confession that it had failed in its commitment: a public confession of failure.

Alison had seen her entire four years work at *Gay News* as a proof that the word 'gay' in the masthead (title) 'Gay News' did include gay women – and had endured accusations from many lesbians that the endeavour was a failure; that the paper was by men, for men, and she shouldn't lend her talents to it, but work solely among women.

She had lent herself to what amounted to a continuing campaign: 'gay' means women who are gay and not only men who are gay.

At this turning point, as well as being cautious about the creation of a special page, her experience led her to be doubtful whether a shift in *Gay News* terminology towards a much more pointed use of the word 'lesbian' wouldn't be divisive.

Running counter to that history and to those doubts were two factors of such concern that it was agreed in the end that they were over-riding. One was a change in the language. The tendency of the homosexual and the heterosexual media to refer only to men whenever they used the word 'gay' was beginning, by the close of the 1970s, to make it a struggle to insist on 'gay' as the term for both sexes of homosexuals. In the USA, still the fount of so much that influenced gay or lesbian thinking in the West, the thinkers and the politically energetic were switching over to the term 'lesbians and gay men'.

'Positive discrimination' put the word 'lesbian' in front of the words 'gay men', to emphasise the politically and economically weaker of the two sexes. Those who had defined themselves as 'gay women' to emphasise solidarity of experience and aims with gay men were being encouraged, in the USA, to accept for themselves the far more distinctive style 'lesbian'.

The development drew its energy also, from efforts to resolve a ceaseless dilemma: homosexual women in the women's movement found themselves submerged in the prevailing heterosexual concerns of a great part of the movement, yet became equally submerged in the gay movement if they defined themselves as gay women; they experienced invisibility in the social and political worlds of both undertakings.

Self-definition as 'lesbian' stopped dead the 'invisibility' in both worlds and in press or other media coverage of both of them. It was a case that Jackie Forster, who had been editor of *Sappho*, had been making for years in the UK. And its merits were being proved in a back handed way in the late 1970s and early 1980s in the emergence of 'lesbian' as a catch-all term of abuse in conservative writings.

Gay organisations in the UK intended for both sexes, such as Campaign for Homosexual Equality and London Gay Switchboard (except that the latter, like *Gay News*, kept to its portmanteau-word title), had been accepting the new thinking and new usage, and those most in touch with developments in homosexual life knew very well by the end of 1981 that the heyday of 'gay' as the description of homosexual men and women alike was over. 'Gay' could continue to be used loosely of both. Precision would require 'lesbians and gay men'.

The other special factor by the end of 1981 that altered the previous disinclination of women at *Gay News* to see a specified women's page was the loss of the magazine *Sappho*. Its very special credibility for lesbian readers, many more of whom passed it from hand to hand than bought it, had been the certainty that its contents were chosen by lesbians for lesbians – nothing filtered to satisfy or to appease the aims or the opinions of gay men.

Sappho had possessed the merit, for lesbians, that *Gay News* itself had for all homosexuals. Just as no heterosexual had any voice in the selection of contents for *Gay News*, so no gay man had any voice in the selections made for *Sappho*. If *Gay News* was to come to the rescue of lesbians deprived of the best known magazine out of the very scarce range of publications available to them, it would have to find a way of inspiring a similar degree of confidence, yet do it inside a newspaper owned and edited by gay men.

The only answer was a page in the paper edited by lesbians only, who must be able to say that there was no interference. Through December 1981 and early January 1982 women worked on the project, retailing the progress of their ideas to Andrew.

The proposal as they finally put it to him for his formal rejection or consent as editor (deputy editor when he first heard it) was for a page per issue provided it didn't mean an absence of material of concern to lesbians in the rest of the paper. He considered that this posed no problem; and when still at the stage of considering it in the role of deputy, knew that the absentee editor had no objections in principle, though he'd voiced anxieties about male readers being 'put off'.

The next element in the proposal was that it should be 'women's work'.

A phrase drawn from the women's movement, 'women's work', signified more than a promise that the results would be unaffected for good or ill by the views or participation of men. A way of working, as between the women taking part, was also promised.

It would be 'non-hierarchical'. Expertise would not be allowed to have automatic sway, or lack of expertise devalue the expression of an opinion. It meant the page would not be prepared under the direction of Alison Hennegan in her *Gay News* rank of literary and joint features editor; nor would its final decisions lie in the hands of the journalist women as a group – Alison, Gill, and Jo – though they would naturally play a key part in the mechanics of sub-editing the page and determining lay-out.

Wendy, Lesley, Amanda, and Jane, would have an equal voice in selection and presentation, as would any other women who might come on staff. Scotty chose not to be drawn in.

Developed to encourage women who had found their feelings silenced when among men, and to challenge the elitism of women capable, among other women, of behaviour defined as 'masculine', 'women's work' wasn't only held to be the most appropriate way that women could co-operate with one-another.

In the women's movement, there were those who claimed it to be the way that men should learn to work with men, and men with women. Some of the women at *Gay News* thought so too, and felt that if it succeeded in the project of instituting a women's page in the paper, the 'model' might encourage a spread of less strictly departmentalised, less vertically organised, ways of working for men and women on the paper alike.

'Women's work' was collective working. The women according-ly also proposed that, in their capacity as a team meeting once a week to organise the women's page in *Gay News*, they would call themselves after the name chosen for the page itself. They would be the 'Visible Lesbian collective'.

They asked that Andrew let them sink or swim doing the page in the way they thought right. No interfering in the preparation (though any comment or criticism after publication of an issue).

Gay News's art-room had no lesbian worker, any more than typesetters had a gay male worker. Union rules of the National Graphical Association (NGA) specified that only union members could finalise artwork for printers, so material chosen by the 'collective' would be readied for the printer by Jean-Claude.

But otherwise, it would be 'women's work', selected and prepared without the collaboration or interference of a man.

All this seemed to Andrew to be nothing less than was necessary if *Gay News* was to try the page at all. His predecessor had consented to the principle of better coverage for women, but might not have let the resulting page go without a departmental editor.

Andrew thought that editorial autonomy to handle it as they saw fit would both give the women the incentive to achieve excellence – for there'd be no excuses whatever if they failed – and give the women's 'space' in *Gay News* equal status with the writings of lesbians in the rare lesbian-only periodicals. He gave a guarantee that the page would have six months to prove itself and that there'd be no prior supervision of contents from himself, unless, improbably, he were compelled for legal reasons on behalf of the paper as a whole – e.g. to prevent libel.

No definite date in 1982 was set for getting going, and then, on January 14, came the announcement that Denis had retired (abruptly, as far as many were concerned) and that Andrew was editor. Sure of their backing, the women decided to produce the first of the *Gay News* women's pages at once, in the very first issue of the new editorial regime, to be in from the printers on February 2.

At mid-day that Tuesday, Bob, the distribution manager, brought into the *Gay News* art-room the first batch from East End Litho. People turned to page seven:

'THE VISIBLE LESBIAN' it read across the top, in leaf-decorated capital letters. And a 'banner' across the centre of the contents read 'This page guaranteed'. The introductory explanation to readers of what the page would be offering said:

'. . . Now, after all the speeches, here's some action: Meet The Visible Lesbian, making the first of her regular appearances in GN (one page every issue, going up to two quite soon we hope).' The collective declared itself to be 'caretakers for the space', and asked for contributions from readers, emphasising 'frivolity's as welcome as seriousness'.

There was a cartoon, a picture of a graffiti on a hoarding by a well known lesbian photographer, Jill Posener, a display ad for a lesbian disco in north London, and a feature about a lesbian's visit to the most sexually explicit film about gay men ever to have gone on public release in the UK, 'Taxi Zum Klo'.

Lacking outside contributors for a brand new page (a lack still being felt four issues later, when Jo began to write her feature on 'The Gateways'), this was by Wendy. She had gone to the screening with Lesley:

'. . . We certainly weren't bored, nor repulsed, nor embarrassed. What can I say? It was funny, it was loving, it was honest . . . .'

Words which demonstrated, if anyone wanted more demonstration beyond the fact that the women were working at *Gay News*, that neither the lesbians on the paper nor the page for which they'd taken on responsibility, felt hostility towards gay male sexuality.

There was an aboriginal feeling about that inaugural Visible Lesbian page in early February 1982, a lack of surface 'professionalism' similar to the early issues of *Gay News* itself ten years before. But it was friendly and it was exuberant.

Most of the men on the staff didn't think much of it, fastening on the 'amateurishness'. One or two people asked if it couldn't be moved further back in the paper, but this would be to demote it at the start before it had had its chance. The paper and its readers' loyalty, in Andrew's view, were fully strong enough to stand one page out of over fifty groping for its identity.

The women's movement terminology by which the preparation of the page was described, seemed 'heavy' to some on staff, and men on staff who went past the typesetters' door when it was closed on a VisLes meeting were sometimes annoyed by this seeming privilege of withdrawal into a form of exclusiveness. According to temperament they were simply curious or they made fun of it out of a reflex fear that somehow they were being put down (Mike did). Peter of features and Chris of the news-room, criticised the prime location and the quality of the page, and as great dislikers of meetings themselves, thought the 'women's work' or 'collective' method of preparation a great time waste, particularly when they wanted to put their own material through typesetters.

Chris and Peter apart, writers who put a high value on uninterfered with personally individual work, it was those among *Gay News'* fourteen gay men who were furthest from the production departments of the paper who were most sceptical of the innovations connected with the VisLes page. For a long time they saw nothing much, only the periodic disappearance of the women to confer in private. They didn't much care for that. Also there was a feeling of unfairness that Amanda, say, from classifieds, should now be allowed to have a share in the editing of a page in the paper, while none of the men in the administrative and advertising departments – Mike, for example, who so much wanted to write – had such an opportunity under the new regime any more than under the old.

Jean-Claude, Glen, and Tony, in the art room, exasperated though they often were by the delays or confusions which every now and again resulted from the 'collective' preparation of the women's page, were growing to be the staunchest supporters of the novel enterprise. They had the closest dealings with the problems encountered by the *Gay News* women, finalising the pages for press as they did.

The Visible Lesbian's first and subsequent issues in early 1982 attracted some thirty letters of protest from male readers, a few of whom said they would be cancelling their subscriptions. Some made it plain they regarded *Gay News* as a paper for gay men and were affronted at the eruption of a page of their own for lesbians, and at the adjustments elsewhere in the paper by which both material for gay women and the word 'lesbian' had started to make a more obvious appearance. Some more temperately (as did some women readers) criticised the idea of the separate 'space' and made the same point that had been made until now by women at work at *Gay News* themselves: that such compartmentalisation implied that lesbians were somehow 'different', different in an unacceptable and divisive degree.

A selection of the letters of protest (and the letters of encouragement that followed) was printed.

The most notable protest letter was one coming from, or affecting to come from, L Markham of London WC2, who in February wrote: '. . . I am no longer proposing to buy your magazine. I found No 232 so full of articles about lesbians that I was skipping most of the paper . . . .'

It was suspected that this was a pseudonym for a London pub, the Markham Arms in Chelsea, which is famous for being packed out with gay men on Saturdays at lunch-time, so perhaps the name was meant to stand for the metropolitan gay male pub crowd. The letter in full was so over the top that it was further suspected that it was by one of the young men on *Gay News* own staff, partly in earnest, partly to be anarchic.

However, knowing it represented a genuine strand of opinion among gay men, even if perhaps no more than a forgery itself, it was printed, and drew a salvo of angry letters from men and women readers supportive of the new approach to content concerning women. The February-March 1982 controversy also drew an entire rumbustious 1,000 word attack on lesbian writing in *Gay News*.

Called 'Dykeshead Revisited', the author's own choice of title, it appeared in the paper in early March and was by Roy Russell-Pattison, marketing director of the UK's best known gay-owned travel agency, Man Around (a frequent advertiser in the paper): 'Oh *Gay News*, this is another fine Ms you've got us into . . .', he wrote.

In answer to the probably pseudonymous L Markham, a guest-writer, Linda Hardy, wrote in a column published April 29: 'Before peevishly bleating on about how much increased lesbian visibility has spoiled his fortnightly read, Mr Markham might have spared a thought for women to whom *Gay News* is their only real link with the homosexual community'.

And in the same April issue, Andrew, in a personal column he briefly awarded himself, attempted a summing-up as the controversy apparently blew itself out: 'I think what the complaining gay men have been feeling', he wrote, 'even if they haven't explicitly said so, is that lesbians turn them off sexually. They expect to get a buzz from the paper, a rush of gay maleness; and this process is badly disrupted by lesbian comments, pages, news, articles . . .'

The Visible Lesbian went from strength to strength, both in terms of having more contributions than could appear, and in terms of winning interest from many different lesbian affiliations who had previously regarded *Gay News* as a men-only affair. During its year of publication, issues ranging from bereavement to lesbian S/M were covered and commented on. Nor was the working method a failure. On the one occasion when the collective was threatened with dissolution, the rift was healed within twenty four hours.

The women at work on the paper and the gay men with the final veto over its affairs had responded as best they knew how to needs not previously met by the paper. It had taken three months, but they had done what they could to fill the void left by *Sappho*.

Internally, a 'collective' had entered *Gay News* in a small way for the first time since 1972: in the midst of a paper privately owned, dedicated to the maximisation of profit (how dedicated, under the terms of the agreement by which Robert had bought it, was still a secret), and run on hierarchical lines, from editor to receptionist.

Very hierarchical, *Gay News* during the spring and summer of 1982.

Not as glossy periodicals are, where the fine furnishings are an editor or publisher's mark of rank. Nor as at large circulation newspapers, where the chauffeur driven cars and lavish provision for pensions are the marks of seniority.

The tokens of affluence at the *Gay News* of Denis's day have been largely got rid of. The flamboyant red sports car bought for his use by the company has been sold. Robert has taken over the sickly green Mini Metro, which Andrew had been driving, and that's now the sole company vehicle, other than the distribution van.

As an editorial prerogative of a rather preposterous kind, Andrew now sometimes drives the company van when it isn't wanted for the fortnightly distribution run; bombing round London with its 'no cruise' stickers on the flank and old heaps of the paper in the back, wheeling himself sometimes to Leicester Square and the Subway all-male club, with its notorious orgiastic 'back-rooms'.

Entertainment and similar expenses are low compared with what Denis, according to Robert, used to spread around. Departments stick close to the various budgets that Robert sets for them.

Everyone's on first name terms, but then that's no indication of a lack of 'hierarchy'.

Policy making is strictly binary. Twin stars, one revolving round the other (who around whom?), Robert and Andrew, or Andrew and Robert, dominate the affairs of *Gay News* no less than its previous owner-editor used to do by himself.

They are invited to a meeting of the London Monday Group, a discussion society affiliated to the Campaign for Homosexual

Equality, and asked how they divide the responsibility between them. Inarticulate in public, uneasy without a prepared text, Robert asks Andrew to give a definition:

'Robert is responsible for *Gay News* as a business', says Andrew, 'and I'm responsible for the quality of the contents. We've got enough to do on the editorial side without interfering in financial matters, and Robert has no desire to interfere in editorial content. He's guaranteed, in fact, that he won't try to impose any views of his own on the paper.

'In a word, it's up to me to make sure people want to read the paper. It's up to Robert to make sure it doesn't go bust. Of course, if he thought that anything we were doing on the editorial side was going to make the paper go broke, he'd have a right to intervene. More than a right – an absolute duty'.

The gays at the Monday group look content with that.

Temperamentally, Robert and Andrew get on fine, though by April, after some four months of the new regime, Andrew is rather missing Denis's kind of gayness, the former owner's appetite for the 'raunchiness' of the male gay world. Asked to a party at Robert's Little Venice home on April 17, he satirically wears a suit, shirt, and tie, in a restless though gentle enough mockery of Robert's 'straightness' – his lack of participation in the naughty world of gays. In advance mockery also of the *Gay News*' owner's taste for 'celebrities'. Kenneth Williams, most outrageous and bravest of Britain's camp comedians, is there, so it's not as 'straight' as all that.

The two men have different ways of being 'hierarchs', Robert liking to operate very privately; making up his mind, and then seeking out one individual to give him or her instructions (on 'his' side of the paper: advertising, mail order, finance, administration). Andrew working in the upstairs news room with Chris and Gill and open doors to Alison and Scotty in their cubby hole, and to Wendy and Lesley in typesetters, likes to get everyone nearest at hand to talk about possible changes, but there are no significant group or 'collective' editorial decisions. In the end, he says what's to happen on 'his' side of the paper: editorial, typesetters, art-room.

There are no all-staff meetings to criticise the contents of the newly published issues as they come out, let alone all-staff meetings to put forward suggestions for the future. The office is in two 'halves', reflecting the binary division of authority at the top. About a third of the staff, those in administration, finance, mail-order, and advertising, are vertically answerable to Robert as marketing director and financial controller, and about two-thirds, those who 'produce' the paper, are vertically answerable to Andrew.

Very important that the two men get on and have confidence in each other. The staff, for their part, give both men their trust. There is no attempt by any of those who were most disappointed to find the paper changing hands secretly, from one private owner to another in January, to oppose either the method of ownership or the division of authority; and no further attempts to find out what Robert agreed to in the financial and other confidential clauses of the deal. What happened, happened.

In time, Robert's offer of a more widely-based ownership, with staff participation, can be brought forward for realistic discussion. In the meantime there are floods of work to be done on the newspaper.

Floods, avalanches. Cramped in the little West Kensington building, staff bring out 'big papers' fortnight after fortnight: fifty-two page issues through March, and from then on a ceaseless fifty-six pages in the spring and the summer, with 'threats' at intervals – though they aren't realised – of sixty pages and even sixty-four.

Art room and typesetters have to meet, to declare that though they'll handle sixty pages if asked, sixty-four is out of the question until and unless *Gay News* moves to larger premises. They give their ultimatum in proper form as union members (National Graphical Association). It isn't an open row with management in the formal sense of head-office union officials coming to speak with either Robert, or Robert and Andrew together, but it's a digging-in of heels. Willing hands can do just so much but no more.

Even with that restriction, *Gay News* is a consistently larger paper throughout the spring and summer of 1982 than it has ever been before – more editorial content, more display advertising. Without question, the most impressive newspaper for homosexuals in the world, for volume, quality of contents, and frequency of publication, other than *The Advocate*, in Los Angeles – and with the advantage over *The Advocate* that while the American national fortnightly for homosexuals is being criticised in 1982 for increasing stuffiness (and specifically for an alleged failure to cover the fast emerging AIDS crisis), *Gay News* is once again showing daring, as it did in earlier years. And not only with the experiment of the Visible Lesbian pages, though that has drawn most comment.

If there's a common denominator in the policies of Robert and Andrew other than their willingness to take final decisions on policy, it's 'outreach', to use the slang of that moment.

Robert believes the paper should and could reach far more gays than the 18,000–19,000 who have bought if for years now: that this 'ceiling' can be broken through. He's negotiating with the country's largest newspaper and periodical distributors, W H Smith, in the hope that if the paper can be got to hundreds (potentially thousands) more retail outlets, the circulation will soar.

He's also – he begins to confide the fact to Andrew during the summer – interested in setting up a distribution company of his own, in partnership with the adviser, Brian Homan, whom he's put on a *Gay News* retainer. He declares himself deeply impressed by how profitable the established distribution chains are. He has in mind a privately owned company of his own, of which *Gay News* would be one of the clients.

Continuing an effort that he was already making after joining the paper as business manager in January 1981, he's also hoping to bring major consumer product manufacturers in as display advertisers, and succeeds in getting Sony. Single gay men doing well in their careers and free of any financial burden from children or from non-working wives are very big spenders on consumer durables. In America, as Robert knows, *The Advocate* has succeeded after years of rebuffs in breaking through the reluctance of 'straight' advertisers to risk tarnishing their product-line by advertising in a periodical for homosexuals.

It's feasible even in slow moving Britain, though Robert faces a great difficulty in making the attempt at a time when recession has hit budgets in industry and when social conservatism is on the upswing after the more exuberant middle 1970s.

Andrew believes that *Gay News* had become an in-turned institution under Denis's last years and urges every kind of outward-looking policy, from suggesting posters – the paper makes no use of its art room talents for this kind of promotion in the places where gays gather – to doing part-publications; and even paperbacks. He urges writers on staff to freelance, if they can find takers, in the general media, and does some himself (only on gay subjects).

The common thread is 'visibility', the word used for the new lesbian pages. He argues that the newspaper's reflection of the growth of the gay male 'commercial scene', honest though it had been in itself, had gone so far that the paper had become positively dim-witted except in the enclave of the literary supplement – on which, he also argues, there had correspondingly been an excessive pressure to do the job other parts of the paper were conspicuously failing to do.

A highly visible interest not only in lesbian issues but in the overseas experiences of gays and in the politics of the early 'eighties, both sexual politics and the impact of Westminster on the lives of gay people, is needed, he says, if *Gay News* is to become a 'sexy' read for the mind as well as sexual in subject matter. (Or, to quote the words of a later commentator looking back on the editorial changes of spring and summer 1982, to escape from the 'sometimes infuriatingly wilful and unwise apoliticism' of the paper's recent history).*

Robert's search for wider distribution and Andrew's for a greater 'openness' to the world coincide very happily in a number of initiatives designed to show the paper is getting energetically back into its constituency. On Gay Pride Day in London on June 26, when lesbians and gay men march through the capital with maximum public visibility, as they're doing in other Western capitals round the world, David Bird organises, for the first time, a *Gay News* float and balloons with a comic slogan 'Out with a bang – *Gay News*'. Almost embarrassingly, it leads the procession.

Robert suggests, and Andrew willingly agrees, that the paper launch an appeal among its readers to finance the post of Gay Rights Worker at the UK's National Council for Civil Liberties – and several thousand pounds are put up by the readership.

Far more photos are being taken for the paper by Bob the staff photographer – and by others, such as Chris in the news-room – than ever get into print. Andrew suggests asking Gays the Word

* David Widgery, in New Society, May 12, 1983

bookshop, in London's Marchmont St, if they'll put on an exhibition of some of them; and the bookshop – where Lesley of typesetters, is one of the directors – willingly does so.

The poster idea has to be deferred when the heavily pressured art room say they can't think of doing it till they're either working on smaller issues or have more space to work in. Publication of special pamphlets on gay issues, let alone paperpacks, has to be put off for the same reason, that everyone in editorial and production is too hard-pressed. But the consensus is there, to break out of the constrictions of the recent past.

Nothing does more to inspire optimism, during the late summer, than the arrival in *Gay News*' offices of some people from a record-company. In suits and with tape-measures they wander through, deciding whether to buy the building.

The 'For Sale' board stuck outside the premises for so long is at last like a fairy-tale coming true.

The rooms that had been rented next door, as overflow accommodation, have long since been lost, the owner having sold the house. The two Peters in 'accounts' have taken the computer with them to Peter Coell's flat, and are working from there, for lack of a spare inch in the West Ken offices. Numbers of staff are up to twenty-three against twenty-one when ownership changed. Overcrowding is so bad that when the proof reader is in to check the pages before they go to the printer, or when John Wilmott, the voluntary worker with the shock of white hair and the stick, is in to send subscription copies overseas, there aren't enough desks for people to work at.

Jo, who often abandons her desk for proof-reading – Jo the first person, always, to put herself out for the sake of others at the paper, and who sends herself up when asked to do something by saluting, and saying 'Aye, aye, sir!' – Jo frequently works from home, or is to be seen moving her bits and pieces from one room to another. It shouldn't be. Hers is one of the most vital tasks in *Gay News*' entire operation: the preparation of the ten pages per issue of Gay Guide and Diary of Events.

But the building suits the record company. If the conveyancing can go through without a hitch, *Gay News* will be free to move to more spacious rented accommodation. Art-room will be able to lift their embargo on the vital role that they would have to play in

128

almost every kind of new publishing departure, from the posters that editorial side are so anxious to see developed, to redesigns of the paper – including possibly redesign of format – to *The Bedside Gay News*, an idea for selections of the best in a year's issues of *Gay News* to go out in paperback form for the Christmas market.

People will be able to breathe and work.

Scotty does a survey of the distances and directions from which everyone comes to work, and it's decided that the Camden or Islington or Clerkenwell or King's Cross areas of London would be fairest to everyone. Robert finds two prime candidates: a well-appointed office in Camden, and a battered but spacious detached building in King's Cross, near the main-line station. Robert is inclined to Camden, Andrew to the somewhat cheaper King's Cross.

Members of staff go off to look at them both. The choice begins to settle on the King's Cross offices (which would amuse Australian gays, whose gay 'red light' district in Sydney is also at King's Cross). An autumn move-in is provisionally agreed, if the West Kensington sale goes through smoothly. It'll be the loss of freehold accommodation, but the gain of proper floor space for bringing out one of the larger periodicals of the UK. There's even some potential free space on the ground floor. Alisdair talks hopefully of expanding his mail-order work in a *Gay News* book and poster shop.

Robert, disconcertingly, talks for a while of using the space to open some kind of discount wine-store.

The 'hierarchs', Robert as owner, Andrew as editor, get on well enough. There's no split at the top. No power struggle of the kind Denis had bleakly forecast late in 1981, when he said that if he didn't sell *Gay News*, he and Robert would never be able to go on working together, both being too 'presidential'.

They scarcely ever meet in private. Each literally leaves the other to run 'his' side of the paper. If Robert has personal friends on the paper, it seems really to be the two Peters in accounts, with whom he spends a great deal of time doing the paper's financial work. Andrew doesn't socialise away from work with any of the members of staff, saying outright that he thinks it a bad idea for an editor.

There are some set-to's.

Robert springs an attack on news coverage at a meeting supposedly called to review future plans, and gets a counter-attack
from Andrew, who tells him he's only succeeded in demoralising
the news room who won't now be sure who they're working for. It
blows over, or is papered over, Robert agreeing that in future he'll
first raise any worries of that kind in private conversation with the
editor.

In early May, Andrew calls joint features editors Alison and
Peter out for a talk in the sunshine on the parapet outside the
church opposite. He insists that they consent to a demand he has
been making that issue 240, to be published on May 13, carry as
cover story a feature on Hollywood's first 'positive' gay movie,
Making Love. The joint features editors hadn't thought the article
good enough and claimed the right to take if off the cover.

The two incidents amount to an assertion by Andrew that with
the sole exception of the contents of the pages for lesbians – and
though generally speaking preferring to let people get on with it on
all the pages in .which they specialise – he sees himself as holding
the same final authority over everything which appears in the
paper as Denis, in his capacity of editor, used to possess.

Robert concedes that, as do Peter and Alison. But the incidents
are symptomatic of strains as the two men sharing control of the
paper energetically 'reach out' in directions which do indeed coincide here and there, but which also collide. They collide with a
thump in the spring, and the reverberations are echoing still
throughout the summer.

Jane lasts just two months as advertisement manager. Squeezed
between space-selling demands that Robert makes on her and
protests from the editorial/production departments as display
advertising pours in at every point of the production cycle she can
take no more of it.

Everyone knows, from the explanations given at the Gloucestershire weekend in January, that *Gay News* has been a loss maker for
three years, and must make a profit in the financial year starting
April 3, 1982. Every future intention, from art room and editorial's
longing for a better quality newsprint to improved wages for the
lowest paid, from special publications projects to such benevolent
notions as a paid 'sabbatical' for JC after his ten years on the

paper, depends on it.

It's no surprise therefore, and fully understood in principle, when, from the moment he's in full charge as publisher, Robert drums up revenue in every way he can, with a cover price increase, a display ads rates increase, and a flat out drive for more display advertising revenue. The problem is, he piles on the pressure so much that the advertising manager leaves, production is thrown into chaos, and many feel that the external effect must be very 'exploitative', *Gay News* seen to be wringing every copper coin out of the community.

The cover-price goes up from 50p to 60p in April, accompanying an issue whose front page pays tribute to London Gay Switchboard as 'the best thing the movement ever made'. On past experience, the increase will push down circulation by about two-and-a-half per cent, but in cash terms that should be far more than compensated for by higher 'net newspaper sale' income as distributors begin to pass back *Gay News*' share (approximately half) of the twenty per cent increase to readers who will still be able to afford to buy.

Raising and re-raising the targets per issue that he sets her, Robert induces Jane to procure £8,600 worth of display ads in the two March issues. To meet targets, she accepts bookings without regard to the usual 'shut-off' points in the production cycle, causing chaos both in the routines that have to be followed if the paper is to come out on time, and in the arrangements already made for editorial space. Both the design look of pages and reading material and photographs commissioned, are thrown into confusion by the unprecedented volumes of space repeatedly demanded by display advertising in the early spring.

The £8,600 worth of display ads booked into the March issues (partly inflated by the rates increase) compares with £6,000 per issue carried on average throughout the last half of the previous year. Though March represents the peak of Robert's pressure on the display advertising department, the paper carries thirty per cent more display advertising in money terms (against second half 1981) through the spring and into June.

It all constitutes the first really serious upset of Robert's new ownership. The two Peters in accounts, who have to meet the paper's bills, are inspired with a respect for Robert's restless energy in tackling the necessity of getting into profitability. The production staff are shaken by the new proprietor's determined indifference to their own needs if the paper is to be produced: so are the editorial staff. He refuses, on several occasions to take up the suggestions of editorial and production staff that he make a real effort to learn what they do, so that he will understand the reasons for production schedules.

Peter, of features and 'scene' coverage, is away for some of the worst of it – in a disgusting incident of 2 am on March 15, on Brighton sea-front, he is 'queer-bashed' by a gang of youths some of whom have acted as 'beaters', as in a shoot, to drive 'queers' into a trap on the darker stretches of sand away from the promenade lamps. His left wrist is broken, the other sprained, and shock keeps him away from work for three weeks, though he still manages to organise his pages from bed, and on April 29, in *Gay News* No 239, writes about the experience:

'Queer bashing was something I'd read about – and now realise, had rather callously dismissed. I can't say what being queer-bashed has done to me . . . but I still keep thinking about it and wondering if it will happen again. Maybe it won't to me . . . but the very nature of our society suggests it will continue to happen to others.'

Without being too pious about it, it was of course from the experience of such violence, sometimes physical, sometimes 'only' a matter of social attitudes, that the paper in which he is writing was born. The fact that those who work for *Gay News* are so enmeshed in the same experiences as their readers is a part of what makes most of the staff so sensitive to the suspicion of 'exploitation' that lurks in Robert's conduct of the money side – no matter how urgent the need to get into and stay in profit.

To replace Jane, Robert promotes Roger Jay, who had been helping on display selling under the style of 'client liaison manager'. An actor, Roger stipulates that he must be allowed to take time off unpaid should he get any engagements. At *Gay News* he uses another name because – as he explains – it does not always reflect well if an actor takes other work outside the profession. In practice, this summer, he stays hard at work through nearly every issue of the paper, in fact turning engagements down.

Self-assured, with a carrying actor's voice and lavish endearments, very 'paternalistic' towards the others who work in display advertising, valuing women's friendship, Roger had watched with horror as his predecessor fell into a dust-up with all the 'creative' departments of the paper. He immediately sets about restoring procedures, and in private session with the owner, tells him that the gay 'economy', and the staff at *Gay News'* disposal, can produce only so much advertising revenue, and no more. He successfully stipulates for a more reasonable display advertising revenue target per issue from May onwards, though it is nonetheless higher, considerably higher, than a year before.

How right he is about the 'pink economy'. The UK recession is bottoming out, but is still the deepest for some fifty years. Even the clubs, pubs, and service industries patronised by gays aren't immune. As the summer goes by, accounts finds an unprecedented bad debt record building up from the lavish space selling of 1981 -1982; UK bankruptcies are at historically high levels throughout industry; some gay businesses that had placed advertisements go broke.

Robert builds up the strength of the *Gay News* display ad department. As an assistant for Roger, twenty-five year old Don Hitchcock comes on staff at the end of April. Tall and slender, Don 'comes out' one day to his mother on the office phone, and arrives in the art room to say so; deeply shaken, hardly knowing whether to laugh or cry, like any homosexual at that moment, often one of the most critical in personal life. Rather startling everyone in quite a different way, he turns up at work in a spectacular Mercedes. It turns out he has a lover, Tony, a prosperous management consultant, who sometimes lends him the car of a morning.

Mike escapes from the reception area to become advertising administrator (one of Jane's bitterest complaints having been the clerical load on top of the sheer selling burden). It isn't a move into writing, the move he so much wants to make, but it's a step up from reception, lowest rung on the *Gay News* ladder. To replace him in reception and on 'box replies' Linda Semple, twenty-four year old lesbian and Socialist with a passion for Renaissance music, joins full-time staff. She had been a part-timer doing proof-reading once a fortnight. Gill also, a year before, had gone from proof-reading to successfully applying for a full time job – it seems to be one of the surest ways into *Gay News*.

There's now a three-man team on display advertising at *Gay News*, plus Amanda handling classifieds, in place of one, Sandy Murdoch, in display advertising when Robert took over the paper. Total numbers on staff, accordingly, have risen from twenty-one to twenty-three. Over in Mount Pleasant, Michael and Graham on *Capital Gay* look at the 'cast list' printed in the front of *Gay News* and comment how high the overheads must now be.

Robert, questioned about the build-up on 'his' side of the paper during another nondescript board meeting, explains that extra numbers in display advertising pay for themselves, thanks to the extra business they drum up.

Andrew, as editor, is full of new ideas. Indeed the two men, Andrew and Robert, share a marked common characteristic. They're impatient, they want what they think right carried out at maximum speed. There's a temperamental divergence – Alison called Andrew 'laid back' in a radio interview in the course of June – and Andrew, unlike Robert and unlike his predecessor Denis over recent years, is physically on the premises and embroiled in the output of the paper for as many hours a day as anyone else.*

But it remains true that Andrew puts up something of a smoke-screen about 'consultation', even among his colleagues on the editorial side let alone consulting staff as a whole. The person on-staff with whom he finds himself in closest agreement about the state of *Gay News'* contents, as Denis has left them is Gill. Both were very anxious through the late part of 1981 to see a revolution in the newspaper's handling of topics of specific interest to lesbians. Both particularly want to see improved coverage of news from abroad.

By late March, a page has been created ('WorldView') to do just this, kicking off (March 18) with items about persecution of male homosexuals in the British Crown Colony of Hong Kong, a South African academic research project into lesbians, and a photograph of two gay men in nun's habits, 'Mother Inferior' and 'Sister Mary Sit-on-my-face', sending up a gay rights conference in Australia. In the next issues, WorldView goes up to a two page spread, and begins to attract correspondents and contributions from round the world.

* Robert works very hard – so much so that he calls himself a 'work-aholic' – but is out of the office a great deal.

134

The pressure Andrew puts on to achieve the innovations in lesbian and international coverage cause two loosely federated camps to emerge at the 'senior' levels of the paper by late spring, if not before. On the one side, Gill and Andrew. Gill runs the international pages for which she herself, Australian born and with a German born lover, has such enthusiasm. On the other side, Chris, who accordingly begins to feel rather isolated in the news room, who has opposed creation of the page (subsequently two pages) for specifically overseas news and news features, begins to feel more at home with Peter, of features and 'scene' coverage.

Alison is not over much interested in 'abroad' and is particularly wary of American gay men's attitudes, unless they're good writers, but broadly speaking confines herself to protecting the Literary Supplement (Andrew, like Denis before him, has fits of wanting to see some aspects of it made more 'populist') and, until the church-parapet showdown over ultimate authority in features, she makes a fiefdom, with Peter, out of the four or five pages of general features now carried with solicitous care about 'gender balance' in each issue. She has had long experience of interfering editors, and is on the defensive, in her own special territories, from the moment Andrew takes over.

Peter, a most punctilious professional, who takes exacting care in meeting production deadlines for the 'Hotspots' column he writes about the social round in the gay clubs, rapidly redesigns the arts and entertainments pages, invariably showing his ideas to Andrew before carrying them out. They have only one conflict over the gay commercial scene, which is when Andrew tells him not to print his own, Peter's, diatribe against one of London's most famous gay male pubs, the Coleherne in Earls Court, until he's commisioned a balancing piece from someone who likes the pub.

In line with what Alison had said at the Gloucestershire week-end in January about the need for the country's national paper for homosexuals to pay more attention to UK cities other than London, a feeling shared by everyone on staff, Peter and Chris take themselves off from time to time to do a major feature on gay life in other parts of Britain. They kick off, in late March, with four pages on Manchester which they call 'City of muck and magic'. Working together in this way brings them closer together, so much so that Andrew enquires of Chris whether he'd be happier transferring to the entertainment and features end of the paper; but Chris prefers to stay based in the news room, where he's highly productive, and where, besides news stories, he writes a regular 'Mediawatch' column. His own idea, it reviews the fortnight's handling of gays and gay issues by the 'straight' press, radio, and TV, and is one of the most popular features in the paper, attacking and sharp.

The editorial 'hierarchy' holds firm, and the conflicts of attitude are no worse than on any paper or journal where people on the whole get on with their responsibilities unhindered, but it's apparent that in his polite way Peter is a constructor of 'gangs', liking to form a like-minded team of his own in which to work.

He runs a sustained campaign to use a freelance photographer friend, Bill Short, to take photos of his pages, calling the work of the paper's staff photographer, Bob, 'sexless'. It's true that Bob is going through a career crisis, after six years on the paper. He works as hard as ever, sometimes producing indifferent pictures, sometimes even bad ones; but it may be that much of his inadequacy is the result of systematic demoralisation from Denis Lemon and now, latterly, from Peter Burton and Chris Kirk. Bob has also run foul of the art room by advising them – in his best 'bad boy of the school' manner – how to do their jobs. Partly it's all because he is excluded from decision making and from editorial discussion. For years he's felt frustrated by having no writers to work with; no 'vox pops' or 'private lives' to do; no 'personality' interviews. He also has no access to the telephone lines, is not supposed to see the editorial mail and is not given a desk in the editorial department.

Bob feels threatened – and justifiably – by Chris, who is developing a taste for taking photographs. In the dark room in his house round the corner, Bob processes everyone else's negatives, including his own, adding wormwood to gall.

In August, the *Gay News* Board receives a letter from a number of lesbian photographers wanting to know why their work is not being used on the Visible Lesbian pages and why, instead, the work of a male photographer – *Gay News*' house photographer, Bob Workman – is appearing on these pages without justification or comment. The Board asks Alison to write back.

This brings into the open the festering wound of Bob's job and the encroachments being made upon it by two of his male colleagues: Chris Kirk and Peter Burton. Alison and Gill discuss the matter with their women colleagues in the Visible Lesbian collective. The matter is also discussed at a staff meeting held on September 3. The minutes of that meeting record the following:

'(1) Finance: If GN is currently suffering financial constraints, it seems odd that money is being spent in fees to freelancers when the house photographer is available to do the same work. It was pointed out that the superficial cost of using freelancers may appear low, but that in fact the invisible costs of processing – in the event of having no house photographer – would be considerable. At the moment, the house photographer processes other people's films, frequently out of office hours, and quickly, for which double rate would normally be charged. He does this for no extra cost.

(2) If freelance photographers are being commissioned to do work which the house photographer is available to do and willing to do, then the cost should not be born by GN. It is an almost untenable position for the women journalists at GN to stick to the principle of using the house photographer, who happens to be male, and to defend this principle to other lesbians, when their male colleagues feel free not to do the same. In addition, at a time of financial anxiety, no employee's position should be undermined by encroachments upon his/her job description. Everyone present at the meeting was unanimous in expressing their fullest support for the principle that colleagues' jobs should not be endangered in such a way.

It was also suggested that the NUJ chapel, the NGA chapel and especially Peter Burton and Bob Workman meet to discuss solutions to the problem of freelancers.'

Most of the principals in this drama are absent from the staff meeting, owing – variously – to assignments, illness, holidays, or work deadlines, Bob, Peter Burton and Chris are not present; nor are Andrew, Tony, Lesley, Roger, Alisdair or the two Peters from the accounts department (who hardly ever come anyway to staff meetings).

As the staff meeting has requested, a meeting of the NUJ chapel is called. Andrew is not a member; nor, yet, has Jo's application for membership been processed. Bob is away. Chris, who is the Parent of Chapel (the official recognised by the union to order the affairs of its members on the *Gay News* staff) and Alison, the clerk, call the meeting. Peter Burton and Gill, the only other two members, are present.

The meeting lasts for nearly two hours. For most of this time, Alison and Gill, both separately and together, try to make their male colleagues understand that Alison and Gill are risking their loyalty to other lesbians by protecting Bob's job in the face of indifference from Peter and Chris. Peter consistently refuses to take Bob on assignments and, instead, uses one of his friends to take photographs for the paper. His friend's fees and expenses are paid for by *Gay News*, without demur either from Robert or from the Board. Chris has taken to photography as a hobby and also refused to give assignments to Bob, preferring to take his own photographs, which appear in the paper, also without demur. Ironically Bob, who processes his own work at home, helps load Chris's camera and develops his negatives for him. If Alison and Gill refuse to give Bob assignments, on the grounds that they wish to support women's work, then no-one except Andrew will be using the full-time house photographer to do the job he is employed to do. And Andrew has been heard muttering his dissatisfaction with the quality of Bob's photographs.

Alison and Gill ask Peter and Chris to consider several things: if there is a consensus that the quality of Bob's work needs improving, then he should be told about it and discussion should begin about what could be done to improve it – perhaps he might value some further training, or perhaps his colleagues would explain to him what their requirements are – but Peter and Chris will not agree to such a process, saying instead only that 'Bob is no good'. Alison and Gill also put to Peter and Chris that if, for aesthetic reasons, they judge their work to need photography not done by Bob, then they should be willing to pay for it, rather than charge it to *Gay News*. Naturally, perhaps, they do not see the force of this point. Nor do they understand at all that Alison's and Gill's determination to use Bob, come what may, is an act of professional solidarity towards a colleague whose job is being threatened in an underhand way and who is being given no opportunity either to discuss his work or to defend himself against charges made against his competence.

It looks to Alison and Gill suspiciously like egotism pure and simple, on the part of Peter and Chris – rather than any attempt at professionalism. Peter just wants what he wants because he thinks he is entitled to do so, whatever the effects on anyone else, and Chris thinks that his judgment is better than Bob's and that he takes a damned fine photograph anyway.

The problem of what is to become of Bob, or what's to be done with him, remains a painful matter throughout the spring and summer, but in terms of the 'gang' formation tendencies in Peter, he's only an instance. By the sheer drive with which he organises forward planning of features, Peter soon has Alison in what seems to Andrew to be a secondary position in the joint features editorship (though Alison perfectly successfully fights the corner of features of particular interest to women – Andrea Dworkin, of the USA, on pornography, and material on lesbian S/M cause particular comment). He draws a willing Chris into his ambïence, and brings on new young gay male contributors for the 'scene' pages.

So he should, though he needs shoving to get lesbian contributors to the pages much space, but the effect is of a shadowy 'Opposition' to the paper's 'Government' as vested in Andrew. The effect is enhanced by occasional remarks from Peter – which don't get back to Andrew – about it being most peculiar that Andrew regards himself as a personal friend of Denis. The implication is that if anyone understands, and can perpetuate, Denis's former achievements on the paper, it's the person who was really a friend, Peter. As a final and significant ingredient in this gradual construction of a kind of alternative editorial approach and grouping, Peter shares with Robert the downstairs office by the front door, and gives him genuinely useful advice on display ad possibilities in the gay commercial world and recommendations for new books that could be taken on to the *Gay News* mail-order list.

Valuing the work done by Peter (and Chris) Andrew doesn't regard this as a power-play. He doesn't believe that Peter wants to become editor (Denis, late in 1981, had gone out of his way to say that Peter wasn't competent to edit the paper) and regards it all as a fairly unsurprising way for a gregarious writer, specialist in the social scene for men, to behave. What does happen, however, is that the emergence of so strong a 'bloc' centred round the *Gay News* coverage of the commercial gay scene strengthens Andrew's determination to force through a much more intelligent handling, as he calls it, of the leading 'movement' and political issues, of which creation of the Visible Lesbian and the international pages are two examples in 1982.

Thus when the Falklands War breaks out, *Gay News* trailers 'Argentina – never mind living under their sovereignty, who wants to live under their sexuality?' on the cover of April 2, puffing two articles about repression of homosexuals in Argentina which Gill has procured for WorldView. The same cover trailers news coverage of the fruits of a long-nursed reorganisation of the Campaign for Homosexual Equality, designed to deal with its dwindling membership and fuzzy campaigning edge. Andrew and Gill don't privately plot the innovations they both favour, but are obviously in sympathy. Both Peter and Chris begin to speak of Gill, who indeed lacks journalistic experience compared to either of them, as 'academic' – the same accusation Peter, and also Denis, had used in previous years about Alison.

As the summer develops, the fact that the *Gay News* editor is in open sympathy both with the aims of lesbians to achieve a better reception of their views in *Gay News*, and with Gill, among the writers, leads to murmurings of an 'L Markham' kind among some of the men on staff.* Peter in editorial, young Mike in advertising, say that lesbians have taken over the paper and its editor with it. It's not an opinion shared by the three men in the art room, who work most closely with all the women on the staff, nor by the new advertisement manager, Roger.

Tensions over editorial policy erupt in the late spring row over news-coverage, when Robert unexpectedly springs his onslaught with a most demoralising intensity. Citing the late 1981 Readers Survey, in which a ninety-four per cent male readership put news top of their list of the valued ingredients of *Gay News* (some 2,000 respondents filled out the questionnaire), Robert says that the news pages are becoming 'too heavy'. And is promptly made very angry by a suggestion that what he really means is that as financial controller he wants to see the paper go 'down market'.

Andrew refuses to budge.

Peter and Chris draw closer together in their vision of a paper with an undemanding approach to news coverage, and their shared personal interest in the entertainment scene, the generally

---

* For the misogynist 'Markham' letter, see the previous chapter.

pleasurable end of life where 'politics', gay politics included, are suspected of having killjoy intentions. Andrew neither reduces the space made available to them both, nor cuts into their 'expenses', which work out higher than for anyone else on the writing staff, himself included, believing that the areas they're interested in are fully as important as they say they are. But he refuses to agree with them that the paper must also, in the run of news pages with which each issue begins, avoid 'alienating', as they put it, the expectations of the male gays who use the 'commercial' scene in the big cities.

Andrew doesn't share their vision of a gay world divided into the 'thoughtful', who don't go to clubs or buy records, and the 'non-political', who do. The two worlds, he says, are one, apart from a minority in the clubs who indeed never want to be troubled with a serious question, and a minority of 'gay politicians', who are hostile to the clubs. Most gays, men and women, he asserts, pinning the paper's colours to precisely that mast, will want to find everything from the deeply serious to the completely frivolous in 'their' newspaper.

To illustrate the point, he prints as 'outrageous' an article as *Gay News* has carried in years: the personal account of a fist-fucking experience. In mid-1982, fist-fucking is still the most extreme and most talked about cult in the raunchiest American gay men's private clubs. Most gay men in England talk about it with awe. The article Andrew puts into the paper tells the true story of a West Country gay whose lover, greatly excited by reading of the practice, demands that he be fist-fucked. It results in surgery, and a most moving account of his remorse and despair by the lover who consented to do it.

Robert continues, at intervals, to ask Andrew in private for 'short', 'snappy', 'human interest', news stories.

Just wait a bit, says Andrew during the course of the summer. It's hard and disruptive, he suggests, over and over, to break a pattern whereby a newspaper has avoided its obligations to a whole array of subjects, and to sections of the potential readership, and it's true it flouts the habits the more acquiescent existing readers have fallen into. But as with the introduction of the Visible Lesbian pages (letters of complaint have faded away, subscriptions to *Gay News*, for whatever cause are going up), people get over the shock of the new where they'd expected everything, in a favourite newspaper, to remain the same.

The paper's reputation and hold on its market are strong enough, the editor says, to survive the jolts of incorporating some less 'safe' material. The only known commercial test is revenue, and as the broadly based board of directors gets told, month by month through the summer of 1982, aggregate revenue from display, classified, mail-order, subscriptions, and 'net newspaper sales' is well up on 1981, ranging from eleven per cent up to eighteen per cent up month on month between April and August.*

Once *Gay News* has proved that it can, despite the lapses of more recent years, offer more material on serious topics affecting the gay world, the paper can try to do it with an increasingly light touch.

By August, Andrew is recommending an overhaul in the autumn to achieve just such a more 'graceful' touch without abandoning any of the commitments to material from abroad, women's coverage, and attention to the political.

Simultaneously, Peter is telling Robert, quite accurately, of complaints he hears in the clubs and by club-owners of *Gay News* being 'too heavy'. Rumours begin to filter back that Denis, returned from America, is telling people how little he thinks of *Gay News* these days, and that he doesn't bother to read it. It is even said that he tries to persuade his favourite local gay pub, the Edward VI, to stop advertising in *Gay News*. For whatever reason they do stop, but Roger persuades them to come back in again.

Andrew says that if it's all true, then Denis is feeling no more than the usual annoyance a past editor feels at changes made by a successor. The two men haven't seen each other since Denis left the paper in January, though they've spoken a few times by phone, most recently in the early summer. Andrew is slightly taken aback that Denis wants to be so permanently detached, but Denis had said, as far back as late 1981, that if he got away from *Gay News* he'd want nothing to do with anyone who had any connection with the paper.

* Not that figures are presented to the board in this comparative form. They are never provided as historical trend lines, but only as compared with Robert's budgets – ie estimates of what he thought they should be. In short, though this isn't clearly apparent to anyone, he's making spending commitments on forecasts of exceptionally high income.

Hazily perceived, there are the makings of an 'in-house' revolt, against the directions in which the new editor is taking the paper.

To women on the paper, who find that the new owner, and Peter and Chris, are all in their different ways very ill-at-ease with lesbians, it's the makings of a gender-based faction – gay men who are drawing closer to one another because consciously or unconsciously they have substantially the same attitude towards *Gay News* that Denis himself had. They see it as an important newspaper, no quarrel there. They're all hard working, no quarrel there.

But the women see the three men as temperamentally hostile to anything at all troubling, anything that isn't reassuring to those expectations that might be attributed to the unthinking, high spending, youthful gay man of the cities. They further see Chris and Peter, popular writers though they are for very many readers, as showing a growing appetite for personal prestige from the paper through their by-lined material, the most costly of any procured by the paper.

Andrew is unworried by the tensions, none of which find any expression in the pages of the paper. He's sure he has a better perception of the future of *Gay News*, editorial and commercial – so far as content will govern the commercial future – than either Peter or Chris. Or if it comes to that Robert, and on the far horizon Denis. In this he's as sure, or as arrogant, in his own judgement, as Robert is on financial affairs.

'FROG TALK'

The aim of getting *Gay News* out of its shell, on which everyone's agreed, succeeds by leaps and bounds during the summer of 1982. For one person the publicity becomes almost too much of a good thing – the editor, who in July seemingly gets burgled by Fleet Street in search of a story.

But first, the past gets laid to rest.

On May 10 the European Commission of Human Rights refuses to forward the 'blasphemous libel' case to the European Court of Human Rights, on grounds which include, unbelievably, an assertion that the rights of the original complainant, Mary Whitehouse, had been infringed, though she was never a reader, when the poem about Christ was published in 1977.

The legal bills, both of the paper and of Mary Whitehouse, now have to be paid. They are settled out of the £26,435 raised in 1976–77 by readers of the paper, well-wishers, and benefits staged by the commercial gay scene. Accrued interest over the years means that bills totalling nearly £30,000 are paid (and leave a £4,700 surplus which can in due course be put to some purpose useful to gays).

No part of the 'quality media', despite press releases from *Gay News*, devotes any space to the constitutional and press freedom issues raised by the peculiar decision of the European Commission.

Better fortune, in terms of some response from the world in which *Gay News* and its readers live, attends an altogether more likeable event on June 22, one day after (it so happens) the birth of a son, Prince William, to that ringing affirmation of heterosexual value, the marriage of Prince Charles and Lady Diana. (*Gay News* notes that the infant would seem to have been named for two sodomites, William I 'the Conqueror' and William II 'Rufus', for a bisexual, William III 'of Orange', and a sailor, William IV).

The event of more immediate concern to *Gay News* is its own tenth birthday. 'Only ten?' says the editorial in the Birthday issue published on June 24, 'We should be 100, or 1,000, but as it is, it's a fantastic achievement. Some credit to us, but far more to the tens of thousands who in ten years have rejected all the misnomers that society had given to gays, and have accordingly bought us – bought us because we took the right to be heard.'

JC designs the cover. Ten years before he had worked on issue No 2 and sold it by hand, like everyone on the collective, during the Gay Pride festivities of 1972. He takes a slip of paper with some wording, given to him by Andrew, and instead of Letrasetting it, photographs it for the foot of the front page. It reads 'Born 22 June, 1972, Place of Birth London W2, Parent Gay Liberation Front'; and accordingly the handwriting of the originator of the paper appears on the commemorative issue.

Chris seeks out all the original members of the 1972 collective he can get in touch with, and does a 'Where are they now?' feature, including what they think of the paper today. JC himself is quoted: 'I think we're lacking a little in political direction, there's not enough commitment. GN tries too hard to be a mirror – I hope we start sticking our neck out more. The big issue? What it is to *survive* in the 'eighties as a gay person.'

Chris tracks down Glenys Parry who had been head of the Campaign for Homosexual Equality when the paper started, and who had played an important role in soliciting advance subscriptions and offering publicity. She says she rarely reads the paper today, but thinks of it as 'commercial and male-oriented'. Another woman of the early days, Suki Pitcher, who had been on the collective, recalls selling copies of *Gay News* every Sunday in London's rich Mayfair district: 'A beautiful Rolls would draw up, and a man sitting with a beautiful boy next to him would buy five copies at once.'

Graham Chapman, of the Monty Python TV series and films, who had put some cash in both at the start and during the 'blasphemy' appeal, is critical: 'I don't think the more informed gays here [in the UK] read GN so much because there's often not enough to feed their minds.' Ian Dunn, of Edinburgh, who wrote Scottish material for the first issues and has just become editor of a new Scots magazine for lesbians and gay men, *Gay Scotland*, says of Denis's editorship that he was 'convinced *Gay News* was going to last, as long as Denis stayed on. The good thing about Denis was that he wasn't allied to any one faction'; but of the newspaper, 'I'm pleased it's now turning away from being stodgy and predictable. It has a new sense of freedom.'

The 'quality' print media again pay virtually no attention to what those who work on *Gay News* consider a fairly remarkable social and publishing achievment, despite being fully informed about it, but BBC Radio, personalising the anniversary, runs a twenty minute 'profile' of the new editor. Those interviewed for it include his sometime employer, former editor of the London *Times* Sir William Rees-Mogg. It appears, says Andrew, that parallel lines can converge after all – for Sir William is a devout Catholic.

Tony, in *Gay News*' art room, does a three-quarter page cartoon mocking the salaciousness of the 'popular' press on gay matters and the censorship on gay issues of the 'quality' press. He satirises *The Guardian*'s failure to cover matters concerning gays despite its 'liberal' pretensions (despite, too, the fact that the *Gay News* Readers Survey suggested that thirty-seven per cent of *Gay News* readers buy *The Guardian*, making it their preferred daily paper).

A paragraph from Andrew's editorial gets reprinted in one of the oldest American papers for gay men and women, *The Gay Community News*, of Boston:

'A free press, they say, is the great defence against tyranny. There is no free press in this country for homosexuals. Apply a simple test: who can you think of who writes for the quality or popular press, whenever it would be relevant, as an out gay? If people cannot be open about their homosexual viewpoint to the same degree that heterosexual writers are open about *their* viewpoint, then a significant section of opinion finds no expression in Britain's "free press", and that press is not free.'

There's a birthday party for staff, lovers, friends, contributors, and members of the gay public who buy a ticket, on the evening of Wednesday June 23 at one of London's most famous nightclubs, The Embassy. A plaque on the wall records that David, Prince of Wales, used to dance there with Mrs Simpson in the 1930s. Plus ça change . . . . Sunday nights at The Embassy now are gay nights, and the club's manager, Stephen Hayter, is interested in picking up publicity by hosting the birthday celebrations of the country's leading gay newspaper.

Gay News says yes to the venue, and yes to Hayter picking up the bill, because as Robert says, and everyone believes him, there isn't the money available for the paper to organise and pay for its own festivities. Nonetheless, it's a bit demoralising, after ten years – *Gai Pied*, in Paris, after only three years, manages to rent a major Parisian building and play host to thousands of ticket-buying gays. The crowd at The Embassy is restricted to about 400.

This, the press do notice. The 'popular' press. The right-wing mass circulation newspapers *The Sun* and the *Daily Express* send gossip columnists. Hayter produces an immense birthday cake. Robert is dressed in 'velvet' smoking jacket, ruffled shirt, bow tie and cummerbund, which conservative, social-climbing garment is to become an obsession for *Gay News* cartoonist Tony Reeves in later months. Andrew is in singlet, jeans and tennis shoes, keys jangling as always at the hip. Together they cut into the cake while the cameras flash, looking like a most satirical bridal couple.

It's an uneasy party.

Gill and Linda, waiting to be let in before the party starts, are confounded to have Robert walk past them without a word, gain admission, and disappear, leaving them shut out, as they say, 'like a couple of ninnies'. Robert gives a halting, poor, speech, which he reads off a piece of paper. Michael Leapman, 'William Hickey' gossip writer on the *Daily Express*, declares himself surprised by the lack of outrage at the party.

He means presumably lack of drag or nudity, but it's a way of voicing what many of the homosexuals present feel and many of those on staff. Where are the spontaneity, the sensations, the fiascos, that ought to accompany anything celebratory organised by the people on the *Gay News* staff? It's as if the paper had elected to go as far away from its constituency as it could at the very moment of patting itself on the back.

Denis, who most certainly should have been there, isn't. Andrew had invited him, but Denis had said he might not be back from America in time.

Another unease is that birthday cake, so generously provided by the Embassy management. Its top is decorated with a pink triangle, the emblem Nazis made homosexuals wear in the concentration camps, and which has been re-adopted by gays of both sexes around the West as a gesture of memory and of defiance. No need to get too 'political' about a birthday party, but is all well when a symbol of suffering and courage dwindles to become the icing on a commercial cake? Maybe that's what liberty amounts to . . .

It's out of its shell with a vengeance, *Gay News*, just one month later, and this time not because of any interior event which attracts (or fails to attract) the attention of the larger world, but because the Home Secretary announces to the House of Commons that the Queen's bodyguard, Commander Trestrail, has resigned after an admission that he'd had a long affair with a male prostitute.

For nearly two weeks, starting Monday July 19 when the 'scandal' breaks, Linda on switchboard is besieged by the whole array of the British 'quality' and 'popular' press, as well as radio and TV. Old hands at *Gay News* say they've seen nothing like it since the height of the 1977 'blasphemy' trial, when Denis and the paper were across the world's front pages.

Trestrail, a man trusted by the Queen (who apparently takes care to leak her annoyance with the Home Secretary for humiliating so publicly someone she had thought a good servant) effectively goes into hiding, and the press concentrates its attention on discovering the name of the male prostitute, whom the Home Secretary omits to identify. The 'popular' press take for granted that the editor of *Gay News* will know it, while the 'quality' press want comments from him as a 'spokesman' for the British gay community.

Most are content with ceaseless phone calls (it is at this point that *The Sun* borrows *Gay News'* story of March 1982, about the gay policeman fired from the Diplomatic Protection Squad, as its own July 1982 'exclusive'). Others perhaps go further. On the evening of July 22 Andrew's flat is broken into. His papers are gone through but nothing is stolen – not the TV, the stereo, the portable electric typewriter, or a moderately expensive brand new Swiss watch belonging to a friend, which is taken out of its case, and left. 'Not', say the police, 'one of your local toerags', by which they mean amateur sneak thieves. It seems perfectly possible that it's a 'stringer' for Fleet Street's sensationalist Sunday papers who can see a few thousand pounds in it – which there would have been – if he can find proof of the identity, and hopefully the address, of the 'rent boy' that every news editor in town wants to discover.

Andrew doesn't know the name, and keeps saying so to the media.

An unexpected by-product of the lamentable Trestrail scandal is that only one month after editorialising, in the tenth Birthday issue, about the suppression of the openly homosexual viewpoint throughout the British print media, *Gay News* breaks through the barrier. The editor is asked to write on 'the Trestrail affair' in the right-wing *Daily Express*, and the left-wing political weekly, *The New Statesman* (which had previously been as obdurate as any other section of the press in keeping out any open writing by homosexuals).

The articles appear, and *The Guardian*, becoming more of a *bête noire* by the minute, not merely fails to commission such writing from anywhere, but contents itself with printing a columnist's attack on the *Gay News*' editor's article in *The New Statesman*. Never mind, the gays' own paper is doing a bit of campaigning, as it has said it would.

The paper plays a part in public affairs in a more terrible, and wholly unannounced, way in the same week of July as the degradation of Commander Trestrail. A double IRA London bombing on July 20 kills Guardsmen and horses in Knightsbridge, and blows up a military band in Regent's Park. The anti-terrorist squad learn that the Park is used by male gays at night as a 'cruising ground' and calls *Gay News* to ask that under promise of the strictest confidentiality readers be asked whether they had seen anything 'out of the ordinary' on the night of July 19, when the band-stand explosives seem to have been planted. An answer is forthcoming.

There had been a shut-in feeling about the run-up to the tenth birthday and its commemorative issue, but now it can be all eyes to the future. New offices to come; 'blasphemy', Denis, West Ken, soon all will be time out of mind, an era of triumphs and failures that can be confined to the paperback history of *Gay News* that everyone keeps talking of doing, and about which nothing ever gets done.

August. Gay men by their thousands wing to Mykonos, to Ibiza, to Key West, pursuing sun 'n sex. Peter and Robert and Roger, separately, have all fixed themselves up for such holidays this month or in September. The editor is going to Israel for the first fortnight of September for sun 'n' sex 'n' history, and says he'll do just one piece of writing, a feature article on Sodom.

Gill takes August off so she can have time with her son during his school holidays having – at some pain – saved up her holiday and time-in-lieu entitlements. She is shocked that Robert seems not to have costed into his budgeting the salary which will need to be paid to the lesbian journalist she has found to deputise for her. The scepticism with which she has all along treated Robert's management is reinforced by this episode and it is only after intervention from Andrew and Alison – and after she has been made to feel guilty for taking her entitlement in this way – that the matter is agreed by Robert.

She returns for the prime date in the UK gay community's calendar for August, the combined Campaign for Homosexual Equality, GayFest, and International Lesbian Information Service conferences booked for the campus of Sheffield University, in the North of England, for the last weekend in August. The *Gay News* presence is bigger than ever before: Robert, Andrew, Alison, Peter (of features), Chris, Gill, Linda, the newcomer on reception.

They're all there not just to report on events for the next issue of the paper, but to attend in their own right as gay people, and to answer for what they're doing with the paper to a 'Readers Meeting'. A feature of the conference agenda, the *Gay News* readers' meeting at this annual gathering of the lesbian and gay clans is the nearest the paper gets to being publicly accountable to its community, face to face.

A gossip-sheet distributed at the start of conference on August 27 carries a satire about Robert forever spending his weekends drawing up endless new versions of the *Gay News* accounts. However, the paper's financial affairs remain confidential, as always, and though there's something unsettling about a satirist choosing just that vision of the *Gay News* owner to make fun of, nothing is known that would justify alarm about the economic condition of the paper.

Display advertising is so much in evidence in issue after issue of the paper, that the 100 or so men and women who attend the

Readers Meeting ask, as they do every year, whether there really has to be quite so much of it. Yes, says everyone, there does, such are the economics of a national newspaper. Will the Visible Lesbian two pages be continued now that their six month guaranteed trial is over? Yes, says the editor, apparently to general satisfaction.

The paper is reproved, as it always is, for continuing to be too 'London-oriented', but Peter and Chris can point to the major features they've done on cities elsewhere in the country, and Liverpool, they announce, is coming up next. And Robert describes how he has succeeded, after long negotiations, in persuading W H Smith Wholesalers,largest distributors in the country, to do a test of *Gay News* in retail outlets in the North West of England during the second half of 1982.

If it works well, Smith's will consider undertaking national distribution from the start of 1983. Since Smith's prides itself on being a 'moral' outfit, supplying to the family, this is a remarkable development for a newspaper whose very masthead proclaims it to be for homosexuals. (In the demonology to which the board of W H Smith are so sensitive, gays are parthenogenetic, neither coming from families, nor having any connection with families later in life. There are lesbians and gay men who wish that were true, but it most certainly isn't true of the vast majority of *Gay News*' own readership).*

Everyone on staff affects to be as enthusiastic about this achievement – it is undoubtedly an achievement – as Robert is, but the first gloss of his efforts in this direction has worn off for, among others, Andrew, Gill, and Alison. They grasp the commercial logic of a sharp expansion in the number of newsagents' premises round the country being induced by Smith's representatives to stock the paper, but have learnt to think Robert altogether too obsessed by the necessity of getting into Smith's distribution chain. Too unreceptive to the various comments and warnings that people on staff do try to give him.

People are known to be timid about going into a local newsagent, where they or their families may be known, and asking for a

* Smith's does NOT agree to sell the paper in its own high-street newspaper shops, only in 'independent' retailers which don't carry the W H Smith name.

copy of the flagrantly titled '*Gay News*'. How sure can Robert be that enough gay men and lesbians are now self-confident enough to overcome that timidity, and dramatically lift the circulation of the paper by buying it through new outlets to be serviced by W H Smith?

Subscriptions, particularly from new 'markets' being opened up by the international and women's coverage, and promotion directly into gay venues where potential readers feel safe in buying a copy (viz by the posters campaign in which Robert is little interested) should be regarded as equally or more important, and yet they seem to be ignored by the paper's marketing director in his passion for the wholesale distribution route.

Raising circulation by getting into new outlets is an agreeable thought, but it's expensive. Not only does it take two to three months for the rewards, if any, in the shape of the *Gay News* percentage of 'net newspaper sales' to come through, but there are start-up costs, the 'repping' of outlets and, perhaps trivially, Robert's expenses on travel and accommodation in going round on tours of distribution areas. (Chris and Peter are greatly taken aback, in the late summer, to run across Robert staying at what they think a very costly hotel in the North of England.) Also Homan costs some £300 a month as adviser.

Sharing in these worries, and voicing them, like some others on staff (including members of the art-room and typesetting room), Andrew keeps to himself the unworthy fear that the personal ambitions to get into distribution which Robert has started to speak about in confidence ('You've no idea how profitable a business it is') are dictating, no matter whether consciously or unconsciously, the *Gay News*' owner's marketing strategies.

Most worrying of all is the question of the impact of W H Smith on editorial content. In the interests of getting the paper into the hands of many more gays, editorial staff are most reluctant to interfere in any initiatives which might improve distribution, and they're quite prepared to swallow a gut feeling of loathing for the W H Smith boardroom, which has had a reputation for rejecting the socially unconformist since the beginning of the century.*

* Smith's has also, most notoriously as far as the British public are concerned, refused to stock the satirical fortnightly *Private Eye* in its shops – a fact that doesn't stop *Private Eye* putting on a massive increase in circulation during the late 1970s.

Perhaps Smith's are changing, perhaps *Gay News* is now too 'grown up' to afford instinctual distaste to rule policy.

But as far back as March 1982, when Robert was in the thick of negotiations with W H Smith, and when Homan was closely advising him, there was a ruckus over editorial interference even before W H Smith had said yes. The intervention didn't come from Smith's, but from Homan. Coming into the art-room to see the projected cover for Issue 237, due out on April 1, he saw plans to use a photograph of naked actors from the British National Theatre's production of Howard Brenton's play 'The Romans in Britain'.

The actors were seated on stage, not even full-frontal. The reason for the cover was that Mrs Whitehouse, prosecutor of *Gay News* in 1977, was now prosecuting the director of the play for a simulated act of buggery, in contravention, she alleged, of the Sexual Offences Act 1956 (whose provisions were aimed at acts of 'indecency' between men in a 'public' place). As distribution adviser to *Gay News*, Homan warned that such a cover might stop dead the deal being slowly struck with W H Smith's.

Editorial staff and art room devised a most adult compromise: CENSORSHIP was printed across the lower extremities of the actors, but the photograph was still used.

At the end of August meeting with a selection of readers in Sheffield, representatives of *Gay News* are united and good-tempered with one another, and are concealing no bust-up behind the scenes, but Peter, already worried by criticisms of *Gay News'* new 'heaviness' in the London gay clubs, is dismayed by arrange-ments Andrew makes with Labour Campaign for Gay Rights in the campus dining-hall.

In 1982 the British Labour Party is making the running, so far as any Party is, in extending civil rights protection for homosexuals. Each of the Parties has its more or less affiliated special interest activists on behalf of gays, and LCGR is the Labour Party's. Andrew arranges for a set of feature articles about the efforts of gay trades unionists and Labour supporters, to be written by them-selves, though edited, of course, by *Gay News*, to appear in a two or three page spread towards the end of September.

His idea is that space be made available to gay supporters of the other main Parties in later issues, both as an editorial response to the round of Party Conferences in Britain in the autumn, and as background for the General Election universally expected (though Mrs Thatcher is denying it) in early or mid 1983.

It is part of the new editor's continuing response to his own sense of the 'infuriatingly wilful and unwise apoliticism' (*see previous chapter*) of *Gay News* in the past. For Peter, and for Chris, and in due course for Robert, it is additional proof that the paper is being given an unduly 'serious' bias which will attract only a minority of readers, or new readers, and may all too easily drive away people who will think *Gay News* has been taken over by academics or 'Lefties'.

The art, claims Andrew, will be in the editing: in a presentation that's visually lively and that makes quite clear that the paper is not itself pushing one Party rather than another – that 'lighter touch' with the serious topic that he's been talking about for the autumn. Neither Peter nor Chris is satisfied with this, though it's out of their power to prevent publication of the material Andrew has in mind and is now commissioning.

They don't like the cumulative effect of changes made to the paper between January and the summer, by which Andrew has introduced or backed not only the two pages for lesbian readers and two pages of news-material from abroad, but with effect from the first issue after the tenth Birthday commemorative one, moved international news up to pages four and five, put a regular news feature (the 'Hot Topic') on page three, and set aside another half-page or page, later in the paper, for a news feature under the heading 'Issues'.

Young gays' campaigns against Britain's age-of-consent laws (no homosexuality for men under the age of twenty-one), 'cowardice' shown by the Labour Party's National Executive Committee over gay rights legislation, the threat posed by the AIDS crisis in the USA, the spread of hepatitis among gay men, and the continuing effort to stop American Immigration officials turning visitors away on the sole grounds that they're homosexual, are among the subjects that have been dealt with since the Birthday issue under these newly created headings.

To make space available for them, even in a continuous flow of fifty-six page issues, the number of pages available for general news stories of no particular description has been reduced to an average of about four. News-tied coverage - incorporating foreign news, lesbian news, and news features – is the opening sequence of twelve pages in each issue, followed by Letters, editorial, and Chris's Mediawatch.

It is restoration of many pages in succession of short news reports that Robert is calling for in his continuing claims, through the summer, that Andrew is asking too much of a readership which wants, Robert considers, as much 'news' as possible. A problem is that Robert, and with him Chris and Peter, regard 'news' as coming in only one form, the short report familiar in daily papers, while Andrew when driven too hard declares roundly that the problem with *Gay News* has been its 'stupidity': trends and developments are also news, he says, and space must be found for them.

The latter case is one that Gill has been making, with her customary apologetic tic ('I know I'm new here, but . . .') since she joined the *Gay News* news team in July 1981. It is true that her background was not that of a professional journalist; but that does not mean that her more experienced colleagues – Andrew and Alison – reject her views as ill-founded. Nevertheless, Peter and Chris – and Robert with them – are inclined to think that the *Gay News* editor – undeniably an experienced journalist – has 'gone over' to Gill's inexperienced ideas in a fit of misplaced radicalism or idealism which in their view can only be damaging to the paper.

By the end of the Sheffield conference, with its evidence of Andrew's plans for 'political' news features in September and October, Peter's feeling that *Gay News* must be protected from erosion of the popular appeal which had brought it to its 19,000 or so fortnightly circulation is very strong, and he has with him Chris and also Robert; though Robert is much impeded by fear of the storm if he tries to force editorial policy changes, and is anyway, despite his alarm about 'news', impressed by Andrew as editor, or personality, or both.

It seems to her colleagues at *Gay News* that Gill – who lives in a household of busy working women and who has a young son still at primary school – already has a full life, quite apart from her job at the paper. She has become a more influential individual at *Gay News* in little more than a year than her rank in the 'hierarchy' would indicate. A later recruit to the news room than Chris by a

155

few months, she's in theory 'cub reporter'. She did indeed spend agonising months in 1981 adapting herself to the smoke-filled wreckage, the phone-battered din, of a news room typical enough of news rooms anywhere. She is no stranger to writing and, with training and experience as a teacher, is used to communicating, analysing and explaining. It is her role as a lesbian news reporter that is new, and she is expected, somehow, to learn it from her male colleagues, since her nearest lesbian colleague, Alison, works in a different form of journalism.

Chris shows her how things are usually done; and Andrew, perhaps like any news editor, glowers at any attempt at being spoken to. Chris, who is temperamentally disposed to being led – and therefore also to leading – finds her mystifying and threatening. Gill suffers conflicts; she cannot forget that her first assignment for *Gay News* – requested by Andrew – was to cover the 1981 lesbian celebration march. At its end, in the University of London Student Union building – where gay men joined lesbians for meetings and fun – Chris was waiting to meet her and to explain which events she should cover for the story. He took her aside, and over a paper cup of coffee, explained to her that Andrew knew nothing about news and that she would need to work with him – somehow bypassing Andrew – if the paper was to have an adequate news section.

Gill was embarrassed. Andrew, after all, had interviewed her for the job and chosen her for it. Was Chris wanting to involve her in some personal disloyalty of his own? Was she to take it that Chris was an authority on 'news' and that Andrew was a fool? 'It's hard to explain,' said Chris earnestly. 'He's so muddled. He gives me the creeps. I know that's an awful thing to say, but I like to be honest. You have to have a nose for a news story and Andrew just hasn't got it. So it'll be up to us – you and me – to follow stories through.' Gill was confused by this. Was it a 'male gay' reaction? A human one? Or a proper journalistic judgment?

Chris had begun his 'teaching' of Gill in this vein and had continued in it. Small wonder that she found it difficult to accept Chris's instructions. But there was another complication as well. Gill understood that her gender was an important part of her job – that at least part of what she was employed to do was to begin an adequate coverage of lesbian news and affairs. Some of that had been discussed in her interview with Andrew. The rest she knew she must learn by trial and error. She is convinced that the views Chris holds about what the paper should cover and what it could leave were such that most things of interest to lesbians would be left out, made silent and invisible, if his criteria were accepted. She senses – although it is not made explicit – that Andrew agrees with her or, at least, is willing to accept that she might know more about lesbian life than he does. As news editor, nevertheless, Andrew's stance is what Alison often called 'laid back'. He values Chris's industriousness and – whatever sympathy he may have for Gill's viewpoint – he does not have 'favourites'.

The ambivalence Chris feels is clear – nevertheless – to both Andrew and Gill, though it is not spoken of by them for a long time. Chris wants, on the one hand, to show affection towards Gill, treating her as he might a motherly elder sister. On the other hand, be beavers away in busy rebuke at enough news stories to fill the section single-handed, as if Gill will let the paper down if he doesn't pour out the copy he feels she won't – or can't – produce. Gill for her part (and she notices the same attitude in Andrew) is not afraid that she can't fill the section – single-handed if necessary – but she refuses to compete with Chris, either for space or for by-lines or for doing the most copy.

If tension is creative, the *Gay News* reporters ought to produce the best news pages ever. But the truth is that Chris – who wants a clear brief and allowance to get on with it – feels put down (and put out) by Gill's wanting to discuss things: from the implications of a news story to working procedures throughout the building, and, not the least of it, the finances of Gay News Ltd. He gets so melancholy in the late summer that Andrew tries everything (short of firing himself or Gill, if that's the real problem) to alleviate Chris's depression. He invites Chris to be a roving reporter outside the office; he asks if Chris would like to move over to features to work with Peter; he tells Chris that he can be personally in charge of the opening pages of news stories in the paper. It is all to no avail. Chris turns down each suggestion, and then, to Andrew's great relief, most unexpectedly announces that he's been unwell for some time but is now better. Depression, he says, had been a side-effect, but now, with the autumn coming up, that's all over.

Gill, by the time she goes away in August 1982 to be with her son for a month of his school holidays, considers she has tried every form of co-operation with Chris. She has concluded that he's much more competitive than he himself realises, and that in part he genuinely doesn't agree with her efforts to expand coverage of lesbian and overseas news through pages specifically devoted to the subjects, and in part he's jealous of the backing she has had from the editor. Chris has moved across to Peter's orbit, she feels, because there he'll hear the sort of dismissive remarks about lesbians on the paper which will shore up his own self-confidence. She's beginning to think that perhaps she'll have to move on.

It isn't only, or most importantly, a matter of a prickly working relationship in the news room with Chris.

At £7,500 (the same as Chris) she's not making enough to pay her way – and could in fact earn more, with her Oxford doctorate and her teaching qualifications, if she took a full-time teaching job. As it is, she thinks she'll take an evening teaching job once a week, to make ends meet. The *Gay News* job has become increasingly demanding. She's afraid her long absences in the daytime and working late in the evening on the paper, are becoming bad for her son.

And perhaps she has done all that she can, according to her lights, to improve matters as she found them on joining *Gay News*. Hers was the main impetus behind the 'women's work' collective system initiated for preparing the Visible Lesbian pages, designed – in part – to raise the self-confidence of women inured to a 'hierarchy' that she had thought, especially under Denis, a near-caricature of the patriarchy, embedded at the heart of lesbian and gay male life in the UK. She had pressed for much greater editorial attention to the lives of gay people overseas (and by no means only in America) and had organised the pages from initiation, though always in consultation with Andrew.

Herself the daughter of a businessman she finds herself unable to believe that Robert is competent, either as a marketing director or as a financial controller, but she's not on the *Gay News* board, and even if she were, has heard enough to convince her that that board is without any effective influence on Robert's financial strategies. (Somewhat shakingly, her father, on a visit to England, briskly says that it sounds to him as if the new owner will bankrupt the paper).

Away on her August holiday, Gill hasn't actually decided to leave, but she's certainly wondering whether perhaps it hadn't better come to that. She feels blocked out from any very real prospects in the future at *Gay News*. She sees the paper as one run by exclusive 'hierarchs', not only Robert doing as he wills with the finances (and with the secret deal before that) and Andrew insisting on an individual final power of intervention editorially (even if he doesn't use it all that much), but Peter and Alison demanding to be allowed to plan and procure general features without any prior discussion with anybody, on mingled grounds of efficiency and of its being their responsibility.

In such a set-up, personally no more than a staff reporter, she defines herself as doing 'alienated' work and tries to achieve change quietly, 'from below'. She has the makings of a spokeswoman for those at *Gay News* who feel that on the gays' national paper their opinions are never genuinely sought, and that in this regard, little has changed since Denis went.

Andrew calls Gill 'Tugboat Annie', after the fictitious American tugboat captain of the 1940s, sole woman owner in the male world of the New York waterfront, forever embattled with the harbour authorities and the other skippers. He values her questioning of the way things are done, or not done, on the paper, but is more often excessively cautious, in her opinion, than adventurous, talking of doing things but drawing back from doing them.

Her word for his behaviour is 'frog talk'.

The phrase had come out of an incident a month before the birth of Prince William on June 21, when Andrew proposed, and then wouldn't proceed with, a cover drawing that would have referred to the fairy story of the princess who kissed a frog to turn him back into a prince. The cover would have shown an appalled nurse leaving Princess Diana's lying-in to tell Charles 'It's a frog'.*

'Frog talk' about editorial independence from the owner is responsible, in her opinion, for some of the divergence of opinion

* It would have been an extraordinary departure for a *Gay News* cover. Andrew was mainly afraid that readers woudn't make sense of it, but also worried that, based on Homan's advice, it would gratuitously wreck the W H Smith deal. As it happened, an immensely successful cartoon cover by Tony in July made mild fun of the Queen. Distributors Seymour Press promptly rang in a panic and demanded no more references to Royalty.

about whether or not Andrew in the summer of 1982 is pushing *Gay News* in so 'serious' a direction that it will drive away readers. True, the paper is rightly or wrongly, commercially or uncommercially, laying very clear stress on meeting afresh what the new editor believes to have been unsatisfied expectations about *Gay News* as a paper for the thoughtful, as well as for those who want to be entertained. But far from sharing the owner's concern, or Peter and Chris's, that Andrew has made the paper off-putting to the average gay man by the time of the Sheffield meeting with readers in late August, with too much lesbianism, internationalism, news-analysis, she thinks that far too much indulgence is shown to Peter and Chris's fear of what they call 'political' and to their personal delight in being 'name' writers.

More important, she thinks that Andrew has been much too trusting of the claims made by Robert about over-riding commercial necessities, and that the freedom of manoeuvre that should be Andrew's as editor, or should be the editorial/production side's as a whole, has been damaged by a failure to challenge Robert's basic competence.

The crux of it has been Robert's behaviour over the drive for revenue in the spring. From Gill's junior position in the hierarchy she saw Robert declare one crisis after another with shockingly disruptive effect. First, the clamour for massive display advertising space in March so that the financial year ended April 2, 1982, could wind out with as low a loss as possible on the books (a loss of £17,000 in the event). Then, without pause, a clamour for unprecedented average revenues from display advertising through spring and summer, so that the new financial year, started April 3, 1982, would instantly show trading profits month on month. Atmospherically it was the economics of hysteria, with Jane pushed so hard that she left, Roger forced to read the riot act about what the 'gay economy' would bear, art-room and typesetters forced into one emergency after another, and the editor wasting his time picking up pieces wantonly broken by a foolish and inexperienced young man.

(It was true that in the spring Andrew, and not Andrew alone, muttered that he spent his time cleaning up after the chaos induced by Robert for business reasons, rather than getting on with what anyone might call editing or writing).

Display advertising wasn't all. Gill also saw an editorial transformation on the paper – one that began in February and by May was praised by Gay's the Word Bookshop in a comparative review of the international gay press – jettisoned because of revenue raising imperatives declared by Robert and insufficiently contested, in her view, by Andrew or others.

The moment Andrew became editor in January he had removed the two-page house Mail Order ad from the position allowed it by Denis, on the centre spread, and put it toward the end of the paper, where 'classifieds' were located. He had also moved the six page Gay Guide and the four page Diary of Events, 'the listings', to the back of the paper preceding the classified. The idea was to free the 'centre spread' for the major feature article of each issue (where it could also be illustrated with 'spot' colour) and provide the reader with an uninterrupted flow of editorial content moving from news through features into 'scene' coverage and arts and into the literary supplement, before the relatively static regular pages of information.

It was this flow, together with such new ingredients as the two pages of lesbian material and a *Gay News* Interview and a personalities page called People We Meet, and the international pages, which Gay's the Word had admired. And it was this flow which Andrew consented to jettison because by March Robert was claiming that vital Mail Order receipts were being damaged by removal of the house ad to the back part of the paper (it followed the Literary Supplement, which seemed a natural place), and because the apparently permanent drive to pack in more display advertising than ever before was making havoc of the designing of editorial pages the length of the paper.

Robert insisted that vital revenue-raising ingredients of the paper, particularly the Mail Order ad, be moved back into the middle.

In a co-ordinated effort between the typesetters, the art-room, Roger as new advertising manager, Jo in charge of Guide and Diary, and Andrew as editor, everything that had been moved to the back was packaged into the middle of the paper as a twenty-four page 'run' of 'listings' and classified and Mail Order with an extensive allowance for display advertising. Andrew demanded it be on pink paper (an innovation in the UK, but already a practice at *The Advocate* in the USA) and that it be lightened with 'sexy' and comic illustrations, which art room readily provided. It was launched with the tenth Birthday issue on June 24.

It went down all right, so far as anyone could tell, both with advertisers and with readers. It was orderly, it stopped the chaos of display advertising forcing itself into every part of the paper, it met Robert's urgent financial demands. Andrew plainly considered that even though he'd never have initiated it as editor except under commercial duress, it amounted to a piece of wizardry as a newspaper 'technician' solution to an acute conflict between editorial and commercial needs. It was presented to readers as if it were a freely chosen innovation for the greater good of *Gay News*.

Gill knew that it wasn't.

Introduction of the twenty-four middle pages of 'pink' from June onwards had divided the rest of the paper into halves; sixteen pages, including the cover, at the front, sixteen pages, including the back cover, at the back; the 'clumps' of sixteen still on white newsprint. Flexibility had plunged. All the news, whether news feature or general news, had to be packed into the front half, together with a fair degree of display advertising, while 'scene' coverage, general features, arts and entertainment, and Literary Supplement remained relatively comfortably off in the back half. Gill thought it unnecessary to look further than the distortion induced by Robert's clamorous demands on space for revenue raising for the origins of the accusation that too much 'heavy' news coverage was being packed into the opening of the paper.

Andrew, she thought, should have been far less attentive to Robert's views. And as to the 'pink pages' solution to Robert's requests, she saw them as the loyal achievement of a very skilful staff driven hither and thither by an owner of far less ability than themselves.

Gay News's trading figures continue to be presented to the board of directors on a non-historical basis through the spring and summer. Had they not been, it would have been apparent by the late summer that on a measure of historical performance, Robert was wrong in saying that the changes made to the paper immediately after the departure of Denis as editor had damaged receipts, except in the shortest term, when readers were getting used to new ordering of contents. Down thirty per cent in the first month of the new financial year (April), mail order receipts were up ten per cent in May, on the equivalent period in 1981, and up twenty-one per cent in June, before they were shifted back to the middle, inside the new pink pages. (They then went down thirteen per cent on 1981 in July, first month in the new position, and up thirty-five per cent in August, second month in the new position).

Receipts from all five revenue earning sectors of the paper taken together (display, classifieds, mail-order, subscriptions, and 'net newspaper sales') were up twelve per cent in April, on the same month of the preceding year, up eighteen per cent in May, eleven per cent in June, eighteen per cent in July, and eleven per cent in August. This bettered the UK rate of inflation. The newspaper was holding its own in the market in time of recession.

Circulation, despite the twenty per cent cover price increase in April, expected to push sales down some two-and-a-half per cent, averaged out at a drop of little more than one per cent in the first six months of 1982 compared with the second half of 1981 – a shortfall of 240 copies a fortnight out of a total sales of over 18,000 a fortnight. Compared with the first half of 1981, circulation in the first half of 1982 turned out to have been over 500 copies a fortnight *up*. This, during the introduction of new lesbian coverage supposedly alarming to the loyal gay male readership.*

Figures are instead presented to the board on an 'as of now' basis only, with Robert's prior budgetary forecasts the only basis of comparison for assessing the paper's performance.

Expenses nonetheless exceed receipts (partly thanks to a higher wages bill) as the new financial year develops. April and May show trading profits of respectively £2,686 and £6,447, but in June there is a trading loss of £2,446, in July of £896, in August of £1,888. Nothing too serious, though of course disappointing. The move to rented premises, instead of freehold ones, will very probably add £600 or so a month to the deficit by the late autumn if something isn't done, though some on staff presume that this will be cancelled out by the end of interest charges on bank borrowings known (though without detail) to have been taken out on the freehold.

At this rate, the financial year 1982–83 will wind out with a

* ABC Audit.

trading loss of about £12,000, an improvement on 1981–82, but not, for all that, desirable, even if it could be covered (as people imagine that if necessary it could be) by some of the capital profit released by the coming sale of the West Kensington premises.

Although neither the commercial performance nor the array of Robert's obligations under his secret deal with the previous owner are rendered to the staff in any clearly comprehensible form, those who physically bring out the paper and its contents, from editorial through to advertising, know perfectly well from the sheer evidence of their senses that *Gay News* is trading as successfully as it ever has in its history as August ends and people prepare for the autumn.

To Robert, however, who has bought it, the paper is not fulfilling his expectations, nor meeting the projections he took to the bank in 1981 to finance his purchase. He knows, as staff do not, that £10,000 must be obtained from cash flow by December to pay the next instalment-purchase sum to Denis. He knows that £26,000 out of whatever net capital profit will be achieved on the sale of the freehold is going to appear in the books as a debt by his own Robert Palmer Marketing Ltd to his subsidiary Gay News Ltd. And he has no capital with which to make good that debt, should the paper stand in need.

The mockery of him, in the Sheffield gay conference 'gossip' sheet, as poring night and day over sheets of figures, is all too accurate. He is badgering Andrew about 'news' coverage because he's so frightened, aided by what Peter says about opinion in the clubs, that *Gay News* is going to attract less display advertising and fail to hold, let alone steeply increase, its circulation.

Peter and Chris very, very, much agree. At the same August NUJ meeting which discusses the position of the photographer Bob there is a discussion, unreported to Andrew, about his editorship. Chris and Peter are at one. Neither trusts Andrew's judgment about the paper, about gay people or about quality and standards. Neither of them likes him, either. Peter and Chris blame Andrew bitterly for what they see as increasingly wrong-headed directions taken by the paper. Gill argues as strenuously as she can that most of the problems as she sees them are caused by Robert's incompetence as a manager of people and his equal incompetence as a financial planner. The two men disagree, rather blaming Andrew by saying he's 'weak' and 'muddled'.

Gill asks the others what they think is necessary for the paper, in their view: the retiring of Andrew or of Robert. Peter has no ambivalence whatsoever. 'Andrew' he replies with a bitter intensity. 'He's a disaster'. Chris, whose chief comment about Andrew is usually that 'he gives me the creeps' wriggles on his chair. He doesn't want to answer directly. 'I think it's rearranging deck chairs on the "Titanic" time', he says. He refers, hoping for a laugh, to those musicians who, knowing that there was no hope of rescue, decided to go on playing as the 'Titanic' sank. For Chris, the writing is on the wall and the paper is already dead.

Gill is appalled at this display of what – to her – is a complete lack of judgment and a wanton display of emotional hostility which seems more personal than either objective or professional; to have as little to do with judgments about what sort of paper *Gay News* should be, or how people should work together to create it, as Chris's other hapless remarks about what he thinks 'news' is or what, in his opinion, 'real lesbians' are.

CATASTROPHE

In Camden High Street, north London, one Alex McKenna publishes *Zipper* and *Mister*, monthly magazines for gay men only, and has just bought the title of his principal rival *Him*, whose owners have gone out of business.

He now, by the late summer of 1982, has a virtual monopoly of 'soft porn' publishing for gay men in the UK. (Denis, dismissively, has always referred to McKenna as 'the pornographer'). Circulations are small, but in revenue terms his operation is perhaps second out of the 'big three' in British periodical publishing for homosexuals, after *Gay News* but ahead of *Capital Gay*.

He hasn't really been in the same market.

With their long monthly preparation periods, their male nude photography, their mildly erotic short stories, his magazines have made no pretensions to news coverage or to 'serious' reading matter. And of course as 'stroke' mags for gay men they've purveyed a fictional universe from which women are wholly excluded.

Nor do any women work in the Camden High Street premises.

Him had been a very brave magazine at the start of the 1980s, admittedly after a fashion disapproved of by those who thought its contents 'sexist' and 'exploitative' of men. It had become 'raunchy', at grave risk from police operating vice laws, and under its previous owners had paid the price in seized copies and distribution troubles.

Having bought the title, McKenna decides in late 1982 how he'll protect his own *Zipper* and *Mister* by introducing more features and moderately 'newsy' material into *Him*, and print only 'tasteful', very 'soft', photos of young men. It will end any claims the magazine had had to courage, but should stop all problems with the police and raise the chance of wider distribution.

He plans to drop the cover price from £2.90 to 90p, continue marketing it to gay men only, and make a promotional drive. McKenna's a man who affects to take nothing very seriously. It soon becomes apparent that he's prepared to use knocking copy critical of *Gay News* in an effort to wean away gay male readers and display advertisers to the new-style *Him*.

It isn't what you ought to do to a 'community paper'. But then who can really tell any longer whether *Gay News* is a 'community paper' or just a commercial leader with no claims to special regard? No-one has been better placed than McKenna to know of the kind of commercial drives Robert has added to, or inflicted on, the national fortnightly.

The gay world being as leaky as a sieve (very properly), advance notice of McKenna's intentions reaches Robert in late summer, and is seen by him as a terrifying development. There has been a pattern, at *Gay News*, of proprietorial fear about competition, and it has always, so far, been misplaced. In 1981, Denis and Robert were deeply alarmist about the plans for the weekly London paper *Capital Gay*. Robert and Peter Burton have only this summer had a scare about what might become of *Gay News*'s display and classified revenue following a decision by the weekly entertainments 'listings' magazine, *Time Out*, to launch a page for gays.

Capital Gay has by September 1982 overcome its financial crisis of the start of the year, and while far from being a money-spinner is stable, and in most issues getting all the display advertising it wants without doing anything to stop *Gay News* reaching far higher display revenues than in 1981. The scare about *Time Out* successfully poaching *Gay News* advertisers similarly comes to nothing. Now there's a new scare, over competition by a monthly for gay men only. If people keep their heads there shouldn't be any very disastrous contest. The USA, Canada, and Australia make room for glossy monthlies with some 'serious' content for gay men only, without destruction of newspapers with all the advantages of shorter 'lead times' between copy date and publication. The new *Him* appears in September/October.

Four days into his holiday in Israel, in the first fortnight of September, Andrew develops the symptoms of hepatitis B.

Instead of being away from the office for a fortnight, he's more or less incapacitated for five weeks into mid-October. Instead of being away during production of one issue of the paper (249, published September 17) he's almost completely out of action for three (up to 251, published October 14). He's back in London, sitting in his London flat from about September 20 and using the phone, but if he were to obey doctor's orders he'd be away for between three to six months.

Robert is exposed to the full fears about the future being felt by Peter Burton and by Chris, without having Andrew's own kind of certainties for compensation. Peter, doing the rounds of the London 'commercial' gay scene from which so much of *Gay News'* income flows, whether by direct sales on the spot or by advertising placed by club-managers, is hearing about eroding profit margins as competition and the UK economic recession worm their way into the 'pink economy' of the gay male entertainment world. By early October (issue 251) he'll be writing an editorial in *Gay News*, during Andrew's absence from the office, lamenting the 'band wagon jumping', the 'beady and avaricious eyes', which in his view have lately tried to exploit a club scene originally pioneered by more daring and able managements.

(An ambiguous editorial, since it names no names, it could in fact be read by those still upset about Robert's display ads drive in spring 1982 as an attack on *Gay News*'s own proprietor, though apparently Peter is really going to the defence of those managements in the club world that he admires.)

Peter takes the 'threat' from *Him* very seriously. So does Roger, in charge of *Gay News*'s advertising department. So does Robert. Unlike Roger, Peter is now very much on the record, away from the paper as well as in the offices, as believing that editorial policy changes at *Gay News* are well on the way to destroying its appeal to male readers. The display advertising cake is about to get smaller, he considers, due to the financial problems of the advertisers themselves – and *Gay News* is wantonly making itself less appealing during hard times rather than adapting itself to fight for revenue. The 'net' message that Robert, with responsibility for *Gay News* finances, is getting from Peter is that Andrew is no good, Alison is no good, Gill is no good, the photographer Bob is no good. Or it might be more precise to say the message is that each of them, with the exception of Bob, might be good for some things, but they're no good when they force their own 'middle class', or 'academic', vision of reality on to the paper.

It is mildly unfortunate, though of no real bearing on the larger battle about to fall on *Gay News* with shattering abruptness, that editorial policy ossifies at the start of September. As the next two in seniority in the editorial 'hierarchy', Alison and Peter, joint features editors, edit the paper in Andrew's absence. Peter, supported by Chris, wants an immediate reduction in the 'heaviness', as he sees it, of the opening news pages of the paper. Alison, though herself dubious about extensive arrangements for 'serious' coverage made by Andrew before departing on holiday, insists that the paper's new commitments to what the straight press calls 'in depth' stories should not be scrapped in the editor's absence.

She is strongly supported by Gill. They make sure that material by gay trades unionists and gay activists in the British Labour Party (mostly commissioned by Andrew at the end of the August Sheffield gay conferences) appears, as Andrew had wanted, in issue 250. It proves timely. Copies of the paper are distributed at the end of the September Labour party Conference, where there's a major row over gay rights, with 'homophobic' representatives of the national press being ejected from a fringe meeting attended by leading Labour politicians.

Had Andrew been present in the office, he wouldn't have dropped the 'serious' comments either. But bound by no loyalty to himself so to speak, he had devised, he believed, a compromise between Peter and Chris's legitimate calls for the less sophisticated reader not to be alarmed, and a continuation of the ability to handle 'serious' issues. It was to take five months, such were the disruptions about to befall everyone at *Gay News*, before they could be successfully tried out, in February 1983. In the meantime, in September 1982, he stares ungratefully at successive issues of *Gay News* through literally jaundiced eyes, but refrains from criticism. He, after all, is doing no work.

He does, however, in the week beginning September 20, ask Alison, Chris, Gill and Peter if they'll visit him at his London flat to bring him up to date on forward planning to Christmas. On Andrew's insistence people fetch mugs and glasses from the upstairs flat, lest somehow they too catch the dreaded disease.

At this meeting a seemingly chance remarks opens a hairline fracture about the state of *Gay News*'s finances. A fracture which within days becomes a yawning fissure, in which it seems that *Gay News* may be swallowed up, and disappear.

Peter and Chris describe how on a recent visit to the northern city of Liverpool, formerly of the Beatles but now of economic depression-induced riots, they heard rumours of deep financial trouble at *Gay News*. They had been up there preparing another of their occasional series on gay life in the big cities outside London (it appears as a five page feature in issue 250, published September 30).

Andrew insists that the rumour must be put to Robert at a Gay News Ltd board meeting set for the following day. Peter and Alison, board members unlike Chris and Gill, will put the question. If they get reassurances will they please, asks Andrew, prepare an upbeat editorial about *Gay News*'s own plans, lest rumour snowball into inducing commercial trouble. Robert is duly asked point-blank whether *Gay News* has a so far undeclared major financial crisis, and denies it. Peter Coell, of accounts, confirms that the books show nothing that could be described in such terms.

The interpretation of financing given is that from making trading profits in the months of April and May, the paper has been making relatively small trading losses in June, July, and August. But though thought must be given to economies and/or higher revenues so that the paper comes into profit, grave crisis there isn't.

Alison accordingly writes an editorial published in issue 250 (September 30) which, without directly referring to rumour or citing actual Gay News Ltd trading figures, stresses grounds for looking contentedly toward the future: the coming move to larger premises (the West Ken freehold is under offer); the fact that display advertising remains unprecedentedly high; the distribution hopes attached to the wholesale 'test' now being undertaken in the North West by W H Smith.

While issue 250 is going through the presses, and even before it hits the streets, Robert changes his mind. Between the prospective shrinking 'cake' of the 'pink economy', the anticipated promotion drive to be directed against *Gay News* advertisers and male readers by McKenna's new-style *Him*, and the 'unpopularity' of *Gay News* which he hears about from Peter Burton, he concludes that *Gay News* display advertising receipts are going to tumble – as measured against his own forward projections – during the winter months, the very time when they should be at a seasonal high.

Since they account for thirty-four per cent of *Gay News*'s total revenues (September 1982) and there'll soon be rent to pay on leasehold accommodation, instead of the office's old freehold base, manageable trading losses could shortly, he decides, be entirely unmanageable ones. He's got £10,000 to find for Denis on December 31, as an instalment on the £70,000 or so he still owes for the purchase of the paper, and, apart from the very risky course of making personal borrowings or juggling the *Gay News* cash flow in hopes of better days, nowhere to look for it but in a trading surplus by the end of the year.

He labours over the accounts and over his own trading projections (as he had somewhat uncomfortably been satirised at the end of August gay conferences for doing). If the sale of the freehold offices is accomplished in October or November there will be a large surplus out of the asking price of £77,000. But of that, £24,000 borrowed from Barclays Bank by Gays News Ltd to pay Denis a 'golden handshake' earlier in the year must be paid back to Barclays. A further £26,000 paid to Denis as first instalment on Robert's purchase of the paper will have to become a debt by Robert Palmer Marketing Ltd to Gays News Ltd – and neither Robert personally, nor RPM Ltd as a company, have any assets with which to repay it to Gay News Ltd.

And what is left over from £77,000 after deduction of the two borrowings amounting to £50,000, will have to be ear-marked for exceptional liabilities, such as a printer's lawsuit outstanding from Denis's day, office moving expenses, and any other urgent bills, including a tax one. There is no way in which the remarkable realisable asset formerly built into *Gay News*' possession of its own premises will solve the continuous trading losses if display advertising takes a dive. Of course, in a well-conducted operation, a balance sheet asset would not be disposed of to avoid taking any action whatever on trading losses. Had Robert any personal wealth, or had his holding company been more than an empty vehicle when he acquired the shares of *Gay News* – had company law not been changed in 1981, and had Denis and Robert not

171

struck a deal whereby *Gay News* was itself to finance everything –
then indeed there would be £26,000 clear from selling the building
with which to promote and improve the paper flat out during the
winter of 1982.

But there isn't. Nothing for it, thinks Robert. He will have to cut
several thousand pounds a month off overheads immediately. Jobs
will have to go. The printers bill, some £3,000 an issue, will have to
be cut, and there's only one way to do that while seeking to
maintain circulation: cut the number of pages per issue. Soon,
Robert is taking Valium to try to keep going, such is his fear and
despair only eight months after completing contracts to buy the
paper.

He calls the Campaign for Homosexual Equality, in the person
of Roy Burns, a friend and a long term unpaid activist for gay
causes (by profession, a lecturer.) He tells Roy that he may be
about to have to do dreadful things at *Gay News*. Would Roy be
ready to help spread the word, when the moment comes, that
financial necessity alone is making him ask for dismissals at *Gay
News* – not some covert aim of getting rid of people he doesn't like
or respect?

Murky waters. It is to become increasingly plain that though
indeed Robert will do nothing to enforce the departure of any
particular individuals on the editorial side, he would like to see
Bob the photographer go and would be far from unhappy if Gill or
Alison left. A past chair of CHE, Robert would prefer to associate
himself with the kind of paper his editor has been trying to create
(nothing angers Robert more than any suggestion he'd like to
'down market' *Gay News*). But he is uncomfortable with both
women – indeed, with all women, in the opinion of those working
on the paper – and if he could bring himself to be entirely open
about it, he now, confronting what he expects to be a trading
disaster, would be deeply relieved if the declaration of a crisis could
lead to a shakeout of those who ask questions.

In truth, he sees the salvation of *Gay News* and of himself as the
entrepreneur of *Gay News*, in an instant capitulation to what the big
wholesale distributors would like (no 'radicalism' and, for technical 'racking' reasons in shops, a less bold A4 size format) and
instant conformity to what Peter Burton says about the opinions of
club-owners and young gay men. His own lawyer will eventually

say that as the financial crisis intensifies, Robert would jettison any obligation supposed to rest on the paper in order to keep it trading. It would be a defensible attitude if it were merely to keep people in work or to keep a title afloat pending better days. Unfortunately his personal finances (his salary, and the personal guarantees he gave that Denis would be paid in full) will soon make it impossible for anyone to know whether he favours his chosen course in the interests of the national fortnightly for homosexuals, or to save himself personally. Not least to save himself from Denis, of whose anger should due payments on the *Gay News* shares not be met he is persistently and obviously afraid.

But Robert will try not to make his own harsh decisions unaided. He will try to shelter behind Andrew, and yet again behind Peter – so much so that as the days go by, Peter comes to *Gay News* to deliver copy, and then leaves, doing all he can to avoid being shut into the downstairs office he shares with the *Gay News* owner. Temperamentally, Robert can't endure to be out in the open enforcing policies. He's a behind-the-scenes manager. Gill says of him that he's suited only to positions of middle management and no more – far removed from that vision of him as 'presidential' which Denis had had when they were negotiating the sale of the paper. As person after person refuses to act on Robert's behalf, he turns to a lawyer. And so at last, in legal form, he gets that 'facilitator' whom he'd wanted, long ago, for the staff weekend in Gloucestershire, in the first days after buying the paper.

Besides seeking, in the week beginning September 27, to influence in advance the CHE attitude should redundancies be demanded at *Gay News*, Robert calls Andrew, apologising for needing to trouble him when he's so ill. He describes his belief that display advertising is going to slump and that jobs are almost certainly going to have to go and the range of contents of the paper be savagely reduced by a cut in the number of pages published. Since Robert's plans require that space devoted to display advertising be as high as the market will bear at all times, through the winter and beyond, and he has in mind a reduction from fifty-six pages to perhaps thirty-six, or at most forty, it is not going to be a matter of trimming what readers have been accustomed to, but of jettisoning whole sections of the paper, most of them only fully designed-in with effect from July. Since the cover price is to remain unaltered, Andrew's personal reaction is that his work for the paper is completely over. The efforts of the past eight or nine months, everyone's not merely his own, will never survive such handling. A paper called *Gay News* can perhaps be salvaged, but not the *Gay News* that he himself, with whatever degree of dissension, had been moving towards.

He also, as Alison does as soon as she is made aware of the situation, feels that by giving erroneous financial reassurances at the previous week's Gay News Ltd board meeting, Robert has led the editorial staff of *Gay News* into publishing a misleading editorial at too late a stage in the distribution cycle to call it back. Of all the various ways in which journalists can be made to feel disreputable, editorialising to meet the commercial dictates of a proprietor is probably the worst.

However, Robert has come for help.

Andrew doesn't question Robert's sudden conversion into prophet of doom. Peter comes with Robert and speaks of his alarm about the capacity of the 'commercial' scene to keep up past levels of display spending. Roger is confirming that the trend for *Gay News* has been downwards since July, even though still far above 1981 levels (thirty-five per cent up on 1981 in July, twenty-four per cent up in August, seventeen per cent up this September). Andrew recommends that, in consultation with Roger, Robert draw up 'worst case' revenue possibilities for the remainder of calendar 1982, and that the scale of economies required be calculated and offered to staff on that basis, not on any estimate of what would be necessary if 'something turns up'. A late learner, compared to many others on *Gays News* staff, Andrew is very afraid that Robert will plunge the paper into one round of economies after another, rather than grasp the whole poisonous nettle in one go. He knows that the paper would never survive bout after bout of adverse changes, though it might survive, as a paper of some sort called *Gay News*, one frightful deterioration, if profitability then opened the way to a climb back.

He emphasises that everyone is warning him about the clinical depression which is supposed to accompany hepatitis. His advice might have to be disregarded, he says; he may, from physical sickness, never mind sickness of heart, be taking altogether too bleak a view.

Those who have control of business, and accordingly of the product and of employees, have only the information to hand and their intuitions from which to formulate policy. They don't have the later commentators' advantages of hindsight. All the same, it is for their calculations of future trends that owners of companies are either rewarded (and their staffs with them) or punished. Robert declares crisis at *Gay News* in late September 1982 in the expectation that the newspaper's display advertising revenue will tumble so much, during the best selling season of the year, that the company will go under if staff are not shed and spending on the product itself is not fiercely curtailed.

Was he right?

Not in terms of cash-flow from display for most of the rest of the year, and heavy display bookings for the pre-Christmas issue. There is a slump to come, so his 'display' fears aren't empty ones, but it will hit the paper in circumstances that have already become shakingly abnormal. The declaration of crisis remains confidential to staff, in theory, for the greater part of October, but is then announced in the pages of the paper itself, and is fully public knowledge from the beginning of November. Even in these circumstances, so destructive of reader and advertiser confidence, *Gay News* display advertising revenue remains higher than in the equivalent period of the year before, until December – by which time even the national press in Britain is running stories that the homosexuals' newspaper may go out of business.

As to sales, Britain's Audit Bureau of Circulations will show that *Gay News*'s circulation edges back 5.2% to just under 18,000 copies a fortnight in the second half of 1982 compared with the first half of 1982.

With his controversial version of what's going on, following so swiftly on his denying a crisis and then acknowledging one, Robert begins a process of cutting away all credibility in his actions to date or in the actions he proposes. Within little more than a fortnight (by mid October) his reputation within the paper has sunk so low that when Andrew, driven to appear in the office by the pace of events, feels obliged to ask formally whether production and editorial staff can stand the prospect of going on working for Robert as owner of *Gay News*, they all, including Peter Burton, say they can't.

But before that happens, he too, like Robert, has lost all credibility with staff. That the editor of *Gay News* survives the debacle, unlike the owner, seems to be due more to the charity of colleagues, who suppose Andrew too ill to know what he's doing, than to his having any less to answer for, in the first onrush of the crisis, than the owner. Or perhaps to his showing that he's capable, though so sick, of grasping criticisms that are immediately made. Criticism not of editorial policy but of the emergency measures he takes part in announcing.

The existence of financial crisis is first formally conveyed to staff as a whole in the last days of September at a 'seminar' in Robert's Little Venice flat, grim parody of the hopeful financial 'seminar' on the Gloucestershire agenda in January, and then at an emergency board meeting on October 4. Persuaded of what is indeed true, that revenues must rise or expenditures sink, staff are asked by Robert to make their own proposals. If they too can't see any solution except lay-offs and a reduction in the contents offered by the paper, would they please make recommendations about who is to become redundant, and plan the reduction in the published paper.

Accordingly, a memo, breaking down the number of redundancies needed from each department, is circulated. To offset a 'lower limit' projected £30,800 loss seen by Robert, savings amounting to two-and-a-half people out of the seven in the editorial department are needed; from the three in the art room, one is required; from the two typesetters, half a job; from the four in advertising, one is asked; and from the seven in administration, two are required. But to offset a projected 'upper limit' 'loss' of £44,800, the cuts are even more severe: four must go from editorial, one-and-a-half from the art room, one from the typesetters, one-and-a-half from advertising and three from administration.

Both sets of savings – the memo says – 'assume cutting editorial, artroom, production costs by twenty-five per cent already'. And a sentence is added at the bottom: 'NB. REDUNDANCY PAY WOULD MAKE THE SITUATION SLIGHTLY WORSE, AS WOULD LONG NOTICE PERIODS'. The capital letters emphasise the implication that even if a member of staff made redundant would seek to be treated fairly according to law, he or she must feel guilty for wanting to have his or her due.

The very next day – October 6 – Chris Kirk, as Parent of Chapel for the NUJ, receives a letter marked 'Confidential' and headed 'Editorial Redundancies'. It states – in contradiction to the memo's £44,800 'loss' based cuts – that, in all, *'no more than seven* redundancies are envisaged'. (Later, at the height of his alarm, Robert is to assert – at an official meeting with Parents of Chapel, national representatives of the NUJ and the NGA, and his own lawyer – that eleven is the real number needed.)

The letter to Chris explicitly states that the reason for the proposed redundancies is the recession affecting gay businesses, which has caused display advertising revenue to 'slide', in addition to an accumulation of bad debts. The letter asks that staff should suggest to the Directors how the redundancies might be achieved: through volunteers, job-sharing, half-time, or voluntary lowering of salaries. If such suggestions are not forthcoming, Andrew and Robert will make recommendations, which, the letter states, will be discussed with Chris before any dismissals take place. (Andrew knows nothing of the letter till some time afterwards.)

Two days later, on October 8, the two Peters of accounts circulate a letter, accompanied by their own set of figures for the staff, suspecting that people may not understand the financial situation. Chris Kirk, they say, has agreed with them to chair a meeting which they suggest should be 'a "round-table" meeting informally run but strongly chaired to ensure everyone's feelings are expressed'. Their letter ends 'let's pull together to grow in the future'.

Whether discussions took place with Chris is not known. The meeting proposed by the Peters does not take place. But a staff meeting does consider the possibility of cutting the total wages bill by radically reducing, or abolishing, wages differentials, ranging from Robert and Andrew's £12,000 per year, through Peter and Alison's £10,000, through the 'middle-rung's' rough £7,500 (Jo, Gill, Chris, Bob, Wendy and Lesley), to the bottom line of £6,000 (Amanda, Linda and Mike). The meeting rejects the idea as unworkable in view of commitments entered into by people on the highest levels. (Andrew later tells Robert that they – at least – must drop their own salaries to £10,000, whatever else is later agreed, and this is done in November. No-one else makes a similar move.) Some make altruistic offers, but are dissuaded by others.

By the weekend of October 9/10, Andrew, immured in his flat, gathers that staff aren't going to reach agreement on any way of cutting their own throats at the owner's behest. He fears that Robert may yet let things slide, and bring about the destruction of the paper from paralysis at the prospect of unpopularity both within the offices and in the larger gay world beyond. He presses Robert to grasp the nettle. He assumes that Robert's figures are right, both in themselves and in the interpretation Robert is putting on them (unlike a number of other members of staff, who are sharing their scepticism with one another).

He encourages Robert to take a decision on which named individuals should be asked to go if seven redundancies out of twenty-three are indeed required. Robert, for his part, asks Andrew to be associated equally with him in making the decisions and in announcing them. He asks if he can come over to Andrew's flat to draw up such a list. He will handle the administrative departments, Andrew the production and editorial ones. Andrew modifies the scheme by suggesting a mixture of part-time-work offers and full redundancies.

By late afternoon on Sunday October 10 the two men have agreed names for immediate redundancy and immediate part-time working. They will each at once contact the people affected in their 'own' departments.

Their proceedings are in contravention of UK Employee Protection Acts (notice isn't going to be given) and of union procedures (unions must first discuss redundancy proposals with their members). Andrew ought to have known as much, or at least guessed as much, whatever the degree of the threat to continuous publication of the paper. Robert did know it. When Andrew discovers as much, a few days later, he declines again to exercise the managerial functions of an editor in collaboration with Robert as owner.* He will edit, if called upon to do so, and so far as editing is possible in the circumstances. He will be party to no more 'privileged' consultations with Robert designed to solve the financial situation.

Into the middle of their weekend deliberations has come a

* NUJ advice is that when there are disputes between owners and staff of a paper, the editor may opt either to 'side' with management or to let management get on with it unaided.

178

bombshell from Chris. He is resigning, he says, on the spot, effective Monday morning. The call comes to Andrew on the Saturday. Chris refuses to give reasons, beyond saying that it isn't because he can't work with Andrew, and says nothing will make him change his mind. His action remains a mystery to staff. On one occasion he says that it was because he was 'parent of NUJ chapel' and couldn't bear, during the week when people at *Gay News* were supposed to be choosing redundancies from among their own numbers, to be put in the position of selecting colleagues to be fired. Later, it is supposed that in his despair about the state of the paper, Chris had called Denis and asked him to intervene over the heads of Robert and Andrew, and feels, by Saturday October 9, that the action would put him beyond the pale, if colleagues knew of it. Chris never publicly confirms what really happened.

Certainly, at this point, a very reluctant Denis re-enters the affairs of *Gay News*. He is trying (as he had said in January 1982 that he would, before leaving for the USA) to launch various media or other projects which have nothing to do with the gay world. They are to be financed, or partially financed, it is supposed, from the payments that Robert is due to be making to him out of *Gay News* funds, from December 31, 1982, onwards. Unknown to anyone on staff, unless to Peter or Chris, Robert calls Denis and tells him that staff must be cut if the paper is to make trading profits. Most unwilling to be involved, and even more unwilling that any involvement should be made public, Denis recommends that Robert leave the production staff untouched and try to make savings on the administrative and editorial payroll.

Sound advice, in its grasp of production realities, and better than Andrew's, who lends himself in the course of Sunday to cuts on the production side. Robert disregards Denis's advice, fixated on maintaining the three in display advertising (as against one in 1981).

The early October exchange between Robert and Denis is the beginning of a sequence of contacts, at Robert's solicitation, between the past and present owners of *Gay News*, tied together as they are by mutual disadvantage should the paper be incapable of financing the deal they have made between them. The fact of contact and the nature of contacts is almost invariably kept a secret from staff, but there is a gathering awareness that it is happening.

A disastrous development. If anything further were required to render it impossible to know in whose or what interest Robert advocates a particular course, it is a generalised and unspecific awareness that he is covertly in touch with Denis. Andrew retains respect for Denis, though well informed, from third parties, that the converse is not true (so far as the quality of the paper is concerned). Others see only that Robert is communicating with a man regarded as having no further use or time for *Gay News* than that it should provide Robert with the funds to meet due date payments on the 1982 share-sale.

Whose – the question reappears with unparalleled urgency, as soon as it is suspected that Robert is talking with Denis – is *Gay News*? And what is it for?

Only those who have worked for a company swept by a redundancy demand can know what such an experience is like. It is only just going too far to say that it's like asking a family to make some of their number redundant. The threat isn't only to people's wages, bad enough in itself in such an economy as Britain's, with some three million unemployed; it's to ways of life as well as to livelihoods, to relationships, to pride of work.

And now this at *Gay News* in its eleventh year, when surely it should have some stability. This at *Gay News* whose pages have so often dealt editorially with the problems of lesbians and gay men in finding workplaces where they can be 'out'. This at a newspaper rightly or wrongly regarded by outsiders, for a decade, as having a 'caring' tradition towards gay people. This at a paper which, whatever its troubles in past years, and whatever has been thought to the discredit of past proprietors, has never before fired people to save money – let alone when revenues are at an historic peak. And this, too, at a newspaper where everyone is not only under the usual newspaper people's pressure to keep the paper coming out, whatever the cost, but under 'moral' pressure to put the needs of the lesbian and gay male community above their own, so that scarce reading matter should not be made scarcer still.

Scotty and Jo both react at once by saying that if anyone is to go, they must; the jobs of younger people must be saved. No word of sorrow, about what is befalling the paper and colleagues with whom he worked for years, comes either first or second hand from

Denis; on the contrary, he is understood to be saying that trouble-making members of staff have themselves to blame. No word of apology is heard from Robert – nothing in his financial projections, his financial management, or the terms on which he bought the paper has any bearing, if he is to be believed, on events.

Financial analysis and the description of contending opinions about the editorial quality of a paper – in *Gay News'* case, contention about the creation and manner of presentation of writing by lesbians, international coverage, and attention to 'political' issues – can only go so far. Character itself is critical. As the staff of *Gay News* come to grips in October 1982 with the crisis described to them by Robert and the steps decided on by Andrew and Robert, the apparently constitutional inability of the owner to acknowledge error begins to play its part in shaping whether the paper can be rescued or not. So, as days grow into weeks, does the coldness of the former owner. He seems unable to demonstrate or even to feign any affection for the enterprise and the people who brought him a measure of fame, and (by the standards of most people) a great deal of money. Between them – Robert directly, and Denis through his rights should Robert fail to pay up – these two have overwhelming authority in law, and had they been other men, making other use of that authority, events would have taken other courses.

The mixture of redundancies and part-time working agreed by the owner and editor by Sunday October 10 very nearly includes Andrew's name. In a telephone conversation with Robert on the preceding Thursday of October 7, Andrew tells Robert that he cannot carry on as editor, since he has no confidence in Robert's management. He tells Robert, also, that there is a widespread feeling among staff that Robert's management is not to be trusted and that it is felt that Robert ducks issues and passes difficult decisions on to others. Andrew affirms, brutally, that failure is failure and that when it is financial, people want to know why. Is it managerial policy? Is it editorial policy? Perhaps both? The paper cannot be brought to such a crisis, he says, without one of the people at the top paying the price, himself as editor, or Robert as financial manager.

Robert tells Andrew that he has no intention whatsoever either of giving up control or of sharing decision-making with the staff. Robert insists on staying on, both as owner and as financial manager. And he insists on staying on the pay-roll himself.

Andrew asks Robert if he has additional financial resources, other than Gay News Ltd, with which to finance his commitments to Denis. Robert says he has none, but that there might be family help if Andrew promises not to tell anyone. Andrew is persuaded that Robert can probably raise the money. At this juncture, Robert is making a three-fold claim: that he will pay Denis without involving Gay News Ltd, that he will not default on those payments, and that he will not withdraw either as proprietor or as salaried business director.

For Andrew, the system of control of Gay News Ltd has completely failed. He wishes not to continue unless it changes. He proposes that four to six of the most responsible staff members take control and report to the board of directors and staff meetings as desired. This idea is rejected by Robert. Andrew tells Alison that if he stays, he will have no confidence in a newspaper run on budgets prepared solely by Robert and Peter Coell.

After this conversation with Robert, Andrew is argued out of resigning by a journalist friend, Sheila Black. She says he's too ill to make up his own mind properly and that it would be a tacit admission that editorial policy has all but ruined the paper. She argues, further, that he will drag down with him all those at *Gay News* who have fought for the same ideas as himself. Does he think editorial policy has brought things to this pass? No. Then he must stay, until and unless Robert sacks him.

In her heart, Andrew's friend is trying to save him his home. On his £12,000 salary he's borrowed 100% of the cost of his £23,000 flat (itself a one room 'flatlet', such are costs in London), and will slowly or rapidly go broke on less. In the UK there are better State benefits for those made redundant than for those who become unemployed because they've resigned. Honour carries no premium. It's a point which will play on the minds of home-borrowers on staff and indeed of virtually everyone, for, with the exception of Robert, who can't up and go of his own free will even if he chooses to, every single member of staff considers resigning over coming weeks, if only to be free of seeing the distress of colleagues. The *Gay News* editor will spend more time over coming months trying to hold the staff together – what will be left of it – than on anything conventionally recognised as editing. Everyone, turn by turn, will spend hours on the support of demoralised colleagues.

From October 10, continuously, Andrew expects Robert to take the earliest chance of dismissing him. Though deciding not to resign, he offers to step down in the 'hierarchy' if Robert wants another editor, but Robert refuses. And never fires him.

Amanda of classifieds, is to go. So is Linda of box-replies and reception. So is Bob the photographer, who has been six years on the paper. Three redundancies, expected to be effective at once. Four full-time job losses, Chris having gone of his own volition.

Six are to go half-time, with halved earnings: Lesley, of type-setters, who has only just learned her craft from Wendy; Jo, of the ten page Diary of Events and Gay Guide, spinal column of the paper with its massive array of facts for gay people round the country; Gill, of the news-room, writer of general news items, of news features of short news items for the Visible Lesbian two pages, and initiator of the two pages of international material; Peter Jones, 'junior' in accounts, a very over-strained department at this time of monetary crisis and JC, who has been ten years on the paper, and who, though admitting to feelings of staleness, has written the regular 'Sounds' column on new record releases (a remarkable feat for a Frenchman who has only learned English while in England and at *Gay News*) besides working as usual in the art room.

Half-time (a point which is of course vital) means no entitlement to State benefits, and none of the redundancy payment rights which can be relatively substantial for long-serving workers in a company. It is financial disenfranchisement, a pious fraud. Andrew's fantasy is that it will keep some skills for the paper and give some income to the affected.

Gill has been away in Berlin during the week leading up to the weekend of October 9/10, attending – at her own expense – the Women's University week held there annually, at which the various strands of the German women's movement are drawn together. She has only been home for a few hours, on Sunday October 10, when the phone rings.

It's Andrew, sounding uncharacteristically solemn and remote. He asks her if she'll accept going on to half-time and half-salary, but won't say who else is to go half-time or be made fully redundant. Those concerned must be the first to hear it, he says, either from himself or Robert. 'Dear Gill', she remembers him saying, 'this is in no way a reflection on the standard of your work or your commitment to the paper. I want to emphasise that.' He for his part remembers ending by saying he hopes they'll remain friends, and feels sickened to hear himself.

She puts the phone down.

It's not just demoralising, she feels, it's incomprehensible. She can hardly manage on her £7,500 before tax. How does anyone imagine she could manage on half of it?

If she says no to half-time work, will she be guilty of deserting the paper in its hour of need? Does the request that she go half-time mean she's being offered charity (some work is better than none) or is it that her work is really needed (please don't go, we need you)? If it's really true that money has to be saved in such a way, what sense does it make to cut off half a low salary, when half of £12,000 or £10,000 would save more?

And is it true, anyway, that money must be saved this way?

The more she thinks about it, the more ambiguous, the more illogical, it all seems. Who else is going half-time, or worse still, being laid off completely? That might give a clue to it all. She picks up the phone again. She calls Linda.

With this call, initiative in the newspapers's affairs passes from the two men hierarchically entrusted with it, the owner and editor, to the staff. Specifically to women on staff, though there are plenty of men on the paper who will fully co-operate with the steps the women advocate, and share their perceptions. If the stray remark about rumours in Liverpool was the beginning of the emergence of the financial crisis, Gill's phone call to Linda is the beginning of an organised rejection, after all the years spent in compliance, of the priorities attributed to the successive owners of *Gay News*.

The open role taken by women as the *Gay News* financial crisis develops will lead within a few short weeks to accusations by some gay men, on the staff and off it, that 'lesbians' (with pejorative emphasis) are responsible for all that's gone wrong. The paper's new competitor *Him*, with its commercial aim of raiding *Gay News*'s readership and advertisers, will fill its editorial pages with such accusations.*

184

If it does nothing else, the trouble at *Gay News* in late autumn 1982 reveals, as never before, that the strain of misogyny in the gay male world is as virulent as it is in the straight male world.

* Visiting staffers from *Gai Pied*, the French weekly for gay men, analyse *Gay News'* error as the employment of women and the aim of reaching a gay readership of both sexes. Some months later (June 25, 1983) there's a scandal as *Gai Pied* itself publishes a violently women-hating cartoon.

DISBELIEF

There are already those, in October 1982, who feel that Robert had never proved himself up to the job he had negotiated himself into, even when he was optimistic and people extended their trust to him. Now, threatened with the unpopularity he dreads, confronted with a most testing array of decisions, he seems unable to do anything that doesn't make a bad situation worse. For some, dormant memories of how he had been accused in his days as Chair of CHE of being incapable of co-operation with any kind of equal, are aroused.

The organisation that Andrew as editor presses on Robert in the first days after declaration of the crisis – a financial committee of senior staff, in which Robert, while being a member, would vest his authority – would have been instituted as a matter of course had Robert, by fortunate mischance, had to go off sick in the autumn. As it is, he holds onto his authority as financial arbiter, and the most unfitted person, it seems fair to say, remains in lawful charge of solving the crisis.

Within barely a month, Andrew is so horrified by Robert's white face, reliance on Valium, and evident tearfulness – by the spectre of ruin and disgrace Robert obviously sees constantly before him – that he says at one of the almost incessant crisis meetings of staff that he's perhaps being foolish, but he fears for Robert's life. By December 15, Robert's lover Alan is writing, without Robert's knowledge, to plead for people to lay off, to be kinder to his lover. Another fortnight, and a friend of Robert's is writing to warn 'my constant feeling is that Robert's incapable of taking a decision . . . .'

But it is truly remarked that others also suffer, and their lovers too have to watch the misery helplessly.

When Linda is phoned by Gill on the evening of Sunday

October 10 it's the first she's heard about planned dismissals. The two women agree to phone as many members of staff as they have numbers for, and then to confer again. Gill calls Bob, who had been quiet and resigned in manner when phoned by Andrew an hour or two before, but is now extremely angry, and puzzled and hurt.

At midnight, when she has already been tipped off by Gill, a letter is put through Linda's door from Robert telling her she needn't report for work in the morning. A similar letter, both of them in terms the recipients find 'heartless', will be handed to Amanda when she gets in on Monday morning. Linda comes into work despite the instruction; Amanda stays in the building. Bob comes in. So does Chris, but for Chris it is to say tearful goodbyes.

It is felt, though such things might seem unimportant in comparison with all that is occurring, that while Andrew seeks to phone all the people on 'his' list, and goes to JC personally in his home, Robert can't show, or worse has no room in his mind to feel, human understanding of what this means to the individuals. He is not – to put it in the mildest language, the language of corporations – a good personnel manager. In ordinary words, he doesn't feel the pain of others or if he does, cannot prove it in words or gestures.

People review what Robert and Andrew have announced. The women point out the degree to which the claimed 'solution' to the crisis protects the gay men and dispenses with the lesbians. On Robert's 'side' – advertising/administration/finance – his only full redundancies are the only two full-time women directly responsible to him, Amanda and Linda. The jobs of three men in display advertising are to be saved. Cost-efficient Amanda, who processes upwards of £8,000 worth of ads a month, is to go.

Hard to shake off the feeling that the *Gay News* owner is taking the opportunity, on 'his' side of the paper, to be served in future only by gay men. The suspicion is deepened for those who know that, in the past, Robert has reduced both Amanda and Linda to tears, behind the closed door of his office, with accusations respectively of inefficiency and negligence. The day he had Linda in tears was one on which she'd phoned in and told Alison that she'd be late because she was unwell with a bad period.

Far from seeming to the women on *Gay News* a shy, boyish, harmless individual, an impression he often seems to make on men, Robert is seen as a weak man who fluctuates between turning a deaf ear (Gill can never get him to arrange a proper typewriter for her to do her work, nor to sort out pay and holiday problems) and bullying, when he can get away with it, which is with women under his 'line' authority – Jane once, more recently the now dismissed Amanda and Linda.

If the weekend's 'economies' are carried through, the overall effect will be that there are two women in full-time work at *Gay News* against eight before (of whom Scotty was not quite full-time), and ten men, against fourteen. The women are shocked and disappointed that Andrew hasn't fought for a gender-balance if there must be such an execution among those who have worked for the paper.

The 'weighting' of the redundancy arrangements on Robert's side of the paper has one most damaging effect. If the arrangements are to be queried, then some of the young men in administration and advertising who are about to scrape through with their jobs intact will suddenly find themselves at risk after all – and at risk, if they choose to see it this way, from women claiming that Robert has shown an unfair bias in favour of males in 'his' departments. Nothing could be better calculated to make 'women' seem the enemy than threats to men's livelihoods.

The staff (excluding Robert and Andrew, Chris who has gone, and Bob the part-time van-driver – though he comes in, and takes the side of disputing the arrangements) divide immediately on Monday morning into those who are heaving a sigh of relief and saying 'thank God someone's taken decisive action'; and those (as many men among them as women) who are at a loss to make up their minds whether unfairness, incompetence, or venality (is Robert saving his own skin and Denis's money above every other consideration?) is the more outstanding characteristic of the decisions just announced.

Such is the vocal scepticism of the doubters, taken with an instant agreement among those who have been sacked or asked to go on half-time that they'll turn up to work normally until there's been a proper enquiry, that the 'decisions' of the night of Sunday October 10 have no higher status than that of 'proposals' within twenty-four hours.

The women now come to the forefront in refusing to accept the weekend's decisions by owner and editor. In their phone conversation on Sunday night, Gill and Linda have already agreed that the three *Gay News* unions must make a 'federated' response to what is supposed to be happening, just as unions would on any other workforce. Gill will have other points to advocate, in connection with the to-date useless Gay News Ltd board of directors; including disclosure of all accounts, and the full contents of the bargain struck between Robert and Denis early in 1982, but the unions are the first 'fight back' institutions to hand.

With Chris's departure, Alison becomes 'parent of chapel' (elected representative) of the journalists and Linda is 'parent' of administrative staff who belong to SOGAT. Glen, in the art room, is 'parent' of NGA members (art room itself and typesetters). So two women, Alison and Linda, come to the foreground during the formal union discussions with Robert and his lawyer over coming weeks. Robert is to come to see Alison and Linda and – though she has no comparable formal role – Gill – as personifying an opposition which is in fact far more widespread, and is to talk of all three of them, to his friends, with the greatest bitterness. It seems, to the women involved, further proof that the man to whom *Gay News* had been sold was never fitted to preside over a newspaper with 'mixed' workforce and 'mixed' editorial commitments. When in trouble, he blames women.

The seven lesbians out of the eight strong female staff come to the forefront of affairs for still another reason. They alone on staff, in the shape of the 'VisLes collective' which in weekly meetings has prepared the two Visible Lesbian pages per issue for nearly a year, have a forum which can be 'activated' to debate events regardless of 'hierarchical' or departmental position. 'VisLes', as both the men and the women refer to the lesbians-in-conference, has never yet been used politically to dispute Robert's ownership, Andrew's editorship, or any of the other apparently immutable fixed interests of the paper. But it has the possibilities of a centre of unity and energy.

The men never meet as a sex. Those disposed to be hostile to any questioning of the October 9/10 arrangements, and who quickly define the women as the focus of discontent, begin paradoxically to feel that they as individual men are weak, and the women as 'VisLes' are strong.

It is a fact which will produce rumours, during winter 1982, of a gender-battle at *Gay News*: of lesbians 'rising' against the owner because he's a man, against male colleagues because they're men. It isn't remotely an accurate vision. Lesbians at *Gay News* do not suddenly cease to be individuals holding the same individual views they've always held. VisLes collective itself almost breaks up on one day in October, as the paper's tensions affect the women's discussions, just as they affect everything else. At all times there are men on the paper who welcome the points about which individual women, or the women as a group, hammer away: can the paper work at all, with the mix of lay-offs and part-time announced? Is the owner right financially in saying he must have the equivalent of seven redundancies (he goes as high as eight or more in his estimates)? What bearing on everything has the money still promised to former owner Denis?

The entire art room, JC, Tony, and Glen – the longest serving departmental group on the paper – side with the asking of these questions. So does Alisdair, one of the youngest of the gay men on staff, in charge of mail order sales and subscriptions (both of which have been doing very well). So does Bob the photographer, who is supposed to lose his job; so does Roger the advertisement manager, who is very much keeping his; so does Mike, whose job is to stay.

As the crisis takes its course, there are aspects of every kind of battle that *could* occur internally on a newspaper, but demarcation is never rigid, to each lining up of forces there are exceptions. There are traces of a gender battle, with David, Mike in display administration (despite his criticism of Robert), the two Peters in accounts, and Peter of features and 'scene' coverage, at times showing resentment of 'the lesbians'. There are traces of a class-battle – in which Andrew, Alison, and Gill tend to be seen by Peter of features, by Chris (now gone), and, come to that, by Mike, as 'middle-class/academic' in their ideas about contents for the paper. There are traces of a departmental battle, with Robert's 'gay male bloc' in advertising, finance, and administration, opposed to Andrew's 'mixed paper' in production and editorial.

Perhaps Don, Roger's tall and youthful deputy in advertising, who by temperament so much wants *not* to be made to take sides about anything, exemplifies the truest divide, cutting (now for one person, now for another) across all other categories. It is the one that was signalled on Sunday evening October 10 when Gill decided not to stay quiet but to call Linda and ask what's to be done – the divide between those who don't want the boat rocked by dispute whatever the management does, and those who say that on the record of years it's management itself which rocks the boat, and now looks like sinking it.

On Tuesday October 12, editorial and production staff meet – as is usual on the first Tuesday of each fortnight – to plan the forth-coming issue, now to be cut to forty pages and supposedly prepared by the reduced staff. Andrew, dragged in off his sick bed to oversee planning of this dramatically cut issue, stands weakly against a drawing board in the art room, his skin yellow from his illness. But try as he might, whichever page he attempts to plan, Andrew is confronted again and again with the unworkability of the arrangements he has shared in.

Just forty-eight hours after drawing up his list of cuts, Andrew sees that his crisis measures are a nonsense. Page after page he tries to plan the issue as if the redundancies and part-time arrange-ments are already in force. Insuperable obstacle after insuperable obstacle emerges. If Jo is only to be present to work on the Guide and Diary on alternate weeks and if typesetters are to be reduced to one on alternate weeks, then the ten page listings and Diary section will only be completed if work is sent out to jobbing typesetters – an economic lunacy with one typesetter being put on half time. 'Well', concludes Andrew, 'That's clear; Lesley must stay full-time, after all, in typesetting'. Typesetting suddenly finds itself reinstated to the level of two full-time workers. 'So', says Gill irritably 'now, presumably, half a job must be lost from somewhere else'.

And so it goes. Jo, on half-time, won't be able to do all her usual revisions to the lists of gay pubs and clubs and other places round the country carried in the Guide. There's silence. Everyone looks expectant. Running his fingers through his hair, Andrew says despondently 'we shall do it in the news room'. Gill is unimpressed: 'I shan't be there in the first week of production', she points out, '*you*'ll have to do it' (Chris having departed) 'in addition to editing the paper, following news stories, compiling the WorldView pages' (international coverage, formerly prepared by Gill) 'and doing all the secretarial work, since Scotty mostly won't be there either. You won't be able to do it. No-one could.'

Perhaps Peter, of features, is going to write news stories? Perhaps Alison will? As for the Visible Lesbian, Alison and Wendy alone will have to do it, since Amanda and Linda are to be sacked and Jo, Lesley, Gill will only be present for one meeting a fortnight. Again, the economics don't make sense in the case of Bob the photographer: if he's to go, and the paper must have illustrations, whether forty pages or fifty-six, how will the cost of photographs from commercial libraries and commercial processing of film that Peter and Andrew might try to take compare with savings on Bob's salary? Everyone knows that the top of the 'hierarchy', Alison excepted, has been gunning for Bob for a long time, but in the midst of such emotion, has anyone costed the loss of his function?

The meeting dwindles to paralysis, to a *quod erat demonstrandum*, QED, silence. 'I see', says Andrew, 'that the paper can't be saved in this way. I no longer trust my own judgement.' He goes to seek out Robert, who now sits with his office door permanently shut when on the premises at all – and is often discovered blankly staring out of the window, or, worse, listening behind the closed door – to tell him as much, and to say that his own place as editor must now be among other employed members of staff, and not as a part of the 'executive'. He asks the editorial and production staff how they feel about working, if they are to remain in work at all, for Robert, and every one of them says they have no wish to. Will Tony? 'No', he says, monosyllabically. 'How can I', says Alison, 'after what he's done to my lesbian colleagues?'

Up till this moment and this meeting on this day, the *Gay News* staff could fairly be described as quiescent, hard-working, low on 'political consciousness' or experience, trade union innocents – well-meaning, highly motivated workers, whose principal concern is to bring out a good paper, to bust a gut, when there's a hitch, as on newspapers there so often is, to get it out dead on time, and taking surprisingly little thought for themselves. Tolerance and goodwill – what many, as they come to hear the whole, bluntly call 'subservience' – has been the truest characteristic.

Now the wages disparities can no longer be overlooked. Even if a 'band' from £12,000 (now to be £10,000) for owner and editor down to £6,000 for Mike and Linda in administration is to be accepted, how is it that Jo, all this time, has produced the vital

Diary and Guide on £7,750 when Alison and Peter, no less, but surely no more, vital, have been put up to around £10,000? How is it that Bob as staff photographer (and NUJ member) has had £7,250, against Chris and Gill on the NUJ 'minimum' of £7,500? In the case of the NUJ, how is it that journalistic wages on *Gay News* are so erratic when Rule 22(c) of the NUJ states that members mustn't negotiate salaries without the agreement of the in-house 'chapel' and of the appropriate Industrial Council? The answer, really, is that those, like Jo, who don't kick up a fuss but are always self-effacing, get as little as possible. Chris, for instance, in his time as 'parent' of the NUJ 'chapel', made it clear that he was satisfied with his own salary, and no meetings were ever called to review the erratic 'wages bands' on the paper.

The same peculiarities are to be found in typesetting and art room, though all in those departments are unionised in the NGA. Glen and JC earn upwards of £8,000, while Tony, newer as a full-timer but doing just as much, gets £7,250. Typesetters are on Tony's wage, though historically they had been supposed to be at parity with art-room. (Wendy has been trying forever to get the matter raised.)

Advertising, accounts, and administration wages are hidden in timeless obscurity, and were further muddled, in 1981, by the allowance of office cars to the business manager (Robert) and the then advertising manager. Peter Coell in accounts earns upwards of £9,000 plus overtime (journalists aren't eligible for overtime, but are supposed to take time off in lieu – which they almost never do) while his assistant Peter (Jones) earns less than £7,000.

Redundancy and part-time 'economies' drawn up against so anomalous a system of rewards serve both to compound, and to make glaringly obvious, that here is a managerial mess which no-one has ever determinedly tackled – not 'management', nor union members through their branches on the premises. People are nearly always embarrassed about discussing their wages, very reluctant to seem envious or grasping. It is so throughout Britain, as if salaries were a matter for shame, the 'private parts' of the modern world. *Gay News* has been no more immune than most other workplaces. But should it be? And has the whole erratic muddle contributed to the overheads crisis in trading accounts?

Late on the next day – Wednesday October 13 – Robert meets

the *Gay News* parents of chapel (PoCs) and Mike Smith, a national official of the NUJ. Robert agrees to withdraw all notices of dismissal and part-time working unconditionally, pending consultation and negotiation. Later he will demonstrate, time and time again, that he doesn't understand that he has, in fact, agreed to do so. The PoCs then go to the newly federated chapel (NUJ, NGA and SOGAT combined) to draw up questions – mainly financial – which they want answered. Robert must, that is, make his case for wanting redundancies and other cuts and must demonstrate it to the satisfaction of the unions concerned. Andrew, not being a union member until much later, is not present at this or any other subsequent union meetings. Other non-members of unions – Roger, of advertising, and the Peters in accounts – are also not present.

Advised by union officials, as well as obeying their own intuitions, staff realise that much hinges on the details of the original deal struck between Denis and Robert, hints of which have leaked out but most of which is still secret. It is because of this deal, clearly, that the imminent sale of *Gay News*'s major asset, the freehold offices, has been announced. (In a shock development, it's learnt that Denis might, if he chose, bring an injunction against Robert for selling the office.) The federated chapel demands to see details of the deal between Denis and Robert. National officers of the NUJ and NGA have already told PoCs that Robert must be made to understand that it is in his own best interest to provide the chapel with convincing and truthful replies. 'If not,' says the NUJ's Mike Smith, 'he will *have* to deal with the national unions, who can match any threat of his with greater threats'.

On the subsequent morning, PoCs present Robert with the list of questions arising from the federated chapel meeting:

October 14th, 1982

From: Glen Platts (FoC, NGA)
        Linda Semple (MoC, SOGAT)
        Alison Hennegan (Acting MoC and Clerk of NUJ)

To: Robert Palmer

At a meeting of the federated chapel of NUJ, NGA and SOGAT held yesterday, October 13, 1982, members requested the following information:-

1.   What legal measures if any are being taken by Denis Lemon about the sale of 1A Normand Gardens?

If he is seeking legal action is it against Robert Palmer, Robert Palmer Marketing and/or Gay News Ltd?

2.   May we please see, and be able to take away to examine, the Conditions of Sale of GN Ltd from Denis Lemon to Robert Palmer?

3.   May we see, and be able to take away to examine, all documents relating to loans made or taken by GN Ltd., Robert Palmer Marketing and Coltsfoot Productions?*

4.   May we see, and be able to take away to examine, documentary justification for the immediate sale of this building and the reasons why proceeds from it must go to the bank?

5.   May we please have documentation on GN's major creditors and sums owing to them. If creditors include Robert Palmer Marketing or Coltsfoot Productions, may we have documentation of that, too? (Or any other company connected with the above.)

6.   We would like a full explanation, with the necessary documentation, of the exact financial relationship between Robert Palmer Marketing Ltd and Gay News Ltd.

7.   We would like documentation about GN's financial position at the time of the sale of GN Ltd from Denis Lemon to Robert Palmer.

8.   We are seeking your agreement to the appointment of such financial consultants/managerial consultants as the Chapels may appoint to examine GN's finances. We are also seeking your agreement to give such a person or persons access to such documents as he/she/they may require.

9.   We would like to know what possible sources of external monies available to GN Ltd at the moment or near future have been explored.

An ad hoc meeting between Wendy, Amanda, Jo, Linda, Peter Burton, Glen and Alison springs up in the art room around JC, who tells them that Denis telephoned him the night before to

---

* A company of unknown purposes understood to have been formed by Robert Palmer.

express his fury with Robert's 'bungling' of the cuts. Denis, says JC, reports having already phoned Robert to 'tick him off' and to tell him what a redundancy list *should* look like. Even later, Alison makes an embarrassing phone call to the voluntary, self-help organisation for gay people, Gay Legal Advice (GLAD), seeking legal advice on behalf of the staff. GLAD recommends three firms from their 'ultra-reliable' list. One of these is Richard Creed's practice.

Staff confidence in GLAD is severely dented.

By Friday, Alison is speaking to a company law expert, found by Gill, to clarify the rights and obligations of a board of directors. The expert makes clear that the directors should call an Extraordinary Meeting to challenge Robert on various aspects of company management. Jo, Alison and JC draft a memo to all directors calling for such a meeting on Monday, October 18 and phone Robert to tell him they have done so.

Directors duly arrive for the Extraordinary Meeting, but are handed notices of dismissal from the board. Only Peter Coell remains a director. With the sacking of the board, the polarity between management and staff is complete. Andrew, the editor, is among those fired from the board.*

Throughout the rest of the day, union meetings and telephone calls take place. The national unions express support for the staff's demands for information and the implications and practicalities of an official strike are explained and discussed. The unions stress that their brief ends with the protection of employment; ideological debates about proper modes of ownership fall outside their lawful scope, *unless the modes of ownership affect the conditions and security of employment.* Until the sale documents are seen, this relevance will remain ambiguous. If the chapel proceeds with a strike, the NUJ will back them and will make sure no 'scabs' (non-unionised strike-breaking writers) are used. With a touch of bitterness, everyone agrees that Andrew should go home to rest and recuperate, so that he doesn't 'FO' the situation into any kind of false calm.

From the next day until the final crisis in the coming spring, an era of extended phone calls begins between (mainly) Alison and

*Hugh Stephenson, editor of The New Statesman, is later to tell Andrew that in his view editors should never sit on a publication's board of directors.

two friends of Robert's whose confidentiality must be kept. They are referred to as 'Mole' and 'Throat'. As they have Robert's confidence and as they have the best interests of *Gay News* at heart, they agree to act as 'go-betweens', trying to get Robert, on the one hand, to see sense, and to tell staff, on the other, what is in Robert's mind.

Simultaneously, friends of Denis try to perform the same service with 'non-attributable' calls to Andrew. As the winter goes by, he is increasingly hearing of Denis's distress about the threat to his own prospects of an income – from any source – to the pitch where the word 'suicide', again, crops up.

It is later revealed that 'Mole' and 'Throat' are – respectively – Roy Burns and Harry Coen. Roy offers to do his own lobbying to persuade Robert to release copies of the deal documentation. One such call between Roy and Alison recapitulates a five-hour conversation between Robert and Roy: Robert says that there is a clause in the deal saying that Denis has to be told if the freehold building is to be sold. Robert has not told him and when asked why he hasn't informed Denis, Robert says he 'forgot'. He now fears the serving of an injunction by Denis and the consequent bankruptcy of Gay News Ltd. Robert says he will be more responsive to staff demands once the building is sold, because that will mark the end of all territorial claims which Denis might make on Robert himself, on Robert Palmer Marketing Ltd or on *Gay News*. He tells Roy that he will agree to let a nominee look at the documentation on behalf of the staff. He also expresses fear of Denis, and makes a claim that the survival of *Gay News* is the only thing important to him.

By Thursday, October 28, Gill suggests in a Visible Lesbian meeting that the paper's only collective should prepare an analysis of what is going on and a statement about the situation be published on the Visible Lesbian pages. The other women agree and work begins accordingly. It becomes a piece called 'The Getting of Wisdom' and will itself arouse almost as much controversy as the crisis.

Robert finally agrees to pass over documentation to a nominee acceptable both to himself and to the staff. The person chosen is Marsaili Cameron, a freelance journalist and reviewer and long-time contributor to *Gay News*. She, in turn, discusses the situation and the figures provided by Robert and the two Peters of accounts with an accountancy and company law professional, who agrees to prepare an independent report for the staff.

Marsaili tells staff of his initial response, which includes the view that *Gay News* is probably trading illegally, being 'hopelessly insolvent'; and that – whatever the provisions of the 1981 amendment to the Companies Act – the deal between Denis and Robert 'sails dangerously close to the wind'.*

He insists that there is no way in which redundancies will solve any part of the problem. Later that evening Roy Burns phones to say that his own partner – after seeing the documentation and some of the figures – says unequivocally 'There's only one solution – liquidation'.

Exhausted from frustration, meetings, manoeuvrings and explanations – not to mention getting the issue out on time – the staff depart for the brief respite of the weekend. Phone calls are made incessantly, even so. On Monday, back at work, a meeting takes place between Robert, PoCs, Mike Smith (NUJ) and John Geleit (NGA). Mike Smith hammers away at Robert's forward projections for the next six months, insists on a proper explanation for why £30,000 worth of bad debts are being written off in a single four week period, and asks 'how the hell' Robert thinks *any* sort of paper – let alone one that is to trade profitably – can be produced with reductions in staff of between a third and a half. Robert is exasperated, flushed and unyielding, handing out yet more figures. Mike Smith looks briefly at them, remarking that, as he didn't like the last lot, he doesn't see why these should be any better. He says, too – as others have said – that the system of accounting used by *Gay News* seems 'weird and wonderful in the extreme'. He points out that editorial and production staff are asked to reduce their staffing level by forty per cent, whereas other areas – notoriously advertising and finance – are to remain relatively untouched.

Mike Smith presses hard to establish *whose* projections these are: Robert's or Peter Coell's. Either way, he says, they're 'lousy'. He queries, for example, a provision for spending between £1200 and £1500 per four-week period on 'advertising and promotion', given that there seems to be very little going on there.

Robert's lawyer, David Warner, intervenes to say that two basic

* For the consultants' approval see p79

198

points seem to emerge again and again: the first is the unions' assertion that redundancies at the suggested level will produce an unworkable paper, and the second, that if Robert's figures are correct, there must be some cuts. What, he asks the unions, is their response to that?

Mike Smith and John Geleit have no problem with that question. It's purely academic, they say, since, with the cuts proposed, there'll be nothing left to impose cuts on.

On Wednesday, November 3, the final meeting between management and unions take place. It takes until eleven o'clock at night, ending with agreement to three redundancies, in addition to Chris Kirk's resignation being counted in to make a fourth. Amanda, of classifieds, worn down with the anxiety, the ill-feeling and – for her – the awfulness of Robert's behaviour, says she wants to go. (She takes, soon after, a job in London with The Women's Press, of which she is still (1983) saying, gratefully, 'It's so nice to work with women'.) JC – also worn down by the neurosis-inducing atmosphere and by a deeply felt disillusionment with Denis, for whom he worked for nearly ten years – decides to go and will not be talked out of his decision. He needs a rest, he says. His redundancy payment will help towards recuperation. About half a year later he finally has satisfying full-time work, though in a non-gay environment. Scotty, too, insists on going, despite anguish that she should not, expressed by editorial staff who will consequently be bereft of any secretarial assistance, and by all her fellow-workers, who regard her with unashamed affection.

Scotty – who is not a union member and who is over retirement age – does not bow to sentiment. Hard-headed to the last, she argues that the others should make use of her going. 'If you do not allow me to be a volunteer for redundancy' she says 'Robert will get rid of me anyway, because I have no legal employment protection.' The point is not lost. If she is not to be one of the three, another must go, and everyone sees that she might then be dismissed in addition.

Robert agrees, further, that henceforth staffing levels may not fall below eighteen without union consent. David Warner, on departure, accidentally leaves behind a notebook in which conditions are recorded, including some that Robert has failed to lay down. One of these is that Linda Semple – the SOGAT PoC who is responsible for reception and box replies – is *not* to be allowed to move over into the editorial department. Scotty and Jo, who, together with many others, have stayed late in the office to receive the results of the meeting, are unlucky enough, on departing the building, to be offered a lift – with what they see as coercive courtesy – by Robert and David Warner. Haplessly, they discuss the Christmas decorations in Regent Street.

Just two days later, a further meeting is necessary. Robert is disputing that JC is entitled to ten weeks' salary in lieu of notice. Robert, Andrew and PoCs discuss the matter. Robert cannot remember agreeing to JC's entitlement, which is hardly surprising, since David Warner had preferred to complete the negotiations without him.

David Warner confirms, by telephone that JC is to have the money.

Even so, staff are still to be tortured with uncertainties. They express disquiet about the conditions which they suspect await them at the new, to-be-rented premises, in Farringdon Road, near the offices of *Capital Gay* and of *The Guardian*, and the *New Statesman*. Robert assures them that all will be well.

Gentle people, most of those who work at *Gay News*. Most people anywhere who work in offices or factories are extraordinarily long-suffering and, in practice, patient both with those alongside them and with those set over them. But not for nothing does *Gay News* constantly receive applications from young gays, asking if they can have a job there. It is a very special kind of refuge in a world where gays must mostly remain so 'closety' at work. Those who work on the paper, knowing how some envy them, can rarely shake off the feeling of 'privilege' that they have a post on the paper, let alone the sense of obligation to those who write most urgently about their dependence on it for support and information. It takes a crisis of the magnitude of autumn 1982 to bring to the surface the unstated compromises, the undealt with conflicts of viewpoint, with which people rub along until the whole venture comes to the brink of collapse.

Fundamental ignorance of the production processes of the paper on the part of the proprietor; wages differentials that have 'grown like Topsy' and become ultimately absurd; a politicised staff (ie one in constant contact with the lesbian and gay movement) mixed in with a staff 'unpoliticised' from ignorance or inclination – these are the realities that become inescapable after so many years, as people fight for control of the title in the literally dark days (the evenings drawing in) of the close of 1982.

The deepest muddle of all thrown up by the varying reactions throughout the paper to the October emergency concerns 'gay consciousness' – one of those phrases filled with significance for those who consider it to have any meaning at all, and empty of significance, merely 'political', to those who hold it to be the passing terminology of the early 1970's, or the self-serving invention of those who want to preach conversion to their fellows.

If it means anything in the context of such a paper as *Gay News*, born out of a liberation movement, rescued by its readership in its time of trial in 1977, served throughout its history by 'voluntary' unpaid workers – still served, every fortnight, by John Wilmott when he arrives to send out overseas subscribers' copies, unpaid – it means clear understanding of the paper's commitments, without which it will have no 'soul' at all and no purposes beyond mechanical production, printing, and distribution. And those commitments are . . .? To serve as a forum of information and opinion for the lesbian and gay male population, to refrain from party-political bias (whether it be the 'straight' politics of Parliamentary debate, or the politics of the contending viewpoints in the gay world), to campaign where a campaign is obviously due, to be a 'caring' enterprise, both where its readers and their community are concerned, and where its own members, the staff and the contributors, are concerned. So much is surely indisputable, from the beginnings of the paper in voluntary dedication of effort until this moment of refusal to take industrial action, ten years later.

But not everyone thinks of it in such a way, or thinks it through in such a way, for it hasn't been necessary to show agreement with these notions in order to work at *Gay News*. It hasn't even been necessary to be 'out' for all and every purpose. It would be very hard, and would go against the grain for many of those who might be thought most 'politicised' on the staff, if recruits to *Gay News* had ever had to prove any further credentials than their goodwill and their homosexuality, as if a 'thought police' were to filter recruitment to the paper and ensure that only the like-minded find work – a certain recipe for the destruction of the paper's capacity to be impartial, and probably for its capacity to be frivolous and amusing. But London Gay Switchboard has found it possible to 'train' new entrants, and sometimes to fail them as unsuitable no matter how eager they are. Was there no way in which a middle ground between indifference to whether people knew anything of the history or individuality of the paper, and compulsory agreement with those already in employment, could not have been found? There was never so much as a pamphlet, 'This is *Gay News*', for the new entrant or interested reader.

So with the roof threatening to fall in, and no general consensus throughout staff about what it means to be a lesbian or a gay man, or about the fundamental drives of the paper, nothing is taken for granted or can be taken for granted as issue after issue bursts upon individuals who had had no share in policy making, merely done their job under directive, and gone home.

Issues such as: is it endurable or even commercially wise, any longer, that *Gay News* remain the property of one man? Is the *Gay News* 'hierarchy' nothing other than an amateurish aping of the way that heterosexual or pretend/heterosexual men have long since organised virtually every paper, and grotesquely unsuited to the ways that gays deal with one-another? Is *Gay News* bound, as it were by charter, or at the least by majority reader expectation, to be in part a campaigning and pioneering one, or can it just be a 'fun' paper, indistinguishable in editorial approach from the entertainment world around which so much of its display advertising quite naturally revolves? Do those who work at *Gay News* have any obligation to be active in the lesbian and gay movement? (Difficult that, for there are eyes which can be open and marvellously observant if they go nowhere but to the most 'commercial' of gay discos or pubs, and others which can faithfully go to 'movement' gatherings, and observe little or nothing).

As argument rages with Robert or with his lawyer about redundancies, about disclosures of information, about new controls over *Gay News*, the strain tells on those who had assumed it enough to do one's job, to be gay, to carry on, and those – regarded as 'the heavies' – who are convinced that there will be upset after upset, crisis after crisis, and never a truly able newspaper under able supervisory methods if what Robert and Denis have done, and what Robert and Denis implicitly stand for, isn't uprooted now and for ever.

'Heaviest of the heavies', to those unfortunates whose only wish is to be 'left alone' to do such work as is allowed them, are 'the lesbians'. It is a ridiculous charge when gay men are strewn across every position of power in the paper's affairs and when legal authority is wholly vested in Robert (except so far as he is subordinated to Denis). But it is also – as which extreme accusation is not? – a true perception, made adversarial. As women who share the common experience of the world of all women, as gay women who are liable to be made peripheral wherever they turn, whether in the women's movement or in the gay movement, they are indeed faster than any of the men in this final crisis of the paper to say that not only has the paper been sold, but that people and principles and all have been sold too. Unwelcome, unpalatable as it is for the gay men to face it, their time has gone, at least by comparison with the early 1970s. They have come near to the kind of 'assimilation' in a moderately more kindly world which unfits them for the task of telling a truth and compelling others to take action about it. The women's 'consciousness', unattractive but meaningful word, is higher than the men's. The Visible Lesbian pages and the 'collective' who produce it are seen as this women's 'consciousness' in action, and admired or hated – and hated, by some in the country's population of gay men, with revelatory virulence – according to preconception. According, indeed, to 'consciousness', whether it be a man's or a woman's. Andrew, for all his time at *Gay News*, has been saying 'the trouble with gay men is 'that we have no [sexual] politics'. He has tried to excite interest in the idea of men's pages, but found no takers among the men.

PUNCH DRUNK

Guy Fawkes Day, November 5, falls on a Friday in 1982, but the *Gay News* staff have no time – and little cause – for celebration on the night of this usually festive anniversary of an attempt at sedition against James VI and I and its putting down. Guy Fawkes, the chief perpetrator of the 'gunpowder plot', was executed and, ever since, on November 5, England's skies light up with fireworks and bonfires. At *Gay News*, however, apart from caustic mutterings about who might do well to be put on a lighted pyre, production grinds on towards the paste-up of the current issue. On the previous night, Alison has stayed behind until one o'clock in the morning, trying to pack her books, pamphlets, files and folders into the tea chests which Robert has had delivered earlier in the week. Indeed, staff have had only this week to prepare to leave the building and they must – in addition to getting the paper out – clear everything away, lock, stock and barrel. Volunteers will move the heavier items, but staff are responsible for their other working materials so they get safely to the new offices.

Rumour is circulating that Robert has not – yet – signed the personal guarantees requisite to the taking on of the lease of the new rented premises. But he is scarcely ever in the office and, when telephoned at home, has his answering machine constantly switched on.

Wearily, staff depart for the weekend, wondering how they are to manage the next issue when they have not yet even moved into the new building. They expect, nonetheless, to turn up in the new offices for work as usual on the following Monday morning. The new premises are in Farringdon Road, EC1 – almost next door to the *Morning Star* and *The Guardian* and near to new premises of *The*

New Statesman; near also to *Capital Gay* and *Spare Rib*. At least it will feel like newspaper-land and there will be many more places for lunches.

But staff don't go there on Monday after all. Everyone receives a phone call saying that the offices are not yet ready, but that they will be by Tuesday. It is not to be. Tuesday brings the same story. It is not until Wednesday – with two days of the ten-day production cycle lost – that staff come in ready to begin work on the current issue in the new Farringdon office.

What greets them is truly horrifying. The premises are on the fifth and top floor of a building housing light industries – and they have not been cleaned. Tea-chests, unpacked, are strewn everywhere; desks – with and without drawers, or tops, or other moving parts, lie upended randomly; filing cabinets are in a similar state. Benches promised to support the expensive and extremely heavy typesetting machines are not yet built; and the person hired to build them, and to provide essential shelving, is not a jobbing carpenter, but an advertiser who – in return for advertising space in the paper – is on the premises to do, single-handed, all the carpentry neccessary.

But the lack of order has one remarkable side-effect. Bob finds himself a desk, a typewriter, a telephone extension in the new editorial space. At last he has that real existence on the premises of *Gay News* that he has been calling for for so long. He promptly organises feature articles for which he himself can do the photography, and so comes into his own at a time when every last ounce of initiative is required of everybody. His own long torment of feeling an enforced 'outsider' is over.

Of issue 254's Literary Supplement, only Alison's regular column 'Between the Lines', remains, since publishers' post and reviewers' copy still lie in GPO sacks somewhere between Normand Gardens, Farringdon Road and the GPO sorting office. In her column she recounts some of the prevailing chaos: the typesetters – their machines having eventually arrived – perch them on a draining board next to the kitchen sink and try to get on with it; for the first day there has been no electricity at all, which has meant no light to write by, type by or design by; for the whole of the first week, the art room has had no copy camera and no dark room; editorial staff have been unable to unpack files because there was no shelving to house the contents. And for more than a week, the part-time carpenter wanders about with a hammer (and a sidekick) through doorways, the doors themselves having been commandeered for possible use as work surfaces. The lack of industrial cleaning means that the air is heavy with metal dust (there has been a jewellery business in the office previously). Many staff soon begin to suffer ear, nose and throat irritations, but the premises are never cleaned. An insecurely fixed, six foot long, strip light suddenly falls across Jo's desk seconds after she has left it.

Whatever misery had been suffered in Normand Gardens is – compared to this new torture – almost a fond memory.

But most calamitous of all is the telephone system newly installed. There are indeed four lines, as promised. Unknown to callers, if the *Gay News* number is already engaged, the call will automatically pass on to the next available of the four *Gay News* numbers. As a result, instruments ring all over the premises, with the wrong person almost always having to receive a call. A call to the news room will go through to the advertising department, at the other end of the offices, so that, physically, the right person will have to be fetched. Calls to mail order ring in Jo and Alison's room, calls for the Diary in the news room. Staff are to be seen, throughout the time spent in Farringdon Road, running perpetually from room to room in order to take calls somewhere else. It is – obviously – both inefficient and infuriating. But more, it means that – in the end – like rats exhausted in their laboratory cages from the whims of experimenters – many of the staff simply take their phones off the hook so that they can get on with their work.

The move to Farringdon Road has all the elements of classic British farce – ('Carry On Moving') – with more than a hint of industrial tragedy beneath the surface. Robert – scarcely by now ever seen – fails to show signs of either remorse or sympathy, nor, indeed, any signs that he even understands the effects on the human beings in his employ – not to mention on the production targets of the paper.

What a disaster. As a result of it, all staff at last unite in feeling that the owner is part of the obstacles, and not the person to provide the solutions. In mid-November, seated on chairs and desks and upturned wastepaper baskets, they confront Robert as once, in January of the same year, they had heard him with delight as he announced his success in 'getting rid of' Denis. This time, in a scene with unnerving ritualistic overtones, he invites the *Gay News* staff's opinion of his management. Everyone at *Gay News*, with the exception of Peter Coell of accounts who isn't present and Mike, who must answer all the telephones, one by one says to him that they can't face the future if he's to personify management. It has come to that, within less than a year of his 'triumph' and within weeks of his late September declaration that people must go if the paper's finances are to be saved.

From now on, Robert declares that he is willing to sell *Gay News* to the staff if Denis will release him from all further personal or corporate obligations (£70,000 or so). And if he, Robert, is assured at least a medium term contract to carry on at his present salary as marketing director. And if staff relieve him of personal guarantees he has given in respect of the new offices and of office equipment.

The same issue (254 – published November 25) which fails to carry a Literary Supplement is perhaps the single most controversial *Gay News* ever published, other than the 'blasphemous libel' issue of 1976. In the hideous chaos of the new offices staff succeed in printing extended thoughtful analyses by Harry Coen, Roy Burns, and others, on the causes and possible solutions to the paper's crisis. Robert is carefully given space to make his own points. The most significant assertion made in the pages of the paper by the outside contributors is that there is now a 'moral obligation' on Denis to give up all further effective claims on *Gay News*.

Chris, opponent of so much on the editorial side, had resigned without ever making clear just why. Peter Burton now goes, stating specifically in a letter to Andrew that, having just seen the November 25 issue of the paper, he is 'frankly appalled. I think the issue is a disgrace – and the level of personal attack on Denis and Robert included therein unspeakable . . . I deeply regret that my name is still on the mast head . . . from this point on, I wish no further association with the paper which calls itself *Gay News*.'

He is in Brighton. He has been fading from the paper and its affairs for some time, through a combination of holidays and a crisis-induced relapse into the symptoms that had been caused by his 'queer-bashing' early in the year. In his fury about issue 254, he writes to Andrew 'what you are thinking of by allowing such stuff to appear in print, I simply cannot imagine. I can only presume that you have no control whatsoever over the contents of the paper.'

In an open letter of reply, Andrew says in part: 'the present row is not of our making. We are in the INTOLERABLE position of attempting editorial planning, and planning of every description, without knowing who the owner of this paper will be as from the end of December. We are in the INTOLERABLE position that Denis persists in calling "private" matters which directly affect the prospects of the paper, of the staff, and of the legal and financial position. If people who are not on staff, whatever their past relations with Denis, submit their views and previously unpublished relevant facts, I would consider it censorship of the most irresponsible sort to deny them column space. You are quite wrong to suppose that Issue 254 was in defiance of my judgement or wishes as Editor – however disgraceful I may think it that we should be placed in the position of publishing such material . . . I work for the *paper*, and not for Robert, or for Denis, or for a faction of the staff.

'There is nothing commercially untenable about the position of *Gay News* the paper, but the company into which it is locked – Gay News Ltd – is in the most disgraceful disarray. It is legitimate to ask "why?", and if we are not to say that the freedom of the press applies to everyone and everything *except* gays who have been associated with *Gay News*, and *Gay News* itself, then the details of controversy must be published. I am completely unyielding on this, whatever the price in friendships . . .

'I would have preferred it had you, and before you Chris, stayed on to fight whatever corners you thought right, than left the paper, and then issued your rebukes. I don't deny you your right to say or print or write to me your opinions, now that you're off the paper – but there is a real fight on, and I had hoped that after your years with the paper, you would have stayed long enough to win, if that were the upshot, the kind of *Gay News* that you have in mind. We who are here have had to bear the torment of a situation which, I repeat, is NOT of our making.'

On Friday November 26 a meeting takes place between Andrew and PoCs. It is part of the remarkable story of the continuing production of the paper – unfailingly on schedule throughout these appalling winter months of uncertainty and strife – that this meeting takes place in the middle of a paste-up Friday, the point in the cycle of production which is – at the best of times – most frenetic. It is a particularly frantic time for the art room workers, who must finish pasting up the contents by the end of the working day in order to get all the material to the printers on time. Nevertheless Glen – the NGA PoC – packs this meeting into his already crowded day.

Andrew tells PoCs that he's asked Peter Coell if there is any chance that Robert can – or will – make the December payment due to Denis out of the *Gay News* accounts. Peter Coell's reply indicates that there isn't enough cash in the account to allow Robert to do so, unless the Inland Revenue can be deferred, which is unlikely. Andrew tells PoCs that it seems clear that Robert will not be able to pay Denis by the due date – December 31.

It is rumoured, also, Andrew informs the others, drawing on his private 'sources', that Denis has spent his £50,000 and has – according to rumour – no livelihood. Andrew speculates that in such circumstances Denis may well want to come back to *Gay News*, sack Robert and take a salary himself. Because all this is so unclear – and a matter of speculation only – Andrew says he intends to pursue the matter with Robert.

If it turns out that Robert expects to default, PoCs need to ascertain from national union representatives what the position will be if Denis returns as proprietor/editor, itching to make a clean sweep of 'trouble-makers'. PoCs take Andrew's point, but the unions are not unduly worried and say such eventualities will be handled as they arise.

By this stage, the staff being exhausted from the ceaseless pressure of not knowing Robert's plans, of suffering the frustration of not seeming to influence events, and – not least – from the never ending job of getting the paper out (which Gill comes to refer to as 'being on the rack'), it is decided to go along with something being urged by Andrew – that the time has come for the *Gay News* problems to be made public in an open meeting. County Hall is the chosen venue, since the incumbent Labour Party administration has made known its intentions of supporting lesbian and gay ventures and can provide a large enough room.

The meeting is advertised in *Gay News* and word is put out in the gay movement that help and feedback is desired by the *Gay News* staff. Accordingly, on the evening of Monday November 29 some (but not all) of the staff make their way to the meeting, to find more than 100 interested lesbians and gay men have come to find out what is going on. Robert Palmer also attends, but there is no sign of Denis Lemon. This – together with a second open meeting held a fortnight later, also at County Hall – is recorded and later edited for broadcast by the London gay 'pirate' radio station, Gay Waves.

Andrew addresses the meeting, before questions begin. He says 'we are in the position of having a healthy, commercially viable newspaper encumbered and trapped by ownership tangles of such complexity, it's difficult to know where to turn for a solution'. Robert sits silently, waiting for questions. One of the first is straight to the point, asking 'isn't the crux of the matter whether or not Denis Lemon can be persuaded to waive his remaining rights?' Andrew replies carefully that 'it's difficult to know what to say to that'.

Just as pertinent is a question from Jackie Forster, who had edited *Sappho*, the magazine for lesbians, and is a very well-known lesbian activist. She asks 'Has Robert Palmer enough in the account to cover all subscriptions, postage, mail and so on for *Gay News* number 256?' (the next issue). Robert replies, simply, 'No'. Jackie responds immediately: 'Then you're trading illegally and are liable for charges of fraud'. People laugh at this, supposing it's Jackie just being right on form and in character, trying to hit the nub of the matter with a histrionic flourish. Few realise that she is making a telling legal point, about which she is likely to have accurate knowledge, since *Sappho* itself had to close owing to cash-flow difficulties. Robert, however, does realise; and replies 'No, that's not actually quite right. Perhaps I could talk to you later?'. (Whether they meet and talk or not is unknown, but unlikely.)

Jonathan Cutbill, best known for his part in founding London's gay community bookshop, 'Gay's The Word', says he wants to know 'why Robert Palmer ever thought the paper *could* generate that sort of profit – it throws doubt on his management ability – and, in any case (addressing Robert directly), – if you're so keen on collective ownership, why did you sack the board of directors?'. Another questioner cuts in: 'Can the paper continue publishing after the end of this year? Can you meet your obligations to Denis?'

Robert replies: 'The company's obligation is just to trade profitably. The obligation to Denis is mine.'

Nick Billingham, gay lobbyist and member of CHE executive, says 'I want to say some hard words. It seems to me that Gay News Ltd has been acquired by a company with no assets and the paper is hopelessly encumbered. The two companies cannot be salvaged in any way. Call Denis's bluff. The shares are going to be worth very little anyway.'

Discussion flows, heatedly, back and forth, some suggesting that the *Gay News* staff should set up an alternative paper, others that Denis should not be paid, and others that Robert's motives should be made clearer. Harry Coen, who once worked for *Gay News* under Denis and now works for *The Sunday Times,* says he has come to the conclusion that 'a national gay newspaper *can't* be commercial. It must be funded in some other way', he argues, 'by a trust, perhaps. The gay male commercial scene has at last been hit by the recession. We need to find something which will run *stably,* not profitably.'

The meeting – which runs till past eleven o'clock, long after other meetings in County Hall have finished – ends inconclusively. Various ideas for how an alternative paper might be set up are put forward and a working party/support group is suggested, but it is clear to staff present that those who have come to find out what is happening at *Gay News* are no more able to break the many deadlocks existing at the paper than are the staff themselves. It is clear, too, and painfully so, that the staff are themselves divided, some clearly favouring some form of forced liquidation of Gay News Ltd, but others clearly preferring to try to find a way of dealing with Denis and Robert which will still allow the paper to stay in continuous production.

Next morning, at the usual Tuesday production meeting, messages of support are read out. They come from 'Women's City' (a feminist project hoping for Labour Party funding), 'Sisterwrite' (the feminist bookshop), the gay employment working party advising the Labour Greater London Council, *Spare Rib* (the women's liberation monthly) and 'Wicca' (a London lesbian social and lobbying group). Lesbian author Michèle Roberts sends a drawing she's done of a dancing woman, with the words 'Very best wishes and SOLIDARITY for the struggles at *Gay News*. May all lesbians always be visible!'. And *Body Politic,* Canada's famous paper for lesbians and gay men, phones wanting to know what's going on.

A week later – also at a production meeting – it is agreed that Denis be sent a copy of *Gay News* number 255 carrying a report of the Open Meeting together with a letter from Andrew asking that he be allowed to state to readers, advertisers, and press that Denis will join discussions about the paper with Robert and the staff (or their representatives) *with the main aim being the preservation of the paper in continuous publication.*

But December 7 is a curious day. Unknown to Andrew or others on staff, Denis's solicitors themselves write a letter to Robert's solicitors – a copy of which is sent to Andrew on Denis's instruction – in which it is stated that 'there have been a number of articles in the press concerning the present financial situation of Gay News Limited. It has been suggested that our client may be under some moral obligation to discharge the indebtedness of Robert Palmer Marketing Limited which exists under the agreement reached by our respective clients on February 22, 1982. We would wish to make it clear that our instructions are that the amounts owing to our client by Robert Palmer Marketing Limited are properly due in accordance with the existing agreement and we have no reason to advise Mr Lemon that any sums due under the contract should be forgiven.' (The articles in the press referred to are those that have started appearing in *The New Statesman, Time Out, The Guardian* and others, but the main article is Harry Coen's carried in *Gay News* itself on November 25.)

Andrew sends his letter to Denis – not yet knowing that Denis has instructed his solicitors that no such proposed waiving is at present intended – and asks Denis to phone his response through to Scotty, still working though now unpaid, as soon as possible. Scotty is duly phoned and told that Andrew's letter will receive a reply from Denis's solicitors. It is relayed – further – that Denis wants to know if Robert is agreeable to negotiations since he – Denis – can do nothing without Robert's agreement. Eventually, on December 17, the answer comes. Denis will *not* allow Andrew to announce in the pages of the paper to the staff, and elsewhere, that Denis is to join discussions whose main aim will be the preservation of the paper in continuous publication. To Andrew, the refusal is incomprehensible, and very damaging indeed.

Alison, Wendy and Linda decide one evening to construct a questionnaire for members of staff to fill in, in order to elicit opinion and form policy considering the possibility that negotiations with Robert and/or Denis may be in the offing. Staff are asked whether they wish to negotiate to the bitter end come what may; or to negotiate and at the same time begin setting up another paper (just in case); what new form of ownership people would want – a Trust, a limited company or a co-operative.

On December 10, staff analyse the results, finding that six think negotiation should occur until the effort clearly outweighs the reward and seven think negotiation should take place alongside the preparation of another paper. Seven want the paper to be owned co-operatively by its workforce; ten think it should be non-profit distributing and thirteen think editorial content should be decided by those who produce the paper. Eleven want to develop ways of ensuring input from gay people outside the paper.

There is also a financial feed-in meeting, but – as is becoming usual – without the Peters from accounts. Staff hear that *Gay News* is owed some £30,000, of which the distributors – Seymour Press – alone owe £22,000. Linda suggests that everyone involved in departments of the paper which bring in revenues should prepare a break down of what sums are coming in: these departments are distribution (David Bird), classifieds (Mike Allaway), subscriptions (Alisdair Clarke) and display advertising (Roger and Don). It is income – not profit – which staff wish to know. Staff agree, and the agreement marks another stage in the general dissatisfaction with the accounting system and with Robert's interpretations of figures.

Alisdair tells others that mail order receipts are rising. Display advertising – averaged per issue at £6,500 – is up by 17.6 per cent on the same period of the previous year and would – it seems clear – be even higher if the paper were not cut back to forty pages.

On December 13 Andrew circulates a memo to the staff concerning the second Open Meeting due that evening at County Hall. He expresses anxiety that so much time and energy are being spent in extricating the paper from its ownership tangles that there may be no paper left worth saving. He suggests, therefore, that outside negotiators be chosen, so that staff may be relieved of the principal burden. Nominations may perhaps be called for from the Open

Meeting. Other suggestions are also made: towards an acting body of trustees, an acting body to consider various suits – including ways of preventing any more payments to Richard Creed, and even towards an immediate cessation of work by the *Gay News* staff in the event that Robert creates any difficulties about making himself available for discussion, or fails to provide financial information required.

Wendy, too, has suggestions for the Open Meeting. She says that the first meeting either should have offered a unified staff view (had one existed) or the differing views should have been described and examined. The current meeting should list, therefore, the possibilities that either the staff wish to set up another paper independently, or offer to buy Robert Palmer Marketing Limited from Robert. If it's true, she argues, that Robert bought the paper on behalf of the gay community, always intending to offer shares to the staff, then he will agree to sell. If not, he'll refuse and Andrew will then 'blast the information all over the press' she concludes. If the staff buy Robert Palmer Marketing Limited, she continues, then Denis Lemon will have to sue the entire staff for his money or will have to liquidate Gay News Limited. Either alternative will bring him a bad press. What must be clear, however, is whether the staff will be working on a *Gay News* owned by Robert Palmer, or by Denis Lemon, or by staff themselves; or whether they will be working on a new paper.

The meeting duly takes place, though is more poorly attended than the first. Rosanna Hibbert, a contributor and well-known 'Wicca' woman, agrees to chair. Andrew explains to everyone that staff have decided there is no point in trying to acquire Robert Palmer Marketing Limited, and that it appears that February 4, 1983 is legally the first point at which Denis will be able, should he choose to, to repossess the shares in Gay News Limited in the event of Robert's defaulting on the £10,000 or so due December 31. David Bird then presents the results of the staff questionnaire and Linda explains the need for an external negotiating body.

Among significant points raised by the meeting are that the very idea of negotiating is controversial, since feeling is high that neither Denis nor Robert are easy to trust and, too, because no agreement seems possible which could ensure that neither man receives money from a settlement. Many urge the starting of a new paper, free of the current financial, legal and psychological quagmire. And open discussion occurs – for the first time in public – about the possibility of a strike.

Barry St John Rivers, a journalist on the *Islington and Hackney Gazette*, (which has just been through a similar agony) advocates a new paper. 'Don't waste time arguing,' he urges. 'Management can always wait. We journalists can't. The title's not that important. It's going to die anyway and you're all going to be out of work. You should be talking about starting a new paper and talking to County Hall about money. And don't underestimate the enormous amount of money in the gay community.'

Paul Walentowicz, a gay socialist activist, says pointedly 'The talk about negotiations is obscuring the fact that the staff hasn't a consensus. This meeting was apparently not important enough for all the staff to come to.' This is a valid enough point with respect to administration, advertising and accounts staff; but as far as absent Glen and Tony are concerned, the pressure on their getting the boards done on time in this second production week – given that disruption has put their schedules behind – has meant that they are working late in the office and are therefore unable to come.

The mood of this second public meeting is, nevertheless, one of gloom and disillusion; there is the anger of impotence and a growing weary awareness that simple solutions – strike, liquidate, start your own paper – are not going to work. Rosanna closes the meeting despite some protest, and staff – still not delivered of a solution to the paper's plight – make their way home. No more Open Meetings are planned or held.

On Wednesday, December 15, two days before the Christmas break, and still with no information about whether Denis will or will not be paid by Robert in a fortnight's time, Andrew, Alison and Gill meet in the news room to discuss the nature and constitution of a negotiating body and who might serve on it. They settle on Barry Jackson, of Gay Switchboard and Arts Council experience, and Joan Crawford (whose name is never believed by some Battersea gays – so rumour has it!), a literary agent with business expertise. Their brief – if they agree to act – will be threefold: to negotiate with Robert and Denis to remove the paper from single ownership; to restore it to a non-profit distributing basis; and to invite, receive and give recommendations concerning the best ultimate form of ownership for the paper.

Barry and Joan later agree – at a meeting at Gill's house during the break – and are asked, in addition to opening negotiations with Robert and Denis, to make enquiries about the state of the *Gay News* 'Fighting Fund' (which holds some £4000), a resource set up with donations at the time of the blasphemy trial. The trustees include Denis and Robert; would negotiators ascertain whether Alison was ever made a trustee and why Andrew, as editor,isn't an *ex officio* member?

To keep revenues at their maximum, it had at first been decided to cancel the fortnight's break for the entire staff usually taken at this time of year. But citing the exhaustion of all concerned, and the rather better trading performance than he had earlier been fearing, Robert suggests that the holiday be taken after all, meaning no issue in the first fortnight of January 1983. It is at last a humane gesture.

Yet art room, though worked into the ground like everyone else, protest. They are frightened for the impact on external opinion if *Gay News* is mistakenly understood to have faltered in publication. However, the break is taken.

Whether because art room turn out to be all too right, or because of the months of adverse publicity, or because Roger now takes a theatrical engagement (as he is entitled to do), display advertising now indeed plummets at the start of 1983. Compared with the same period of the year before, it drops forty-four per cent, to £6,600 in the first two issues of the New Year combined. It takes until March, and Roger's return to work, for signs to appear of a slow recovery in display advertising.

By then – indeed with effect from February 3 (issue 258) – the paper, including its cover, will have been very considerably redesigned, drawing a great deal of praise from the outside world – and wonder from those who know the circumstances in which this is being done. Thanks to the efforts of the negotiators, Joan Crawford and Barry Jackson, freeing the editorial/production staff from the direct burden of negotiation with the owners, it becomes possible in January 1983, for the first time since October 1982, to work on creative issues of the paper, rather than one emergency issue after another.

Since the paper obviously cannot hire any new writers, 'commercial scene' coverage, with all its appeal to display advertisers and many readers, vanished from the paper with Peter Burton's departure. A recommendation of Gill's that a collective modelled on the Visible Lesbian now be formed to handle the work that Peter had done, is taken up enthusiastically by many members of staff from all departments and their joint efforts begin to appear in the paper under the new heading of 'Scene and Heard'. The paper's handling of theatre, film, music, consumer developments – also left up in the air by Peter's departure – is also retrieved by the forming of an 'Arts and Leisure' collective.

Through it all, *Gay News*'s regular contributors, shorn of space and paid next to nothing, continue to provide copy and to make every possible gesture of support. One of the paper's best-known former writers, Keith Howes, at this point undertakes to do full-length interviews on demand, regardless of whether or not he gets paid.

Early in January, staff reassembling after their uneasy fortnight's holiday, a meeting takes place in the advertising room. Roger is absent on acting engagements, so the display advertising effort at this crucial time is at fifty per cent strength, with Don carrying the whole burden. Andrew repeatedly and openly wonders why Robert does not fill in the gap left by Roger and get on the phone to advertisers. But Robert does not take up his suggestions.

The meeting is attended by Don, Robert, David, Andrew, Alison and Gill. It ranges widely over the size of the paper. Must it stay at forty pages? Andrew demands tht it go up to forty-eight and insists that redesign is desperately needed, either way; but it is essential that the size is decided on proper grounds and it will be vital that whatever decisions are taken remain constant.

Editorial staff ask the real state of competition and where else customers are advertising; they ask, too, whether *Him*'s propaganda that *Gay News* and *Him* are in direct competition should be given any credence. Is *Gay News* really a national paper or just a London paper making gestures towards national coverage and relevance? Writing staff are – effectively – reduced to three: Andrew, Alison and Gill, though Bob has begun writing features in addition to his photographic assignments.

Robert reveals that the W H Smith trial run in the north-west of England is unlikely to be extended or continued and begins to talk – rather wistfully – about *Gay News* embarking on its own distribution system and perhaps setting up a distribution company. Andrew, who had heard too much of that in summer 1982 and is impatient of schemes at a time when more immediate solutions are needed, asks how much time and money it would take.

In response to the fact that display advertising revenue is slumping Andrew reiterates, as he has been doing since October, his horror that neither he nor any of his colleagues has been able to take any steps to retrieve the quality of the paper since September, though carrying editorial responsibility, thanks to the managerial/ownership crisis. And as special factors notes that it is 'seasonal blues' time, since, after the Christmas spending period, there is always a slump and, in addition, Roger is away. Further, the chaotic state of the telephone system means that people can neither get in or out on the lines most of the time. Gill asks why the advertising staff are so office bound, if new clients are needed and if old clients, who have dropped out, are to come in again. And Andrew adds that Peter Burton used to keep contact with many of the gay club advertisers by spending time in their premises; but there is no way that present editorial staff can do the same with all the other demands on time being so unyielding and – anyway – it means staying up until two in the morning and it means being male. Gill suggests using the range of in-house space selling skills in the short term. She argues, too, as she has for some time now, that diversification is vital; gay people don't only buy night-life; they also buy all the things anyone buys – furniture, clothing, insurance, leisure materials and so on. Familiar – because it is part of her job – with the foreign gay periodicals and papers coming into the office, Gill argues that gay papers elsewhere seem to have a wider advertising clientele than *Gay News*. Robert had tried to achieve just this from 1981 onwards, but from whatever cause it had proved a very hard ambition to realise.

Don says that the advertisers *Gay News* is losing are going to *Him*, to which Robert adds that *Him* started gathering momentum in the autumn. Gill says it must be clear whether the paper is in competition or not, since different strategies follow in each case.

Discussion passes to the extent to which the ownership tangle is making it impossible for anyone to function; planning ahead can't happen and commissioning articles is beset with doubts about whether the paper will still be coming out and whether or not the writers will receive payment.

Andrew says that a forty-eight page paper is needed in order to make the white section 'wrap-around' look less pathetic than it does in the forty page paper. And he tells Robert that the present staff have the resources to do it, with the exception of the art room workers, who are pressed in any case and have no spare time either to re-design a 40 page paper or indeed a forty-eight page one.

Robert asks how the extra pages would be used in order to make the paper more commercial? Andrew explains that interested and informed staff members can work together to produce a 'Scene and Heard' night-life coverage, while others on staff can do the same for 'arts and leisure' entertainment. Both collectives can, therefore, replace the coverage formerly provided by Peter Burton at no extra cost. There can also be coverage of 'What's New' and of regional news (which eventually becomes 'Cross Country'). Robert asks how the advertising department could sell to lapsed advertisers. 'By selling the new look paper' says Don, 'whether it's forty pages or forty-eight'.

Fundamental to the whole discussion, Andrew insists, is that editorial and commercial aims *must* be unified, or splits open up between editorial direction and financial priorities. Robert asks who the readers are whom the paper must reach? Andrew replies that they are spending gay men, non-spending gay men, and women, an obvious enough definition of the newspaper's needs and responsibilities. Robert argues that his marketing/financial aims and editorial/production targets are now understood and agreed, and must be run as one.

Through January and February the paper keeps its own rhythm, its fortnightly cycle. It is brought out, over and over. The inexorable rhythm is hypnotic; the staff are mesmerised by it, behave with total professionalism. Some call it loyalty, some dedication. Some call it masochism, or cowardice. Some call it an ostrich act. Some see it as an act of continuous grace, offered, where there is no comparable gift, to the despised and rejected, the lesbians and gay men who deserve, at least, their own paper.

Despite meetings, paste-up is completed every second Friday. Despite memo after memo, explanatory papers running constantly through the photocopier, written by many, but mostly written and circulated by Andrew – despite this pouring of words to heroic proportions – copy for the paper is produced. Despite hours that stretch into days of telephone calls, attempts to explain to Robert what the paper needs, attempts to reconcile deep divides among each other, the staff bring out the paper.

Above all, Andrew presses, the paper needs redesigning and the art room – strung on the fornightly rack – cannot take time to do the job.

It is put to Robert that the art room cannot function with only two full time workers. A third is needed. And so – with horrid irony – only weeks after JC's redundancy – a third worker for the art room is agreed. Lesley Wilson – known as 'Jo's Lesley', since they are lovers of long standing – is chosen for the job after it has been advertised according to NGA rules. She is already doing part-time work for *Gay News* and it is agreed that she will start in February.

As had for so long been feared or anticipated, December 31, 1982, goes by without Robert paying Denis £10,000 out of any private resources. Through January, everyone waits to hear whether Denis will exercise his right to sue for recovery of those shares in Gay News Ltd, which had been called, in public meeting on November 29, 'valueless'. He doesn't. The utter uncertainty about who will own, or effectively does own, *Gay News*, persists.

ASHES

On Monday morning January 31, 1983, members of the now eighteen strong *Gay News* staff arrive in their 5th floor Farringdon Rd offices to be told that every question about who does own *Gay News* or who should own it has been resolved. Denis has taken employment under Robert; he will be in charge of editorial policy at *Gay News*; they have renegotiated their 1982 deal on terms which are to remain secret: Denis is already on the premises, in Robert's room.

The press in general have been informed.

The office notice board has been cleared: all material related to the financial and ownership crisis has been removed, a symbolic declaration that proposals by staff to buy the paper will no longer be welcome, if 'welcome' is quite the word, and that the five month struggle to extract information about private arrangements governing the future of the paper is over. Staff will return to their desks, the turbulence is over, Robert is in charge. Denis ceaselessly repeats that he is 'only an employee', and that Robert is the shareholding owner.

Arriving employees are asked to come into Robert's room individually to hear the news, in the presence of Denis. Some refuse to do so. Wendy, on her way to the typesetting room, says no point blank. On top of her opinions about what Robert and Denis have now done, she sees this method on Monday morning of 'picking off' the staff one by one as they enter the premises, instead of organising any kind of general meeting, as a return to the 'divide and rule' practice of earlier years. It seems to her to be explicitly designed to signal the end of such capacity for joint agreement, and joint action, as those who actually bring out the paper have achieved over the long months of crisis.

The interpretation seems to be confirmed by Robert's failure to notify the 'parents of chapel' (PoCs, or elected representatives of unionised staff) of this 'settlement' between himself and Denis. Alison, in Cambridge this Monday, as usual on the first day of a new production fortnight, has neither been informed as a senior writer on the paper, nor as PoC for the journalists. Glen, of art room, has not been formally notified as PoC for art room and typesetters (NGA), nor Linda, of box-replies, as PoC for administrative staff (SOGAT).

As conveyed by Robert and Denis to those who do go in to hear their explanation, the new deal means that the confidence of readers and advertisers in *Gay News* will be restored. Denis's name and reputation will by themselves reassure everyone that the paper will be back on a proper footing. The former owner and editor had, after all, been quoted in *The New Statesman* in November 1982 as saying of himself and *Gay News* 'I created the thing and ran it, I hope, rather successfully for ten years'.

Neither in statements to the general press, nor within the office, do Robert or Denis pay any tribute to the choice consistently made by staff, against expert advice given to them, to keep the newspaper in continuous publication throughout the fearfully adverse circumstances from September 1982 onwards, or to the skill with which they managed to do it. In that same *New Statesman* article of November 1982 Denis had, after all, also been quoted as calling *Gay News* 'rather substandard' since he left it, and that he then saw 'no reason to read it'.

However hostile the two men may be to various individuals on staff, and however little difference generosity or courtesy might really make at this moment, it is an omission which seems to show no understanding of newspapers. Anyone with adequate knowledge of periodicals, especially of periodicals in the UK, would know how remarkable the *Gay News* failure to strike has been. Expert after expert had told members of staff to strike, to break Gay News Ltd, and to pick up the title (the right to publish) in bankruptcy proceedings without any of the encumbrance of Robert's claims and Denis's claims. 'You must get rid of those two, and it's the only way you'll get rid of them', had been the advice from accountants and lawyers both gay and straight.

If the past and present proprietors could only quieten their emotions for long enough to see it, continuous production of *Gay News* has been the most remarkable feature of the entire contest of wills. The industrial power latent even in a community newspaper with an extraordinarily high sense of obligation to readers hasn't been used for so much as a 'go-slow'. Internal struggles in UK publishing as complex as those at *Gay News* haven't gone by at *Time Out* or *The Times*, and won't go by at the *Financial Times*, without loss of production.

Andrew, informed of the new deal a few hours before the rest of staff, had specifically told both men that if they seriously expect their arrangements to work they must not fail to give proper notification to the representatives of the unions and must not fail to thank those who have kept the paper in being. It is without the slightest surprise that he finds on Monday morning that neither of these things has been done. He has learnt that both men cease-lessly need to be told what to do, but unfortunately they take direction, so far as anyone can see, only from lawyers.

Will the staff consent to this new 'settlement', as they consented in the past to Denis's editorship in 1972, to Richard Creed's shareholding in 1973, to Denis's complete ownership in 1979, and to the sale of the paper by Denis to Robert (not that 'consent' really applied on that occasion) in early 1982? The pressure is very heavy to regard it as offering the 'best hope' for the future. If consented to, it means the wrangle over ownership so infinitely damaging to that elusive confidence of readers and advertisers in the paper, will be over. It means that those in the gay world and among the readers who hold Denis in high regard, and undoubtedly there are those who do, despite (or because of) recent revelations, will be pleased.

It is a fact that, as of January 31, 1983, Robert has not received a formal bid for the paper from staff, whether meeting all his terms or bargaining to meet only some of them. It was scarcely possible that he should have done so, given that his indications that he was now approachable had been made in November and that removal of Denis's claims on him, a salary for himself, indemnities for all guarantees he had given, and procurement of substantial working capital were a part of his conditions. Nonetheless facts are facts, and he has had no bid. Andrew as editor has been telling Robert that swift improvements to the paper, new blood on the editorial side, an 'injection' of working capital, a return to hard daily work by Robert or by someone doing Robert's salaried tasks, and a resolution of the ownership struggle, are the urgencies as of New Year 1983 without which the paper won't make it. Does this new deal in any real way meet those conditions?

The 'outside negotiators' elected by staff in the first week of January, Barry Jackson (of London Gay Switchboard, and the Arts Council) and Joan Crawford (literary agent), come to the offices by urgent invitation on Monday evening. On the continuing supposition that *Gay News* staff won't strike, they advise that there appear to be three courses of action. Those who are appalled by the reassertion of power over the paper, both editorial and managerial, by Robert and Denis can just give up, swallowing the pill. They can keep their heads down, in the expectation of an eventual falling out between Robert and Denis. Or staff can turn their attention flat out to constructing an offer to buy the paper.

Or those who can face no more can resign.

In their state of shock that such another 'secret deal' can be sprung on them without notice or consultation, many individuals in the production and editorial departments are wondering on the Monday if there's anything left but to resign. The absence of formal notification to PoCs, the absence of any tribute to efforts made over recent months, the known personal hostility of the restored 'management' to such persons as Bob, Gill, Alison, and Linda, result in its being understood throughout the building that Robert and Denis are expecting resignations – indeed, 'they are bound to happen', Robert is quoted as saying in response to questioning. The presumption is that Robert and Denis are hoping, by speed and the kind of determination symbolised in the clearing of the notice board, to see a 'clear out' of the dissidents to their regime, and particularly of the 'troublesome lesbians', so that only those who might be regarded as 'unpoliticised' (both in the gay and in the trades union senses) will be left. And new, equally 'unpoliticised', people can be hired to replace them.

Resignations by long serving individuals on staff would mean personal forfeiture of redundancy and other accumulated financial rights in law. Again, in his conversation with Robert and Denis some hours before the rest of staff learnt of the new 'settlement', Andrew had told both men that they were plainly seeking resignations. And, further, that this was cowardice. An essential ele-

224

ment in any such new deal between themselves, he said, should have been the procurement of suffient new capital to make proper pay-offs to people they had decided to be rid of.

All thoughts of individual resignations, which would unquestionably have involved Jo, Lesley (Wilson) in art-room, Lesley (Jones) in typesetters, Wendy, and Andrew, and possibly others from art room and elsewhere, had Alison, Gill, Bob, and Linda felt that in these circumstances they must go at once (ie at least half the staff and very probably the entire production and editorial strength), have been adandoned by Monday evening. People will face the matter on the premises.

Glen, as the longest serving member of the art room – and in fact, of the entire staff of *Gay News* – says that he will tell Denis to his face that whatever other interventions in editorial policy he proposes, he is not to set foot in the art room. And tells him.

Though not informed of anything by Robert or Denis, Alison at home in Cambridge, working on the next issue's Literary Supplement and features, has of course been informed by colleagues, and takes the train to London. She is in the office by late afternoon. With her fellow PoCs, Glen and Linda, she agrees that if a secretive and self-installed 'management' is to be reimposed on *Gay News*, then the federated chapels, dormant in large degree since the settling of the redundancies battle in November, will handle the management as just that: management. It will be made to face its obligations.

Memoranda are despatched late Monday to Robert insisting on immediate discussion about holiday entitlements, about a relocation payment of £250 to each member of staff for the disruptions occasioned by the move of offices in November, and for modest pay rises geared to the conventional 'London weighting allowance' (made to workforces who have to meet the costs of working in central London).

Robert and Denis are refusing to say whether any additional working capital is going to be forthcoming from any source as a result of their 'settlement' (they reply that this is a confidential matter – in fact, it will later transpire, there is no extra working capital). However, the latest four week trading period (to February 4, 1983) is apparently going to show a profit (of £7,143) and money is being found it seems, to put Denis on a salary alleged to be £1,000 a month. Robert must show in proper form, if it is the case, just why the standard of living of staff must continue to fall.

There is also an unresolved matter concerning Mike. In December Robert had unilaterally awarded a £250 a year pay increase to Mike alone. As soon as he realised that the individual and eccentric award broke every agreement Robert was supposed to have made about conforming to usual procedures over wages negotiations, Mike wrote formally to Robert refusing the pay increase.

Those whom the gods would destroy they first asphyxiate. It is almost unbelievable, but with so much else on their plate, those who are at *Gay News* in these early weeks of 1983 are still being poisoned by fumes, apparently from some light industrial operation on a floor below or from some sanitation disaster on the roof. About a third of the staff suffer intermittently from sore throats, streaming eyes, and labouring lungs. On one famous occasion Roger is found lying on the floor of the advertising room, not unconscious, but incapable. Robert is sharply informed that if he wants to consider himself 'in charge' he had better resolve this matter fast and once and for all.

Denis has shown up this Monday morning (travelling no further within the office, once others have come in, than Robert's room and the administrative offices) in a smart fringed suede waistcoat, 'good' jeans tucked into light brown, knee-length, leather boots, and tinted glasses which are not, he crossly says, 'shades'. It is, someone rudely remarks, all puns pejoratively intended, a 'cowboy look'.

Andrew has not been removed as editor. He turns up in an expensive dark suit, dark blue shirt, tie, and black shoes, an ensemble bought long ago when he was a journalist who might be called on to visit City of London boardrooms. Few on staff have even seen him in such an outfit, though he had once, intuitively, worn it when asked in early 1982 to one of Robert's moderately grand parties. He expects to be asked why on earth he's looking like that, and is. 'What has been done', he says, 'means that this paper is forcibly to be run on straight lines. A straight suit for a straight paper'. 'He is very angry indeed. The gesture is camp-theatrical, but as Alison perceives it, and says of it, it is one filled with a sense of outrage and disdain.*

No title has been announced for Denis, though some advertisers, it transpires, are told by phone that Denis is to be 'Editor in Chief'. Robert and Denis have both stated that they wish Andrew to remain in title, and in fact (to whatever degree practicable), editor of *Gay News*. His own advance information about the existence of a new 'secret deal' and Denis's return in some capacity or other to supervise editorial direction had come to him on the Sunday night of January 30. Robert had come over by car to his flat, and then revealed that Denis was sitting outside, still in the car. Could he come upstairs?

There ensued an appalling discussion, civil on the surface but ferocious, on Andrew's side, in the comments made by him on the conduct and intentions of the two men.

In the months since his participation in the impracticable and lawless redundancy/part-time measures of October 1982, Andrew has increasingly been reawarded the trust of all the departments of the paper. With Robert's near abdication of day-to-day workload from November onwards, the paper's editor has been a 'clearing house' for virtually the whole of its affairs, referred to for decisions by any of the members of staff, and not only by production and editorial staff. The widespread loss of credibility by both Robert and Denis has left Andrew as the only person at *Gay News* with adequate legal status, as editor, and adequate 'moral' authority, to be treated both internally and by the outside world as a kind of acting chief executive.

Another consequence of the crisis has been a newly widespread awareness of his original role as the person who conceived and laid down the idea of *Gay News*. He has the repute of 'the founder', and in crisis-consultations with the country's gay organisations, interviews with the press, and dealings with Robert no longer hesitates to use it. There has been no lessening of the desire of many on staff and off it to see full editorial 'collectivisation' of the paper as well as staff ownership, but until and unless authority can be removed from Robert and Denis, he has been given extraordinary trust and confidence by the desperately hard driven and perplexed staff.

*Andrew's gesture partly backfires. Plenty of people tell him he looks a great deal better and sexier in his traditional get-up. For a couple of days there's a humorous discussion about the women on staff adopting high heels, short skirts, and full make-up, to present themselves as traditional secretaries. Or perhaps the men would like to . . .

227

In such circumstances, he has had to invent a role. There is no clear-cut tradition, naturally enough, for what an editor does on a commercially based paper whose entrepreneurs are in the state of disrepute with the greater part of the workforce and contributors and news-sources that Robert and Denis are. Andrew accordingly considers, and has been saying since October, that he regards it as his first obligation, for as long as he remains editor, to seek to continue bringing the paper out. It means that he can't lend his voice to those on staff, foremost among whom is Gill, who recommend taking the outside experts' advice, and going on strike to break Gay News Ltd. On the contrary, he spends much of December and January trying to wring from Robert the necessary financial consents for an overhaul of the look and contents of the paper which is in fact achieved with effect from the start of February 1983 – in time, as fate has it, for Denis and Robert to claim the credit under their new 'settlement' if they choose to do so.

If readers come first, staff come second. His second obligation, he considers, is to try at every turn of events to forward whatever consensus can be discovered among the staff. Robert has made plain that he won't as owner fire any member of staff. Therefore the paper will be brought out by the qualified existing workers at the paper, or not at all. Their wishes, so far as they can reach agreement, must take precedence over any policies desired by Robert, or by Robert and Denis in tandem.

It is against this background, of real-life conditions and of personal decisions, that he talks with Robert and Denis a few hours before the full staff are informed of the new (or restored) order. If in the course of Monday and succeeding days, the staff reach a *modus vivendi* with Robert as reinstalled owner-manager and Denis as editorial authority, then Andrew will do what he can to help the 'settlement' along before seeking means of removing himself entirely from the newspaper, where he sees no future for himself, whatever Robert and Denis wish, under a system he believes has already proved a failure.

The meeting of Sunday night January 30 is the first time for more than a year that Andrew and Denis have spoken in private circumstances; the first time since Denis ceased to be Andrew's own editor at *Gay News*. As to Robert, Andrew has reached a point of feeling absolute contempt for him as proprietor of a newspaper.

228

As to Denis in his public capacity, Andrew hasn't recovered from the December 1982 refusal, by the man who had been editor of *Gay News* for nearly ten years, to permit a public announcement that he regarded 'preservation of the newspaper in continuous publication' as the first priority in any discussions about future ownership or management or financing. In Andrew's opinion, a consent from Denis at that point would have averted ceaseless confusion and damage to confidence in the paper through December and January, and averted also this desperate new 'secret deal', whose very secrecy must begin the cycle of early 1982 all over again. But there is also Denis in private capacity – Denis as a friend, Denis of whom Andrew had been very fond, and whom he had taken, despite Peter Burton's widely voiced scepticism in 1982, to feel equally close. As the fearful conversation goes on, both men, Denis and Andrew, plainly feel the tug of that affection that goes back so far, to the origins in 1971 of the newspaper now so close to ruin.

Robert and Denis don't ask for Andrew's approval or consent to what they've organised. They refuse to answer questions about the re-negotiated terms on which Denis is still to be paid upwards of £70,000 for his former shareholding in Gay News Ltd. They won't say whether their new deal brings in extra working capital. They simply state, over and over again, that they are now on the best of terms, that all differences have been patched up, that Robert is uncontested and sole proprietor of *Gay News*, and that Denis, with effect from the next morning, will regard himself as Robert's employee.

Andrew retains a respect (not shared by others, such as Graham McKerrow, now at *Capital Gay*, who had worked under Denis) for what he believes to be Denis's capacities as journalist, and says that he can imagine Denis making himself useful in gay 'commercial scene' coverage for the paper. Other than that, he voices nothing but scepticism. Voices it so brutally (it seems to himself) that he can't understand why the two men sit and take it. Has Denis any idea of the opinion people on the paper have formed about Robert's ways of dealing with people and with management? The two men may try to fool a distant public, but do they think that anyone who has been close to events sees them as anything other than enemies? How do they think a newspaper can survive in a situation where Robert has abused Denis, where Denis has abused Andrew as an editor, where Andrew has declared neither man competent to run *Gay News*, where Denis has been heard to say that he never again wants to take part in publishing for gays?

At one point, the nearest to a renewed closeness that Andrew and Denis reach, Andrew says that his own experiences of the last year had led him to understand why Denis made his autumn 1972 ultimatum, that he either be appointed editor, ending the 'collective' system, or he would leave *Gay News*. Andrew means that he has now seen for himself, as he has, what strains are caused by opposed factions on the staff, from Peter and Chris's opposition 'bloc' during 1982 to the inability of the staff in the last few months (much commented on in the County Hall meetings of November and December and again by the 'negotiators' Barry and Joan) to arrive at a unanimous set of objectives. Andrew supposes he can now see why Denis did it *then* . . . but now, with a staff immensely more skilled than it had been back in 1972, the recently exhibited inability of staff to reach unanimity other than on Robert's shortcomings has resulted from genuine conflicts of principle about such matters as whether to keep the paper going under any circumstances or to stop it and start it again. And has resulted, if from any one overwhelming cause, from that unilateral and secret decisiveness which produced the early 1982 sale of the paper and all the subsequent mystifications and turmoils.

The two men leave the flat.

There's a sad and loving story behind the deal being kept so damagingly secret. Robert's lover Alan has finally sold his own flat. The two men are now living together in Little Venice. Alan, unknown to anyone, has lent Robert some £4,250 which Robert in turn has paid to Denis. The money, it will later be understood, constitutes partly salary in advance and partly an instalment on the rescheduled capital payments still due for Gay News Ltd, and is therefore the 'sweetener' which has allowed the new deal to happen at all. It is also said to include payment of Denis's legal bill.

Alan isn't rich, any more than Robert. It's a generous bailing-out of one member of a gay couple by his partner. And a risky one, for clearly the paper must get into, and stay in, substantial profit over coming years if further capital payments are to be made to

Denis and if Robert is to repay his lover. It isn't only from affection that Alan has stumped up the money to pay over to Denis. Alan is a voluntary worker for London Gay Switchboard, a member of the 'gay movement' himself, and he has said more than once that quite independently of his connection with the proprietor he too wants the paper's troubles to be sorted out.

His appeal by letter to Andrew on December 15 to get staff to lay off Robert, to stop 'attacking' him, has fallen, so far as Alan is concerned, on stony ground, even though Andrew answered him by letter at great length in the same month. From Alan's viewpoint (so at least his manner to staff and staff's advisers seems to indicate) Robert is a person of perfectly honourable intentions who has been shamefully harassed and vilified and made to take the blame for disasters in which he may share, but for which he can't possibly be as much to blame as has been said.

Knowing nothing for the moment of the money Alan has put up some members of *Gay News* staff briefly discuss whether a lover should support his or her partner right or wrong in time of crisis, or should challenge the partner's conduct, if necessary to the point of breaking off the relationship. It's an extraordinary brief instance of a Socratic moral dialogue about gay relationships coming wholly to contemporary life, but there's a most uncomfortable air about setting out to criticise the decisions made by anyone's lover in such conditions as those that have been going on for months at *Gay News*.

Nobody is ignorant of the pressures Robert has been under, from individuals or groups of staff, from the 'gay movement' of which Robert had been such a figure when chair of CHE, from the alarming cash-flow/accumulated indebtedness problems since September (indeed, since long before), and perhaps more than anything else, from Denis. For months until this 'settlement' of January 31 he had been at his wits end to know how to find some £10,000 of purchase price money due to Denis on December 31, or to guess what action Denis would take during January if the money wasn't forthcoming.

During the winter months he has tried to raise working capital, as so often demanded by the editor, to replace the £26,000 of proceeds from the sale of the old West Kensington offices borrowed by Robert Palmer Marketing Ltd to cover money already gone out

231

to Denis early in 1982, and which he cannot conceivably put back into *Gay News*' coffers. He simply doesn't have it. The efforts to raise outside capital have failed. In some instances (it is said) potential investors have thought the *Gay News* staff too 'rebellious' or, falling for the extraordinarily misleading propaganda about the personal and political beliefs of the members of staff, too 'Socialist'. In other instances (it is said) potential investors withdraw when they see something of the books and when they form an opinion about Robert's management of the business so far.

The latest secret deal doesn't, as everyone rightly suspects, let Robert off the hook so far as his liability to pay Denis another £60,000 – £70,000 for Gay News Ltd shares over the next five years is concerned. The payments timetable is merely revised. The paper's former owner is sticking to his assertion, as set out in formal correspondence from his lawyer in December, that he recognises no 'moral obligation' to forego any further payments for his former shareholding.

So, just as everyone assumes, Robert remains personally liable for this astonishing total sum of money. Unless, improbably, he can earn it over time from some new venture of his own, *Gay News* is going to have to do it. Secret the terms of the new deal may be, but no-one on the staff or near to its affairs doubts that the paper is once more formally committed, by the actions of its proprietor, to pursuing whatever commercial and editorial courses of action will yield thousands of pounds every year for a man whose fitness to derive any money at all from the paper, whether as capital or by way of salary, is widely and sincerely questioned.

Any sympathy for Robert's various quandaries is squashed by the sheer fact of what is supposed to be enforced on a *Gay News* reeling from six months of troubles and only now painfully beginning to claw back a high standard of contents and reasonable display advertising revenue: salaries for the two men who put it onto the financial footing imposed in early 1982, and a 'mortgage' for years to come, in the interest of their joint deal, on any trading profits that may laboriously be achieved. There is quite genuinely no element of envy in the sense of outrage widespread through staff. The burden on the paper is what seems to most so absolutely intolerable.

It is said that the renegotiated deal of January 31 makes one other change in the bargain struck early in 1982. Staff are led to understand that Denis is no longer bound by contract to refrain from involving himself in any other gay publishing venture besides *Gay News* should he ever choose to do so.

From the moment of the general press announcement by Robert and Denis on the Monday morning of January 31 the media take a resumed interest in *Gay News*' affairs. The London weekly 'listings' magazines, *Time Out* and *City Limits*, erratically beginning the process of developing coverage of gay affairs, give coverage. The country's leading Women's Movement magazine, *Spare Rib*, organises an interview with Gill and Alison of the *Gay News* 'Visible Lesbian' collective, and experiences severe internal strains about the nature and extent of its own lesbian coverage. *The Guardian* is ceaselessly inaccurate, thanks to the lack of proper control over its news-desk sub-editors.

Advance information about the contents of *Him* No 51, out in February, the monthly for gay men only which publisher Alex McKenna is marketing with 'knocking copy' against *Gay News*, discloses that the magazine is placing the blame for *Gay News*' problems largely on the shoulders of the women on the paper: '. . . the only-too-visible Lesbian collective . . . There's always a re-sounding silence from lesbians – they wouldn't even support their own *Sappho* paper because they wanted to get in on *Gay News*' act . . .' Protest against this interpretation and this onslaught comes from within McKenna's male only organisation as well as from without. And *Gay News* itself, having endured *Him's* hostile propaganda to its advertisers and its readers in silence since September 1982, at last editoralises in the issue of February 17 (No 259), not merely about *Him*, a gay publication, but also about *Time Out*, meant for the general reader, both of which seem to have constituted themselves an 'axis' for defining women as the cause of *Gay News*' past and current miseries.

Has it all been good clean fun, the way *Gay News* lesbians have been 'satirised' in recent weeks, asks Andrew as editor in the pages of the paper, and answers 'no'. The women themselves, on page 11, right hand page of the 48-page issue's two pages of lesbian-only material, write: '. . . The charge seems to be that we *Gay News* lesbians are somehow both the cause of *Gay News's* recent troubles and the obstructors of a good solution. The facts are that without our labour the paper couldn't be done at all . . . Misogynist gay men have never resented lesbian labour at *Gay News*. After all, lesbians have worked here throughout the paper's existence. What enrages them is not our labour, but our voice . . .' The item concludes with a list of the fortnightly contribution made by the seven women on staff, ending that 'In fact (without lesbian labour) there'd be no paper at all – because Lesley Jones and Wendy Simpson typeset it all'.

Whatever the effect on external opinion of this cry of anguish from women whose whole commitment has been to working with gay men, internally it produces a major row. As the paper goes out through London and around the country, Peter Jones, Peter Coell's deputy in accounts, seeks an urgent meeting with Andrew. What the lesbians have written in their 'space' in the paper is grossly defamatory, he says, of the equally essential work ceaselessly done by the men on the paper. The publication of such a women only statement is open evidence that Andrew is biased as editor, letting the women print what they please, but interfering, in the traditional mode of an editor, in anything the gay men on staff may choose to write. The argument is strengthened, in Peter's mind, by an editorial decision by Andrew to remove from Mike a column he has recently been doing (Chris Kirk's innovation, *Mediawatch*), on the general grounds that it isn't good enough, and the specific grounds that it is repeatedly offensive, as Chris's columns never were, to women readers of the paper.

Shuttling like Kissinger between a regular meeting of the women on staff on the morning of February 16 and Peter as spokesman for a number of the men in the administrative and advertising departments, Andrew suggests that the men meet to discuss everything, just as the women have been accustomed, for over a year, to holding their own gender-specific discussions. For the first time in the history of the paper such a meeting is held, and seems to be thought rather fruitful. It's agreed that they should become regular, and David says at last, perhaps, the paper can turn its attention to the 'sexual politics' of being a gay man in a very 'straight' world. In an appraisal of a year's publication of 'Visible Lesbian' pages, published in the next issue (GN 260), Alison writes '. . . We rejoice each time gay male readers – whether as groups or individuals – offer their support and show clearly that they understand what it is that we're trying to do and why it matters. And, strange though it may sound, even the lesbian-bashing which these pages have aroused in a very different sort of gay man has been helpful. It's flushed misogny out of the closet. It's made well disposed gay men who count lesbians amongst their friends think about the general phenomenon of anti-lesbianism in the gay world. And it's made the Visible Lesbian collective even more determined to do our part in creating an integrated' (designed for both sexes) '*Gay News*'.

This issue, published on March 3, is the last in which Gill, so formative in the creation of the Visible Lesbian pages and the international pages, works for the paper. She has carried on until Andrew believes he can spare her, but has long since felt that only open confrontation, perhaps through a strike, would have any chance of shifting the balance of power at the paper; and that is the course which the majority of her colleagues have resisted. Staff's efforts consistently seem to her doomed by the internal divisions of attitude towards fully 'collective' working, the ending of wages differentials, the ending of 'hierarchy'. And she feels there is little room for her to develop further as a writer or in other directions at *Gay News*. It is a decision filled with pain for her. Even as she reaches her decision she is told by her family in Australia that her father is desperately ill and that she may have to fly out at a moment's notice. She would inevitably be away for weeks, and it is difficult to know how in its economic difficulties, with a truncated editorial staff, the paper could cope with a long absence.

Linda moves across to the editorial side not as a listed journalist, but to do the tasks that Scotty had done, and which Jo has since done (in essentials) out of goodwill but adding intolerably to her own work load. Her arrival relieves Andrew and Alison of the fearsome filing and correspondence burdens which have for months been theirs on top of their other functions, but no news reporter can be hired. Andrew is now the entire news desk.

Meanwhile, incident has been piled on incident as Robert and Denis seek, in the week starting January 31, to install themselves in command of the paper. On the Monday which has closed with the 'federated chapels' seeking formal negotiations about long deferred pay questions, Denis has told Andrew, in Robert's room, that he has no intention of interfering in the next issue of the paper, nor of trying to scrap the Visible Lesbian pages, but will be devoting his attention to forward plans. On the other hand, Robert and Denis both ask what is going into the next issue of the paper's news pages. With a fortnight to go before publication, Andrew says he hasn't the faintest idea – an exaggeration, but intended as a reminder that news is a last minute operation.

Denis informs outsiders that one of his main aims is to find out 'who edits the paper'.

The phones have been going non-stop on Monday with largely hostile enquiries about what on earth Robert and Denis think they're playing at with this latest 'secret deal', and by the end of the day it is clear that the building will be picketed or invaded in the course of Tuesday by irate lesbians and gay men well known to members of the staff. Forewarned, Denis doesn't arrive on the Tuesday, but intermittently rings Robert from a call box to find out what's going on. The office is duly invaded by some twenty-five people. *The Guardian*, whose building is only a hundred yards up the street, and which has just misquoted Andrew but correctly stated that he has respect for Denis's journalistic capacities, sends over one of its writers, Martin Walker, who subsequently does a good short piece about the situation on a feature page. The angry gay people (who aren't, in fact, invaders, for Robert has consented to their coming in) include Anna Durell, the only paid worker CHE can afford, and some of the volunteers who work for London Gay Switchboard.

Unable to meet Denis, they demand a meeting with Robert, who after some hours receives them in his office. He has asked Alan to come to the office to be with him, and Bob makes an intemperate verbal attack on Alan in which he says 'I suppose you're Robert's heir'. Some others present are shocked by it, and apologise to Robert, and yet (as will be seen) it turns out to have an odd prophetic accuracy, though mercifully not because of any deaths.

On Wednesday, Denis comes into the office again. He walks up the five flights of stairs (a thing people are always having to do anyway when the lift is out of use); so it is said, to avoid anti Robert and Denis graffiti which have been sprayed in the lift. In mid-morning he comes into the news-room with the stated intention of hearing what the plans are for the forthcoming issue (No 259, coming out February 17). Bob, who has written and taken the photographs for a feature about holidays for gays, which has drawn in over £1,000 of display advertising from the gay travel companies, and whose work Andrew praised to Denis on Monday morning, is not there. Gill is. So naturally is Andrew, still dark suited. And so is Alison. With wonder, Alison says of Denis afterwards, 'I wasn't afraid of him. For the first time he didn't frighten me'.

The point has been raised of whether Denis is in good standing with the National Union of Journalists. Since *Gay News* is supposed to be a 'post-entry closed shop' it is legitimate (though in no other circumstances would it have been made a letter-of-the-law matter at *Gay News*) to insist that he be cleared by the NUJ before anyone listens to any interventions he may wish to make in editorial content. Andrew has asked Alison, as parent of chapel for the NUJ, whether Denis's position has yet been regularised, and she answers, correctly, that it hasn't.

Andrew informs Denis, 'I have no objection, as editor of *Gay News*, to your sitting in this morning and hearing anything that is said, but you are here on an information basis only. I will accept no directives from you, and I will not allow you to give directives to any member of the editorial staff'.

'OK, Alison, what does it all mean?' demands Denis, smoking a cheroot. 'In union terms', says Alison, 'you don't exist. You aren't here.' 'Interesting situation,' he replies. 'Fascinating,' she answers.

Robert then appears, and has to ask questions for both of them. He demands to know what intentions there are for the news pages in the next issue (not due to be written or 'pasted up' for another eight or nine days). Andrew is patient for about two minutes, explaining once again that while there are of course various events which will have to be covered, the lead stories, and the relative 'weight' to be given to various items, are still quite unknowable. He then loses patience, and in public, breaking all previous 'codes' of self-restraint, demands that either Robert fire him or leave him to edit the paper. He cannot, he says, allow Robert to go on interrupting and sabotaging, whether he's conscious of what he's doing or not, the crucial editorial and production work of the paper.

Robert should go to his own office at once, Andrew says, to get on with his own job which in recent months he has 'shamefully neglected', not least get on with responding to the union matters that Denis's advent have once more provoked. Robert laughs nervously and Andrew tells him 'stop giggling'. It's the nadir of a professional relationship which had started so hopefully in January 1982.

Robert and Denis duly do leave the room. Denis comments afterwards that he was delighted to see Andrew being so forceful. Presumably he has reassured himself as to who does actually edit the paper. Not 'the visible lesbians', not some ill-defined grouping of 'radicals', but the man paid to do it. It doesn't say much for future relations between Robert and Denis that Denis can profess himself pleased to see the proprietor handled in such a fashion.

However at 3.28 pm everyone on staff gets a memorandum requesting their presence at 3.30 pm in Robert's room to hear Denis outline his ideas for the future editorial policy of the paper. The parents of chapel, Glen, Alison, and Linda, promptly meet and agree to advise their members in all departments that Denis as yet has no status with the NUJ branch that he must belong to, and staff should not at this point respond to any such summons. They find that not a single person on the production and editorial staffs of the paper had any intention of going to hear what one of the men in the art-room calls 'the opinions of a stranger about what should be printed in *Gay News*'.

Most of the administrative and advertising staff, though, have already gone into Robert's room before Linda, as their PoC, can give them the verdict of the federated chapels. In a most remarkable step, coming as it does from one of the members of staff who could least of all be called by anyone 'a troublemaker', Jo asks that her own parent of chapel, Alison, register a formal complaint with Linda, as parent of chapel for SOGAT members, 'about the action of some (SOGAT) members when they agreed to have talks with management without first seeking clearance with you'. Most of Linda's SOGAT members in fact explain that they'd merely walked into Robert's room without fuss just to hear what Denis had to say for himself.

What he had to say for himself is distributed in written form on Thursday morning, with a request from Robert that those who hadn't attended the meeting give their written comments.

It reads:

'Into the Eighties

To sustain its life, *GAY NEWS* has to appeal to a broadly based cross-section of people; as it were – everyone from a reader of *THE TIMES* to a reader of *THE SUN*.

'To reach those people, growth is needed – a sense that the paper is evolving along with the readership and constantly striving to achieve a reputation which will make it essential reading to those who already purchase it and, because of that, attract a new reader-ship – a great part of which, not unnaturally, would be drawn from those just entering gay life.

'It is currently all too obvious that *GAY NEWS* has neither evolved nor moved with the times. In many respects, the paper has stagnated. It has become dull and desperately in need of revital-isation to both keep those readers it presently has and to attract new readers. The paper has become introverted and that intro-spection is destructive. No newspaper should be inward looking; at all times, every attempt should be made to maintain a broad over-view which encompasses as many aspects of gay life and gay life in relation to the heterosexual world as is humanly possible.

'*GAY NEWS* has become long-winded – too often dealing in armloads of words where but a handful would do. It has become elitist – by presenting itself as intellectually superior and politically biased. For the paper to survive, these things must change.

'New readers must be won; new advertisers wooed – and the current financial situation indicates that unless *GAY NEWS* re-establishes credibility with both the readers and with the adver-tisers (who have to see that the paper is appealing to and reaching an audience who are *at least* potentially interested in their pro-ducts) it cannot continue.

'It is vital at this stage in *GAY NEWS'* life that the paper re-establishes the bond of trust between itself and the readers – convincing them that the paper is for them rather than being a convenient platform for the views of the staff and the contributors.

'*GAY NEWS* today is limiting its audience – increasingly large areas of gay life are ignored or treated with no more than a contemptuous nod. What reason, for example, does any young gay have for reading *GAY NEWS*? What reason does any person who inhabits the commercial scene have for reading *GAY NEWS*? Precious little.

'Yet the young and the scene person are every bit as important, as much a part of gay life, as is the lecturer in semantics, the lesbian feminist, or the Marxist art historian. They have their place, they should not be ignored or, worse, sneered at. It is always worth remembering that a paper which tries to reach a wide number of people needn't be a tawdry rag.

'Now is the time for *GAY NEWS* to move forward into the Eighties. If it doesn't, it has very little chance of survival.'

Gill, who has not yet quite taken the decision that she cannot continue at *Gay News*, writes comments as requested, but prefaces them by saying that she doesn't understand why she's to take seriously the views of a man who has been publicly declaring that he doesn't read the paper. (Denis informs Andrew that he has done a rush-course reading up back-numbers).

Andrew puts his own comments on the notice-board. New features, columns, overhauling of the Gay Guide, all are in hand already. What's needed, he writes in a cold fury, isn't rhetoric, but practical proposals and sheer hard writing and design work, and such proposals and work, if forthcoming, are welcome from any source. In the meantime, if Denis is to make himself useful, his talents plainly lie in gay commercial scene coverage, and perhaps he'd kindly get down to some writing or procurement of material.

If *chutzpah* was supposed to carry the new secret deal through regardless of internal or external opinion, *chutzpah* has failed. Some in administration and advertising wonder whether the strength of the reaction is an unworthy perpetuation of old battles; some feel that Denis would counterbalance what they see as Andrew's lack of support for gay male needs in the paper. But the production departments of the paper, whose consent is known by Denis, none better, to be absolutely vital to any effectiveness that he might once again have at *Gay News*, are solid against both the deal and against Denis's intervention in policy.

On Thursday night, February 3, Andrew off his own bat phones Robert at home and says that as the man still charged with editing and bringing out *Gay News* he must inform Robert as owner that in his, Andrew's, view the latest 'settlement' has collapsed. It is, he says, quite unworkable. Later in the evening, Denis phones Andrew. 'This is not, repeat not', says Denis, 'a call about the state of affairs at *Gay News*.' The purpose of the call, which Denis has wanted to make for some time, is to say that he wishes and hopes that when all the dust and misery has settled, he and Andrew can still be friends. Andrew says that that is very much his own wish as well, but that there can be no friendship for practical purposes, no socialising, until the questions that lie between them over *Gay News* are concluded. Denis suggests having a drink to talk about other projects that he has in mind. Andrew says that he can't, can't possibly.

As to *Gay News*, says Andrew, it is quite evident that though he and Denis had once liked working together, too much has happened to make it possible ever again. Neither, says Andrew, can work under the editorial direction of the other. Further, Denis has been out of the daily workings of the gay world for too long, and said too often that he's had enough after his long career at *Gay News*. 'I'm a better editor of *Gay News* than you could be', says Andrew. 'In that case', says Denis, neither man speaking with animosity, 'we'll just have to put it to the test. It'll be creative tension'.

On Friday Robert gives a formal answer to union representations about office re-location grants and 'London weighting allowance' and says there isn't the money in the kitty to make any increases. In that case, the point is again made, where is money coming from for Denis? To show what would happen if staff 'worked to rule', though it is stressed that no decision has been taken to do so, Robert is called in to hear the assembled staff describe what the consequences would be. They would amount to missing the publication deadlines by days, for the first time in the paper's history. At last, in a well enough received gesture, Robert in a memorandum writes 'May I put on record my appreciation to *all* the staff for their work on the paper in extremely difficult circumstances in recent months'.

During the afternoon a majority of staff vote that Denis's appointment should be withdrawn, and the show of hands is relayed by Andrew to Robert and Denis. 'Well, we all know how people can get swayed by the vocal minority', says Denis. 'True', says Andrew, 'but I can only assure you that I've said to every individual on the staff, all through this week, that they must speak and do as they think right. What more can anyone do?'

On Monday morning February 7 Robert and Denis jointly announce that Denis's appointment has been withdrawn, and that they will co-operate fully in a transfer of shares in *Gay News* to staff 'before considering any other proposals'.

A fearful timetable is imposed. If staff want the paper, they're to produce a detailed bid by mid-March, with completion by the end of that month, i.e. April 1. Meantime, of course, they have to bring out the paper, and they may not use Gay News Ltd funds, such as they are, to purchase any professional advice. Everything must remain confidential, otherwise neither Robert nor Denis will open himself to the necessary negotiations. They, for their part, continue to have access to lawyers: Denis to his personal lawyers, Robert to David Warner, who had appeared for him during the redundancy negotiations of October/November. As the weeks go by, Warner is to share in that distress experienced by so many of good will who have tried to lend their expertise to the perpetuation of the newspaper under proper forms of control. He is obliged to guard his client's interests, and does his utmost to do so; but his wish is to see the paper safely conveyed to those who produce it, and his sympathies are so much with the eighteen fearfully beleaguered people who maintain, and are now improving, *Gay News* that he is as torn as any lawyer ever was in a painful case.

The demand for confidentiality is agreed. How not? There will be no negotiations at all, otherwise. It means, beneficially, that apart from stating the facts about Denis's arrival and departure, and the offer to staff, in the issue of February 17 (No 259), there is a moratorium in the pages of the paper itself about the questions of ownership. As everyone wants it to, the paper can concentrate on events in the outside world, and do the job for which people buy it. Less beneficially, and adverse to the interests of staff and those such as the 'negotiators', Barry and Joan, who have come forward to help them, the 'confidentiality' rule means that the paper can't itself be used to make any appeals for funds. The 'failure' to launch a fund raising appeal through the pages of *Gay News* is much commented on, but the general feeling is not only that 'confidentiality' makes this impossible until and unless ownership rights are fully relinquished by Robert and Denis. It is also felt that the whole situation is too discreditable for readers and the gay world at large to be asked to put up money – money that 'voluntary organisations' are always urgently seeking – whose purpose, in part, would be to 'buy out' Denis and Robert from their rights and obligations. The situation is too far removed, too different, from the one in 1976–77, when the newspaper was so obviously threatened by the legal powers of the alien 'morality' invoked by Mrs Mary Whitehouse. Once the ownership has been vested for good in some form of non-personal ownership, then, as they see for themselves that *Gay News* is well-conducted under the proprietorship of those who create it, readers can be approached for loans or equity investment to strengthen the working capital and spread the 'stake' in the paper.

Yet another gruelling sequence of weeks is in prospect. All the usual amenities of life must again be shelved – no holidays for anyone, no recruitment to ease the strain that is particularly appalling on the editorial side, no private life worth the name for the majority. But the telling of the events of a persistent crisis can be very misleading. Visitors comment on the gales of laughter. One visitor in particular, Brian Kennedy, a co-worker on the Labour-controlled Greater London Council (GLC)'s project to establish a London Lesbian & Gay Centre, says 'You're all so amusing, why doesn't it get into the paper?' Back comes the answer: 'We're *trying* to get it in.' People in every department are greatly cheered by the participation they now have, through the 'Scene & Heard' and Arts collectives, in writing for sections of the paper. The 'young gay men' are especially zestful about their new chance to break out of the narrow confines of only doing their administrative tasks. And the decision by Robert and Denis that they are now formally open to a bid has ended the muddle. There is a clear cut situation for the first time since September 1982.

If the paper is to be acquired, there are practical problems and, for lack of a better word, ethical problems.

Where's the money to come from, and through what sort of legal vehicle is the paper to be bought and owned, are the practical questions. The ethical ones include: should staff seek 100 per cent control of the newspaper, or make themselves in some way formally answerable to trustees or other representatives of readers/ the gay community? Should equal pay for all (pay parity), collective working, and a legal co-operative be the aim? A sub-group of staff sets out to find the advantages and disadvantages, legal, financial, and managerial, of the different modes of ownership allowed for in UK law. The staff-controlled London weekly 'listings' magazine, *City Limits*, formed as a breakaway from the personally-owned 'listings' magazine *Time Out*, readily gives advice on the pitfalls of modes of staff ownership that they examined and discarded. Hugh Stephenson, editor of the weekly political paper *The New Statesman*, comes to the *Gay News* offices at the request of the sub-group to share his own experience, both on *The Times* and since, of mechanisms by which staff can run their own newspaper.* The essence of his advice is that virtually any form of ownership (limited liability company, company limited by guarantee, co-operative, etc) can be adapted to the agreed purposes of a workforce, so it is unwise to get too preoccupied with the legal form under which the enterprise is acquired. The vital necessity is for members of staff to reach open consensus on how they will wish to operate internally after they have succeeded in the take-over.

Given the variety of backgrounds and attitudes with which people have approached their time at *Gay News*, such a consensus is not, of course, to hand in the first days of preparing the bid. There are those who say that the whole recent experience of the paper proves that unless there is collective working, pay parity (eventually, if not immediately), and co-operative ownership free of interference from 'outsiders', the paper will carry forward, even when shorn of both Robert and Denis, the seeds of further dissension and catastrophe. Linda, Wendy, and Bob (a convert to this view), go still further, saying that the quality of the paper can only reflect its internal mode of operation: it will never sustain its high standards if it isn't organised internally in the most explicitly non-hierarchical manner. Others are open to persuasion, rather than already convinced in such beliefs. Estimates of what strict pay parity would yield per person indicate a possible £7,000 a year (on the trading profits projected through 1983-84), which is below what many on the staff need if they are to pay mortgages or rent, or raise children, and unquestionably a wretched wage for people of any ability – indeed, for anyone regardless of ability – in the London of the 1980s. But it would be a higher wage than some are getting on the staff. For most people on the staff, several of whom suspiciously

*Stephenson had been on *The Times* in the late 1970s when staff sought to buy the paper from the Thomson family. In the event, Ruport Murdoch was the successful purchaser.

regard all such terms as 'co-operative' or 'collective' or 'pay parity' as belonging to Socialism and of no evident relevance to the strictly non party political editorial objectives of *Gay News*, any option is worth considering if it can be proved helpful legally and financially. Several say that they will definitely go on with their hard tasks of bringing out the paper until the negotiations are completed. They will then, please, review what the new era offers, and take their personal decisions on whether to stay, or to seek work elsewhere.

In the event, aided by a London solicitor, Mike Seifert, who favours such efforts as those now being made by the staff of *Gay News*, the sub-group proposes that *Gay News* should in the future be owned by a trading company that will issue shares fifty per cent (or possibly fifty-one per cent) to a staff co-operative in the form of a company limited by guarantee, and half (or forty-nine per cent) to groups or individuals not on staff. Representatives of both staff and of outside shareholders would sit on the board of the trading company. After successful transfer of the paper from Robert and Denis's authority to the trading company, non-voting Preference shares would be made available to readers and any others by way of an appeal in the paper. The model is very much that which had been adopted by *City Limits*. Given this structure, staff will be able, as the editor of *The New Statesman* had indicated, to organise the internal running of the paper as they think fit. A trading company is bought off the shelf. (Between the costs of this, and of the expert appraisal of Gay News Ltd's affairs procured during the redundancies tussle of autumn 1982, staff find some £500 out of their own pockets).

The most practical of the practical questions, where is the money to come from, is in fact bedevilled by the worst of the 'ethical' problems. Very few who would be prepared to invest in *Gay News* under the new ownership would produce so much as a penny if they thought it would be of personal benefit to either of the recent proprietors, to either Denis or Robert. Potential private backers make this absolutely plain. Yet, as both Robert and the staff's 'negotiators', and common sense, indicate, Denis must be 'bought off'. He must be brought to accept a once-for-all sum, far below the full £65,000 or so still owed to him by Robert personally, but no doubt still substantial, if Robert is to be freed of all debt to Denis and free, therefore, to sell the newspaper. Robert himself seeks no 'premium' on his shares in Gay News Ltd (no 'profit'), but total release from all financial obligations. The latter include his personal guarantees in respect of the now leased premises, and leased equipment, and he insists also that he be repaid the £4,250 or so that he had paid over to Denis under the short-lived January 31 'settlement', so that he can return the money to that innocent party, his lover Alan. Staff accept that if possible Alan ought indeed to be reimbursed. And accept that an offer must be made to Denis. In arduous discussions, Barry and Joan, as 'negotiators', win Denis's verbal consent in the course of March to £8,500 in full and final settlement of all his claims against Robert.

With remarkable rapidity, the funding aspect of the bid begins to stitch together. Onerous work on the actual indebtedness of Gay News Ltd as it will be taken over from Robert Palmer Marketing Ltd, on its working capital needs, and on associated promotional, legal and other costs, together with projections about future staffing needs and eventual improvements in wages, all linked to conservative estimates of revenue prospects, yield an estimate that some £100,000 is needed for the staff to take over the paper as a running concern from Robert. Barry through the wide knowledge of discreet gay philanthropists he has gained in the course of his own voluntary work at London Gay Switchboard, procures promises of some £25,000. Bank financing is cleared by slow and difficult stages in the course of March-April. None of this could go to Denis. Staff themselves see their way, through personal borrowings, to providing another £5,000 towards the total needed.

Still to be found, or purchase of the paper cannot be realistically financed, is another £50,000 or so. Another sub-group of staff goes in search of it. Linda, the only member of staff who is an active supporter of and worker in the British Labour Party, proves invaluable in pursuing the only prospect now open since it's agreed that readers and the gay public at large cannot at this stage be approached. That prospect is public finance from those Labour-controlled authorities which in the course of 1981-83 have declared, in defiance of 'old guard' Labour politicians and of the other mainstream British political parties other than the Liberals, that the aims of lesbians and gay men are as eligible for public support as the aims of other minorities who have suffered extreme historical liabilities. The new Farringdon Road offices of *Gay News* happen to be in the Labour controlled borough of Islington, which has a strong declared policy of helping worker-controlled enterprises. Discussions are opened with Islington. And from several directions comes advice to apply for finance from the Greater London Enterprise Board (GLEB) just set up by the Labour-controlled GLC. The Leader of the GLC, Ken Livingstone, a vocal supporter of the rights of gays though not himself a gay man, personally recommends the GLEB to Linda. If its officers approve financial statements and forecasts laid before them by the staff of *Gay News*, the GLEB has power, and quickly, to make loans of up to (and indeed, far more than) £50,000.

It is with reluctance, with a feeling of being driven into the arms, however helpful, of that larger outside world which has been so untrustworthy to gays so often, that most concede to the plain good sense of making a submission to the GLEB. *Gay News* could so easily be self-supporting; it should never be in this position. But it is. And so an approach is made to the GLEB, and those members of staff who go to the preliminary appointment return grinning from ear to ear. Jo has been one of the delegation. 'For the first time', she says, 'I really feel we've met complete understanding' (she means from outside the gay world). The GLEB officer concerned, a Mr Dinsdale, has been most encouraging. A further sub-group of staff applies itself to drawing up 'cash-flow projections' (revenue and outgoings estimates month-by-month for three years ahead) and 'position papers' for presentation both to the private gay backers found by Barry, and to the officials of the GLEB. Andrew as editor writes 'position papers', defining how *Gay News* operates and what the staff's expectations and intentions are, for every aspect of the newspaper's activities, from distribution to mail-order to advertising income to the nature of the readership; Alison writes a prospectus for a revenue-earning Book Club project. Aided by outside advisers, staff draw up a new system of historical and forward-projection accounting for the newspaper, replacing the management accounts on which Robert had relied. Peter Coell puts in hours of voluntary work on behalf of everyone transferring historical financial data onto the new system, so that a clear record of the paper's, or rather Gay News Ltd's, performance over recent years can be read off for comparison with future projections.

In principle, as March goes by, the thing is done. If the paper strikes the GLEB as a potentially viable enterprise worth a relatively small £50,000 investment, then the £25,000 or so of private gay money will be forthcoming, and so – when Bob Workman, through his family, comes forward with the promise of a personal guarantee to the bankers – will £25,000 of clearing-bank finance should it be required. Then, in an abrupt phone call which leaves Joan, as 'negotiator', as angry, she says, as she has ever been in her life, Denis says that £8,500 will not, after all, be enough to persuade him to lift his claims against Robert. He later refers to the sum as 'peanuts'. To Joan he indicates that £25,000 might possibly interest him, but otherwise the staff can forget it. David Warner, as Robert's legal adviser, immediately says that for legal reasons he would prefer not to have made public at this stage, but which relate to the original 1982 deal between Robert and Denis, he considers it would be both safe and advisable to completely disregard Denis from now on. He discloses to Andrew and Barry that he is quite certain Robert has grounds for bringing a suit against Denis for considerable sums of money. If Denis seeks to make any further intervention in the sale of the newspaper by Robert to staff, Warner will advise Robert to bring the suit. For those who had always presumed that Denis's legal rights over Robert were unassailable, and who for months have been struggling to find some way to accomodate the claims that Denis would not relinquish in the early stages of *Gay News*' crisis, the development is almost unbelievable. Unbelievable development or not, there is no question but that Warner's advice must be accepted. Denis's claims are cancelled from all further discussions, and negotiations continue with the GLEB. Mr Dinsdale, of the GLEB, assures Robert that prospects of a substantial loan to the staff are excellent. He promises the formal GLEB decision by April 11 (a Monday). Robert grants the ten-day extension from the former completion date of April 1.

There is as buoyant a mood through the offices, by this first week in April, as there has perhaps ever been at *Gay News*. There is now every reason to think that the nightmare of ownership and managerial confusion, of financial instability, of damaging public comment, is coming swiftly to its end, and a clear picture emerging on which people can sanely estimate their personal futures. Right through February and March the flat out work on the rescue of the paper as an object in the hands of readers has continued. In all the periods of working hard on the paper, can people ever have worked as hard as now? Most of the officially non writing staff – Roger, back in harness as display advertising manager, Wendy in type-setters, Bob the photographer, David in distribution, Don and Mike in advertising, Linda on box-replies, Peter Jones, virtually all the depleted staff – spend evenings on theatrical events or on covering the clubs and pubs and consumer developments for gays. Through the collectives, material is decided on and work allocated. Art-room transforms the covers, making them 'busy' and colourful in complete contrast to the 'emergency' covers that ran from October 1982 through to February 3, 1983. At forty-eight pages with effect from February 17 (No 259) in place of forty pages, news-space is retrieved and features are restored. Jo works at home in the evenings on a transformation of the 6-page Gay Guide, plans which had been shoved into cold-storage when the financial crisis was first announced in October. Roger and Don, fighting off the acute depression they've suffered from the sight of the slump in display at the start of 1983, work on restoring this vital sector of the revenues. By late March they are seeing prospects of over £4,000 an issue, low by 1981 standards but well up from the slump and offering trading viability on the forcibly slimmed down, relatively low overhead, *Gay News* of spring 1983. Box-replies, driven into chaos by heavy selling of the service and by lack of physical facilities in the new office, are overhauled by Gill in consultation with Linda; and Jo's lover Lesley, now third in the art-room, designs a proper physical system for doing the box-replies, and offers to carpenter it.

Five months late, killed in the interim by the battle to get the newspaper's affairs in order, that light touch with serious matters which had been intended for autumn 1982 is now at last made a reality. Alison, as sole remaining features editor following the departure of Peter Burton, coordinates with Andrew in a flow of news and general feature material which handles the 'hardest' and the 'softest' topics in each issue. The paper becomes the first in Britain, gay or straight, to pay serious attention, fortnight after fortnight, to the approaching menace of AIDS. It carries material on the homosexual informant to the Soviets, Anthony Blunt. Blunt's own brother calls it the best he has seen anywhere.

There are personality interviews with comedian Kenneth Williams, with novelist Simon Raven, with playwright Martin Sherman. Human-interest features (several by Bob) on topics as diverse as foreign lovers, gay people and their pets, gay life in one of the republics of the USSR, Estonia. On top of running the Literary Supplement, Alison, inspiring in Andrew the greatest admiration, edits feature after feature as well as herself writing celebrity interviews. Jo introduces a nationwide page of disco information as the first stage in her coming transformation of the Guide. A column for gays in prison to write of their experiences (which they're now allowed to do under a European Court ruling) is introduced, and a page for the experiences of gays living in small towns or rural areas. Former features editor Keith Howes provides features, regardless of whether he is to get paid or not.

A New Yorker now resident in London, David Dubow, comes in one day a fortnight to help out on the critical news press-day. though highly paid in his work elsewhere. All the regular contributors continue to provide material for the paper.

It is a newspaper again, alive and ambitious, no longer the publication barely treading water, produced by a fortnightly miracle, that it had been through the appalling months of winter. Longer term planning might make anything of it yet. But for now it has broken the back of the task that some at work on it set themselves in January 1982. It has the trust of lesbian readers, it has the admiration of overseas buyers (overseas subscriptions going up), it has the capacity to be 'political' and 'serious' and to be entertaining at the same time. An interview with Michael Heath, one of the cartoonists of the 'queer-baiting' satirical fortnightly, *Private Eye*, yields a sophisticated heterosexual man's comment that he doesn't so much think that 'straight' men disapprove of gay men, as that they're envious of gay men's sexual freedom. And he informally offers to do for the paper a regular strip-cartoon 'The Straights' . . .

It would all be impossible if it weren't for the work of the 'negotiators' – Barry Jackson, and the Canadian-born literary agent, Joan Crawford. None on the paper could take the psychological strain of dealings with Robert and Denis, let alone the endless hours that these two negotiators devote to preparing for meetings with the two who hold the legal powers over the paper and over one-another. The negotiators advise and cajole, they obtain further specialist advisers, in law and in accountancy, and in their labours they become the British gay community, the readership, the 'movement', personified. If anything were needed to prove, by selfless effort, that the paper had grown to be deeply valued in its decade of life, whatever the inadequacies or the failures, it is the disruption to their personal and professional lives that Barry and Joan endure without relief from early February into April, without so much as their expenses paid, let alone any other fee.

But at last it is Monday April 11. The GLEB is to confirm this morning that Mr Dinsdale's recommendation of a £50,000 loan package towards a staff take-over of *Gay News* as going concern has been approved.

The phone doesn't ring. As the day crawls by, enquiries to the GLEB disclose that Mr Dinsdale is inaccessible, away on a train journey, and that all other executives are 'tied up in interviews with prospective recruits to the GLEB'.

Only on Tuesday does Mr Dinsdale get in touch after further badgering. He says there will be no loan. It transpires later that he himself didn't even forward the investment to his superiors. His given reason is that if revenue projections made by staff and advisers are not met, there could be further calls on the GLEB funds, to totals that could be wholly unacceptable.

The entire package of proposals to Robert collapses: no private gay money if the GLEB isn't going to make up the sums necessary for *Gay News*, with its accrued indebtedness, to be a viable proposition. No bank financing. Advisers try to reach senior councillors at the Greater London Council from the Leader of the Council, Ken Livingstone, downwards, and everyone is unobtainable.

It is hard to escape the supposition that a political decision has in reality been taken. The popular press has been besieging *Gay News* by phone for confirmation that large sums of 'ratepayers' money' are to be 'given' to the homosexuals' national newspaper, and for months the GLC has been coming in for crude and ill-informed abuse about its policy of admitting homosexuals to the lists of those eligible, like others, for calls on the public purse by way of loans, grants, or equity.

Robert, his lawyer David Warner, staff 'negotiators', members of staff try every avenue to transfer the paper to the employees despite the absence of the investment capital that everyone knows to be necessary. Offers and counter-offers are made in the course of the week up to Thursday April 14, but none are acceptable to both sides.

On Friday April 15, at about 6pm, David Warner on behalf of Robert Palmer tells the assembled staff that the paper as of this day ceases publication. Robert is at risk in law if he allows *Gay News* to continue trading, and incurring debts, without any prospect of new sources of capital. The paper is closed. Everyone will be made redundant.

In a tailpiece, a coda, Warner states that in consequence to today's decision, the title of *Gay News*, or right to publish a newspaper under that name, has been sold by Robert for a small sum to his lover Alan. Bob's peculiar question of February I, 1983, as to whether Alan regards himself as 'heir' to *Gay News*, has proved bizarrely prophetic.

It is legally a perfectly proper step, says Warner, and should serve to guard the right to publish from falling into unsuitable hands. For 'liquidators' will now be called in to throw the company, Gay News Ltd, into bankruptcy. All assets will eventually be sold.

'I heard the sorry news at about 2 am in one of the most remote parts of Lancashire . . . the National Committee has asked me to write to you to express our deep regret . . . the last edition was, to my mind, one of the best I have ever read in the six years I have been a regular reader . . .'

So writes the national secretary of a British gay organisation on Saturday April 16, the morning after closure of the paper. Others write too. From Sussex, a reader says 'O dear! All is over now, or is it? The fact that *Gay News* has come a cropper is no surprise to me, I was very doubtful about renewing my subscription. I like many others had become so disgusted with the increasing space and activities of the lesbians, two of whom actually run the paper, or did . . .'

From London, another: 'Well, I am bitterly angry. Down through the last ten years one has sensed the eddies and under-

currents, the suppressed coups, the manoeuverings and manip-
ulations . . . But I have invariably assumed an underlying
honesty, impeccable intentions and – more or less – altruistic
objectives. What, then, a shock the revealed truth turned out to
be . . .'

From Australia, one of the gay male correspondents of the
international pages ('WorldView') introduced early in 1982: ' . . .
I have received personally and through other people here some
very positive responses from gays in the UK, in the USA, and in
New Zealand. They had read about what had been happening out
here in *Gay News* and were made aware for the first time that there
really was an active gay liberation movement in Australia . . . I
think it's important for you people to be aware of this fact that *Gay
News* enjoyed unique international standing . . . I would like to
add that in my opinion one of the best new features that the *Gay
News* staff came up with was the section entitled 'The Visible
Lesbian'. The staff are to be congratulated on its introduction and
for the strong political nature of so many of its other recent features . . .'

From another reader, in Britain: 'As a subscriber to *Gay News*
and reader since its beginning I would ask you if you would
forward me details as to what the *hell* has happened . . .' People
look in vain for explanations from the general British media, print
or broadcasting. *The Times* refers to the death of *Gay News* in one
sentence tacked onto a frivolous paragraph in its gossip column.
The Guardian puts onto the story a reporter who has to get to a first
night at the theatre and can't spend much time on it. No background or explanatory feature is subsequently published by the
country's leading 'liberal' daily newspaper.

The oldest Sunday paper in the country, *The Observer* (also
self-defined as 'liberal') prints 5 paragraphs which include easily
avoidable inaccuracies. *The Sunday Times*, owned, like *The Times*, by
Rupert Murdoch, whose own staff describe him as frightened of
the subject of homosexuality, prints nothing. Harry Coen writes or
encourages the writing of pieces, which are suppressed. The BBC
and the commercial television franchises have nothing to say. The
commercial radio station, LBC, in London, is alone in the electronic
media in doing an item including an interview with Andrew.

'It is hard not to detect,' writes the weekly periodical *New Society*, 'in the deafening silence of the liberal establishment a private relief that yet another of those damned hornets that escaped the Pandora's Box of '68 has been eradicated.' Of the three leading 'contemporaries' of *Gay News* around the North Americas and Europe, *Body Politic* of Canada phones to ask for full detail of what has happened. *Gai Pied*, of Paris, arranges interviews. *The Advocate*, of Los Angeles, largest selling gay fortnightly in the world, makes no enquiries whatsoever.

Parties. A member of London Gay Switchboard reports that on the night of April 15, the day *Gay News* was closed, he attended a party at the *Gay News* owner's flat in Little Venice, on the understanding that it was being thrown by Robert's lover Alan, not by Robert. On arriving he discovers to his fury that Robert is hosting the party. His fists 'clenching and unclenching' he hears Robert being 'sympathised with' by 'rich queens', who are saying 'but darling, why didn't you tell us the paper was in trouble? We'd have helped out'. A contributor reports that he has been invited by Denis to what he's told is to be a party in a London restaurant to celebrate the death of *Gay News*. He indignantly refuses to go.

The staff turn up at the offices on Monday morning April 18 and begin a process of sorting correspondence that will have to be answered (and which is answered not only unpaid, but with editorial staff paying the costs of the stamps as well). People empty their desks, answer phone calls. Copies of the staff statement of April 15 describing the closing of the paper are sent out to gay organisations around the country and voluntary worker John organises a large duplication of the statement, at his own expense, so that it can go to overseas subscribers. To everyone's mystification, there's no sign of Robert on the Monday. People haven't been dismissed in proper form, he remains the employer. Where is he? A phone call to his lawyer David Warner produces a promise from Warner that though he's no longer being paid anything for his services, he will do his best to track Robert down. The result is a phone call from Robert at about mid-day on Monday. He's in a call-box. 'I'm at the London Graduate Business School', he says, 'where I've been lucky enough to be accepted for a course, I'm just popping out between lectures . . .'

No doubt he had legitimately enough fixed up this return to school in anticipation of a successful staff purchase of the paper, and so that he can eventually start a career in business all over again. But as the word goes out through London of what the man who operated *Gay News* is up to there's a sense of bafflement at the sort of mind that can calmly attend courses in business management when the enterprise of which he is still the legal director is foundering, its readers, its creditors, its staff, its debtors at sea. Those who have been closest to his performance on the paper see an almost fantastic obstinacy in pursuing a career for which they themselves have concluded he is wholly unfitted. Mixed, for a time, with that bafflement and incredulity is outright hatred. His lover Alan, a long-time voluntary worker with London Gay Switchboard, resigns from Switchboard.

So far as anyone knows, Alan is left some £4,250 out of pocket – the money he lent his lover to pay Denis in February.

On Tuesday April 19, Robert accompanied by David Warner as his unpaid lawyer comes to the *Gay News* offices to introduce the 'liquidators', Leonard, Curtis & Co, a firm of specialists in bankruptcy. The representatives of this firm are so calm and informative about the very complicated legal consequences of the liquidation, explaining the personal and corporate consequences to the staff, that the editor grimly remarks that so far as he's concerned it has taken bankruptcy to introduce good management to the affairs of *Gay News*.

Seeking a private interview with Andrew, the 'liquidator' states that he recognises a 'journalistic province' at such a moment as this, and will do his utmost to co-operate so far as creditors' claims allow him in any arrangements that the editor and/or journalistic staff of the dying paper think proper.

He formally recognises an action taken over the weekend. In consultation with available members of staff, Andrew had entered the office on the Saturday, opened the safe, and removed computer copy-discs and print-outs detailing the 15,000 or so names and addresses of homosexuals confided to *Gay News* over the years and constantly updated. He had transferred these to the custody of three 'outsiders': the 'Chair' of the Campaign for Homosexual Equality, and the two former negotiators on behalf of staff, Barry Jackson and Joan Crawford. In a last service to the readership he had laboured so long to serve, Barry comes to the office and is shown by the Peters of accounts how to change the password into the computer's on-line lists of names and addresses, so that only he and the two other custodians should be able to release them.

The theoretical value of the lists to an unscrupulous popular newspaper, private individual, or even Government agency with exposés, blackmail, or concealed pressure in mind, is explained to the 'liquidator'. He gives a ruling that they are in effect unsaleable, with a nil value. He will not ask to seize them as an asset on behalf of creditors.

The opening of the safe discloses a Zeroxed booklet. It is Alison's 'contact book', a voluminous record of names and addresses compiled by her in the course of her years of work at *Gay News*. Names and addresses of personal friends are in it too. From internal evidence, Alison deduces that the laborious photocopy must have been made – completely without her knowledge or consent – before Robert bought the paper. Informed of the find, Robert says he had never known what it was. In its small way, it is one of the most unattractive discoveries made in the whole course of bringing to light the inner workings of the paper.

In a sad scene, the two Peters, opening correspondence day after day in a deserted office as their 'accounts' responsibility, have to stop the box-replies that still pour in from classified ads in the March and April isues. Instead of forwarding envelopes, for which there is no workforce, they have to open them and then destroy them. On their table a great heap grows: a heap of photographs. They are the colour photographs gay men had had taken of themselves to forward to 'men's personal' advertisers, who usually ask 'photo please'. A great heap of photographs of men's faces. They are the faces of some of those who read *Gay News*.

Since leaving *Gay News* in November, giving as his reason his disgust at the 'treatment' of Denis and Robert, Peter Burton has worked for a short-lived gay newspaper called *Lavender Letter*. After its collapse, he joins Alex McKenna's monthly magazine for gay men only, *Him*, procuring features and writing the same 'Hotspots' column about the 'commercial scene' that he had done for *Gay News* and for *Lavender Letter*. He is there throughout the onslaughts on the conduct of 'the lesbians' (pejorative) at *Gay News*, and through the crude campaign that seeks to erode the commercial base of the national fortnightly.

Months of rumours that he and Denis are trying to get one joint project or another off the ground are now confirmed with the news that Denis too is to join Alex McKenna's group. He and Peter are to co-edit a new national fortnightly for gays to be launched in late May or early June and to be called *Gay Reporter*. Work on it, says their promotional material put out in May, has been going on 'for months'. It is accordingly supposed by many that Denis's *volte-face* from verbally accepting £8,500 from staff in settlement of all his claims against Robert, to calling that figure 'peanuts', and speaking vaguely of £25,000 as more like it, was prompted by a moment of agreement between himself, Peter, and Alex McKenna (as publisher providing necessary services and finance) that they will go into direct competition with the stumbling *Gay News*.

Denis and Peter announce that it will be 'the biggest launch of a new gay publication the Continent has ever seen'. They describe themselves s 'the team which created the original *Gay News* and brought it to its circulation peak'. The new production will specifically be for gay men only. In knocking copy clearly drafted before news came in that the Greater London Enterprise Board had torpedoed staff's purchase of *Gay News*, the two men write: 'Of course we all feel sentimental about the old *Gay News*, but it isn't the paper it was: The staff is different, the content is nothing like as good as it was, and in the end, people just got bored with it and stopped buying it.' The promotional leaflets carry an imaginary question-and-answer between two men about the new paper: 'I bet it's all boring' (the coming *Gay Reporter*, that is) 'and political and full of stories about lefty lesbians'. 'Not so', comes the answer, . . . it's very unbiased. It's a news magazine for gay *men*. So you needn't worry about them preaching on things that don't interest you.'

While people wait to view this demonstration of all that Peter had been advocating before leaving *Gay News*, and that Denis has ceaselessly been reported as saying through late 1982 and early 1983, the only regular valuable source of news actually in publication, *Capital Gay*, arranges to get copies up to urban centres round the UK which are bereft of news material thanks to the collapse of *Gay News*. Pressed to enlarge their weekly paper, to make it 'fill the gap' completely, Michael and Graham steadfastly refuse to abandon their commitment to a fast service newspaper for the Greater London area. But they consciously extend the information from elsewhere in the country. •

Nothing is heard of the money, some £65,000, that Robert is understood still to owe Denis personally for the 1982 purchase of the shares in Gay News Ltd. Nor of the lawsuit he had apparently contemplated for recovery from Denis of sums comparable in scale to the debt still outstanding. It all remains a mystery, 'private', as so much always was, to the pair of them.

The 'liquidator' pays the two Peters of accounts to help him investigate the affairs of Gay News Ltd, according to normal practise, and three weeks after closure of the paper, on May 4, a creditors' meeting is summoned at the West End premises of Leonard, Curtis & Co. Robert nominally chairs the meeting. A number of former members of staff are in the audience, creditors themselves for unpaid wages and redundancy and notice monies. Denis, whose new paper is now known about but not yet launched, turns up and sits to one side in the front row. None of those who had formerly been his employees speak to him; nor he to them. He and Andrew have nothing to say to one-another.

An 'Approximate Statement of Affairs' read out by the 'liquidator' shows *Gay News* going down with an estimated deficiency of £51,000 in regard to unsecured creditors. The largest such creditor is the printer, to the disgust of those in the former production and editorial staff who had had the closest personal and professional relations with a printing firm they had greatly admired. One of the largest assets of the company, in theory, is entered as £31,782 owed by Robert Palmer Marketing Ltd to Gay News Ltd. It comprises the £26,000 borrowed by Robert Palmer Marketing Ltd from Gay News Ltd out of the proceeds of the sale of the West Kensington office in November 1982 and, according to Peter Coell, as Company Secretary, interest never paid on the borrowing. The 'liquidator' informs creditors that he doesn't expect to retrieve a penny of this sum.

To raise what money he can on behalf of creditors, the 'liquidator' arranges for a firm of auctioneers to sell the title, which he has successfully demanded be returned from Alan's brief ownership, and any other assets such as disposable physical equipment on May 23. This ceremony of dispersal, this rite of ruin, will be at the Dickensian-sounding address of Quality Court, Chancery Lane, in the City of London.

As the weeks tick past to the moment when the question of who has the right to publish a newspaper called *Gay News* will be settled in law, under the auctioneer's gavel, for all time, the contending forces make their arrangements. It is learned that Denis and/or Alex McKenna will be attending the auction, hoping to buy such equipment as the copy-camera and art-room equipment, and possibly the title as well. A magazine report guesses that McKenna will want to buy the title *Gay News* in order to reduce competition for the new *Gay Reporter* he's employing Denis and Peter to launch. He certainly indicates that he will be present at the auction.

The former staff of *Gay News*, though enmeshed in all the awful bureaucracy of seeking their state benefits and the money owed them by the bankrupt Gay News Ltd, hold meetings to decide on their own next moves. Former contributors ask for a large-scale discussion, none of them caring for the sound of the new fortnightly announced by Denis and Peter, and this is held, attended among others, by invitation, by Gill, who remains very close to the efforts of her former colleagues.

Preparations for the auction branch into two distinct approaches. Linda, Wendy, and Bob hold urgent discussions with the London borough of Islington (Labour-controlled), in which the former Farringdon premises lie, and set in motion the creation of a wages-parity staff co-operative to republish *Gay News* if the title can be secured, with start-up finance (hopefully) from the borough. The 1983 British General Election is announced in the midst of these negotiations, and the borough's financing projects are 'frozen' until after the Election – which means also until after the auction: no money in time to make a bid.

In a different approach, Andrew talks to those who had formerly been willing to put up private funds towards the proposed staff purchase of *Gay News* as a working concern from Robert in April. His recommendation is that sufficient funds be promised to ensure buying the title and its 11 years of copyrights, so that a small publishing house, both to produce paperback 'offtakes' from the archive and to re-publish the paper, be launched, without dependence on 'public money'. Some £21,000 is promised by the time of the auction, 'movement' money.

There are some strains between the two approaches, but Bob, who pledges £5,000 of family money towards the bid at auction, is involved in both, and so is Alison. The sudden announcement of the General Election means that both approaches resolve into one: a bid at auction with the private money of five or six gay men prepared to back the former staff with no probability of an adequate return on their investment; no certainty even that they will ever get their capital back. It is proposed that if the staff bid at auction succeeds, the private backers will own the title and assets through a company of their own, and lease them to a publishing enterprise to be set up by former *Gay News* staff. It is a concept which the gays have come up with for themselves, but which within a few weeks – in July, 1983 – will be advocated by one of the legal advisers of *The Times* for the entire newspaper publishing industry in Britain.

Michael and Graham of *Capital Gay*; Gill, who had been on *Gay News* staff; the private backers of the staff bid, who are to be represented in the bidding by Bob and by Nick Billingham (who back in November, at the County Hall public meetings, had said the only course for Gay News Ltd was to go into liquidation); Alisdair, Alison, Andrew, Bob, Jo, Lesley (Wilson), Linda and Wendy – crowd into the Quality Court offices of the auctioneer. Staff have arranged with the former printers that they will undertaken the new *Gay News*, and with *The New Statesman* – helped by David Bird – that that paper's distribution company will handle distribution. Nothing is left but to win at auction.

No Robert. No Denis. But Alex McKenna is there as promised. And there is an unknown, a further bidder whom neither the 'liquidator' nor the auctioneer will name. Proceedings are very swift. The auctioneer starts the bidding at £13,500. Staff's backers take it to £21,000 against bidding from a thick set middle-aged man who is plainly the auctioneer's 'unknown'. He then jumps to £25,000. It's more than the supporters of the former staff can match or top. McKenna makes no bid at all, driven out at the earliest stages. The paper is sold. The right to publish *Gay News* leaves Denis, who has no say any longer in the matter, leaves Robert, and leaves those, the staff, who had never had the right in law – yet without whom it would never have appeared when Denis and Robert were entangling everyone and everything in the complexities of the deal once struck between them. It leaves the staff without some of whom it would never, in the whole course of its existence, have been the paper, good and bad, that it had been; leaves the founder, its last editor, without whom it would probably never have been conceived, for good and ill, in the form that became familiar for more than a decade; leaves those readers who had valued it for what it was and for the kind of fame that it had achieved.

The new owner, 48 year old heir to a family fortune made in the British cinema industry, launches The New Gay News *in the autumn of 1983. He is called Nigel Ostrer, and had conceived the idea of buying the title after hearing of the paper's difficulties both as a reader and because he's a friend of Tony, lover of Don who had been deputy to Roger in* Gay News *display advertising department. He promotes* The New Gay News *as being 'aimed at the average gay man and woman with interests in travel, fashion, gossip, entertainment, information and classified ads' and 'who appreciates a political unbiased* (sic*) approach to the news coverage'. He meets representatives of the London gay organisations, who come away dismayed. He invites none of the women who had previously worked for* Gay News *to join the new staff, nor are any women at all working for the new project at the time of its promotional material stating that it's to be for women as well as men, or when the first issue appears, 52 pages in A4 format, on August 18, 1983.*

Ostrer is learnt to be asking whether Glen, who had worked nine years for the old Gay News, *is 'a radical'. Only the Peters who had been in accounts, David Bird who had been in distribution, and Mike, who briefly joins and then resigns, are either invited to work for the new* Gay News *proprietor, or consent to work for him. Invited to be editor, Andrew concludes after a one and a half hour meeting with the man to whom* Gay News *has passed that there is no continuity whatever. Ostrer apparently feels the same, for he marks the first issue of* The New Gay News *as No I.*

Ostrer apparently sees himself as being in contest for the same market and the same kind of reader as Him *and* Gay Reporter. *Before his new* Gay News *has come out,* Gay Reporter *has disappeared. It lasts four issues before McKenna closes it with the explanation that 'sadly the recession made it difficult for the paper to attract enough advertising each fortnight to break even'. Peter Burton reverts to being solely a writer and features editor on* Him. *Denis departs from McKenna's offices.* Gay Reporter *is incorporated into* Him *as a title for the monthly news coverage. As 1983 goes by,* Him *goes from strength to strength in numbers of pages and advertising carried.*

261

Tony the former Gay News *cartoonist, Andrew, Alison and Linda amuse themselves by bringing out the first issue of what is intended one day, if possible, to be a regular funny paper for gays. The 5,000 print-run of issue No 1, financed and distributed by well-wishers, is a gleeful send-up of* Gay Reporter's *publicity material and first issues, of* Him's *misogyny, and of Britain's ridiculous legislation controlling the activities of gay men. It comes out in June, in the course of 'Gay Pride Week', the same month in which, 11 years before,* Gay News *had first appeared. Some think it very undignified for former staff of* Gay News *to bring out a funny paper. But generally it's very well received, with requests for more and offers of advertising. In the other, the 'caring' tradition of the newspaper, four former members of staff, Alisdair, Wendy, Alison, and Linda, plan publication of* The Guide, *a re-creation of the old* Gay News Gay Guide and Diary. *Interim finance is offered by the same gay men who had been prepared to put up their private money towards purchasing* Gay News *from Robert and Denis. Jo, who had brought the old* Gay News Gay Guide *to its essential place in the paper, offers help but doesn't want to work permanently on a new* Guide.

Tired of all that she had been made to endure, roundly and repeatedly declaring that as far as she's concerned Gay News *had been 'hijacked', she and her lover Lesley want to put it all behind them. They go looking for a new home in the West Country, in Glastonbury, where Joseph of Arimathea is said to have planted a thorn tree and where King Arthur and Queen Guinevere are said to have been buried. Tales of passion turn to legend.*

ACKNOWLEDGEMENTS

It was always said, and those of us who worked on the paper supposed it to be true, that more than two people read every published copy of *Gay News*. That made some 50,000 gay men and women in the UK and abroad every fortnight. Though not an official history, with all that that implies of access to all documents and sources, this book has been undertaken as an 'accounting' to readers for the loss of the paper. They paid the bills for over ten years, whether directly by buying the paper or indirectly because they were the market sought by advertisers. And the readers gave their trust to those who brought out the paper, whether as staff or as owners. Its loss, we have every reason to know, was more deeply felt in Britain than we have had space to prove; more deeply felt with every succeeding month after April 1983, as nothing comparable replaced it. For the preparation of the book, we would particularly like to thank the many former members of staff who spent an entire Sunday, in the most uncanny absorbed silence, reading and commenting on the bulk of the text. We would like to thank our publishers Brilliance Books for their patience when the exhaustion caused by a year's events finally caught up with Andrew as one of the authors. And Alison Hennegan, who gave up many days to retrieving factual information from notes she had kept throughout 1982-83 and who travelled repeatedly from Cambridge to help in the final stages of preparation, without stinting her time or her energy. We would like to thank Bob Workman for taking the cover photograph. Those who had valued *Gay News* as readers were foremost in our minds, and for their sake we embarked on the narrative. But of course those who worked for *Gay News*, and who contributed to it over the years, were also in our thoughts throughout the work. Everyone suffered, whatever view they took, and whether they are to be regarded as coming out well, or coming out badly, from the fight for the heart of the paper. With every respect for the efforts of other able people still involved in areas of gay publishing in the UK, we think it fair to say that the most skilled team ever to have emerged in the field of newspaper publishing for gays in Britain was dissipated on April 15, 1983, when *Gay News* was closed within weeks of starting the 12th year of continuous publication. What a waste.

Gillian E Hanscombe
Andrew Lumsden
London, September 1983

Brilliance Books is a totally lesbian and gay press and welcomes manuscripts from lesbian and gay writers on all subjects.

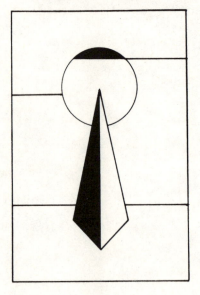